# The Ancient Andean Village

# The Ancient Andean Village

## Marcaya in Prehispanic Nasca

Kevin J. Vaughn

*The University of Arizona Press   Tucson*

## THE UNIVERSITY OF ARIZONA PRESS

©2009 The Arizona Board of Regents
First issued as a paperback edition 2011

www.uapress.arizona.edu

Library of Congress Cataloging-in-Publication Data
Vaughn, Kevin J.
The ancient Andean village : Marcaya in prehispanic
Nasca / Kevin J. Vaughn.
p. cm.
Includes bibliographical references and index.
ISBN 978-0-8165-2706-9 (cloth : alk. paper)
ISBN 978-0-8165-1594-3 (pbk. : alk. paper)
1. Nazca culture. 2. Marcaya Site (Peru). 3. Excavations
(Archaeology)—Peru. I. Title.
F3429.1.N3V38    2009
985'.27—dc22    2008050880


Manufactured in the United States of America on acid-
free, archival-quality paper and processed chlorine free.


15   14   13   12   11     6   5   4   3   2

# Contents

# Figures

# Tables

# Acknowledgments

This book originated as my doctoral dissertation for the University of California, Santa Barbara (UCSB), though it has undergone many transformations as the pace of research in Nasca has accelerated greatly in recent years. Obviously, an undertaking of this scale results in indebtedness to a number of people and organizations too numerous to list here . . . but I'll try.

The three members of my doctoral committee at UCSB deserve special mention, as they are the reason that this work came to be in the first place. All were instrumental in me attending Santa Barbara to study archaeology, and each provided mentorship and guidance resulting in my professional development as an anthropological archaeologist. Mike Jochim invited me to Germany for my first summer as a graduate student and was an incredibly supportive and encouraging mentor throughout my graduate studies. Mark Aldenderfer consistently gave me much-needed advice throughout and after my graduate career. Both Mike and Mark always kept me thinking about my assumptions and concerned with the "big picture."

Katharina Schreiber, the chair of my doctoral committee, was ultimately responsible for my interest in working on the south coast of Peru, and particularly in Nasca. While always encouraging me to pursue my research goals, she eventually convinced me that I would find a project focusing on Nasca villages interesting and rewarding. Her continual guidance in overseeing my fieldwork and writing, and her always-constructive criticism, enabled me to think clearly about the research problem and to eventually accomplish the task. I will always appreciate what an excellent advisor she was. Since I graduated, she has continued to be a source of inspiration in my professional development and has become a close colleague as well.

Permission to conduct fieldwork in Nasca, Peru, and to bring archaeological specimens back to the United States for analysis was generously granted by the Instituto Nacionál de Cultura (INC). The provincial museum and the local INC in Ica provided a great deal of assistance as well. José Cahuas, Fernando Herrera, Susana Arce, and Liliana Huaco were invaluable to me throughout the field season. Then director of the Museo Paracas, Rubén Garcia, was also very helpful.

Funds for fieldwork in Nasca during 1997 and 1998 were provided by a Fulbright-Hays Doctoral Dissertation Research Abroad Fellowship (#P022A70041), and a Wenner-Gren Foundation for Anthropological Research Small Grant (#6227). Dr. Sydel Silverman and Mara Drogan of Wenner-Gren, and Dr. Marcia Koth de Paredes of the Fulbright Commission in Lima, Peru and her excellent support staff were particularly helpful. The original compositional analysis of artifacts from Marcaya was provided by the Missouri University Research Reactor (MURR) through a National Science Foundation (NSF; #SBR-9503035) supported program. Subsequent compositional analyses were provided by a MURR NSF grant (#SBR-9802366), as well as an NSF grant (BCS-#0211307) and an H. John Heinz III Fund Grant Program for Latin American Archaeology grant.

I owe much to my friends and colleagues in Nasca and Lima, including: Josué Lancho Rojas; Olivia Seguro (and the Wasipunko family); Jonas Mendoza; Carlos Valdivia and his family; and Lucha, Cesar, and Wilma Burgos of the Restaurant Huarango, who in the last few years have tolerated with great patience my curiously un-Peruvian vegetarian diet (*"Un lomo saltado sin lomo, por favor"*). Alberto Segura, a Nasca potter who has honed his craft over many decades, was a valuable source of information about Nasca pottery. When I first came to his workshop as a naive young graduate student asking about Nasca pottery and technology, Alberto was understandably skeptical of me. Eventually, though, he was generous with his knowledge and I will always appreciate his advice and support. While I didn't get to know him until after my fieldwork at Marcaya was complete, Moises Linares Grados and his family have been great friends to me. I especially extend warm thanks to Carmen Garcia and her family, including her husband Nicolas, daughter Karin, and son Jefferson, who provided us with warmth and hospitality during those first few months in Nasca.

Discussions with many colleagues were critical in the development of my thoughts on Nasca and how it fit into wider Andean and global prehistory. In particular, I would like to thank Patrick Carmichael, Helaine Silverman, Donald Proulx, Johny Isla Cuadrado, Charles Stanish, Markus Reindel, Karsten Lambers, Anita Cook, Barbara Wolff, Lisa DeLeonardis, Michael Dietz, Ryan Williams, Donna Nash, Richard Burger, Karen Wise, Jerry Moore, Brian Billman, John Janusek, Patricia Knoblach, Darrel Gundrum, and Pat Lyon. A special thanks goes to Patrick Carmichael for his generous offer to teach me what he knew of the Nasca ceramic sequence, and to Elizabeth Carmichael for her hospitality while visiting in Calgary. Hector Neff and Michael Glascock convinced me to submit samples to MURR. Correspondence with them and R. Jeff Speakman greatly influenced my interpretations of the results of the compositional analyses. I also thank Denise Pozzi-Escot and Sarah Cross, who reanalyzed the faunal material from Marcaya in 2007 as part of a broader faunal analysis of materials from Nasca. Sarah Cross also provided assistance with several figures.

I will always look back at graduate school as some of the best years of my life. Friends and colleagues that I made continue to be great friends and colleagues even though we have since scattered all over North America. Discussions with them have been stimulating and have been enormously influential in my thoughts on how Nasca fits into the wider global context. In particular, I thank Jelmer Eerkens, Anastasia Panagakos, John Kantner, Justin Jennings, Hendrik Van Gijseghem, Elizabeth Klarich, Karen Anderson, Corina Kellner, David Crawford, Douglas Kennett, Sarah McClure, Nathan Craig, Cynthia Herhahn, Dennis Ogburn, Cindy Klink, Brian Haley, and Peter Paige. I especially thank Christina Conlee, friend and colleague. Christi and I were in Nasca doing our dissertation fieldwork at the same time, and in many ways, we "grew up" together archaeologically and professionally in Nasca. Here's to you, Christi: We both survived the "*tierra del dolor*!"

I am very grateful to the colleagues and students who contributed their time and energy to the project. Jason Adams and Nadeshna Molina assisted in the initial stages of excavations. Barbara Wolff visited for several weeks and enthusiastically excavated. Brian Stokes and Matt Evans arrived around Christmas to provide some valuable assistance in the field and lab (as well as some comic relief!). Although we had finished much of the fieldwork by the time she arrived, Becky Paulson stayed with us in Nasca for almost three full months. Becky cheerfully and fastidiously helped in the lab.

Julio Niñapaita deserves special mention as a field worker. Julio became the project's most consistent and reliable excavator. Not only did he ride his bike twelve miles along the Pan-American Highway from his home in Taruga every day to meet us in Nasca, he never stopped working and was on the project from day one until the day we backfilled. His strength and endurance never ceased to amaze us. Once, our truck became stuck in the Tierras Blancas riverbed. After the rest of us failed to move it through a combination of pushing and shoveling, he became frustrated (perhaps with our incompetence?) and simply *lifted* it out of the sand!

The writing of this manuscript has taken place at three different institutions. At Pacific Lutheran University I thank Jennifer Hasty, David Huelsbeck, Laura Klein, Elizabeth Brusco, and Carlton Benson. At Purdue University I thank Richard Blanton, Viktor Gecas, Myrdene Anderson, Melissa Remis, Evie Blackwood, Andy Buckser, Brian Kelly, Sharon Williams, O. M. Watson, Michele Buzon, and Ian Lindsay. I extend additional warm thanks to friends at Purdue outside the department: Jeni Loftus, Kris Skjervold, Darren and Debra Dochuk, Mike Ryan, Jen Foray, Talin Lindsay, and Kory Cooper. I also thank the Helen Riaboff Whiteley Center at Friday Harbor Laboratories, University of Washington for providing a spectacular and tranquil location to write the first two chapters of this book and to finish revisions once the manuscript had been accepted. At the Whiteley Center I thank Dennis Willows, Ken Sebens, Richard Strathmann, Scott Schwinge, Billie Swalla, Aimee Urata, Vikki Dauciunas, and Kathy Cowell.

The University of Arizona Press, and especially Allyson Carter, Acquiring Editor, has been a pleasure to work with. Allyson was professional, helpful, and most importantly patient throughout the entire process of submitting, revising, and completing this manuscript. I also thank three anonymous reviewers who reviewed the original manuscript. Their careful and thoughtful comments were very helpful as I revised the manuscript. Obviously, I am responsible for any mistakes or omissions in the final product.

Of course, I would also like to extend a warm and special thanks to my family. Both my mother and father have always encouraged me to pursue my goals (though I'm sure they didn't expect me to become a professional archaeologist). I thank them for their love and support. Special thanks also goes out to my brother Danny, who also has a keen interest in archaeology. He visited me in Nasca to check out sites and hang out with friends. *Es bueno*, Danny!

Finally, it seems that in every research project there is always a single person who is responsible for much of the outcome of the work, but receives very little "official" credit. For this project that person was my wife, Dawn. I cannot adequately express the gratitude that I have for her support. When she decided to accompany me to Peru for the better part of a year, not only did she put her own studies on hold and generally uproot her own life, she immersed herself in the project and was pivotal to its completion. Dawn ran the lab in Nasca and was responsible for many organizational aspects of the project. She spent much time analyzing the architecture of the site with me and drew many maps and profiles. Her participation in the project continued once we returned to the United States. Not only did she deal with a husband who for a good year and a half did little more than analyze minutiae of data and write his dissertation with all the usual neuroses and irrational behavior that accompany this period of time, she gave me constant feedback, advice, and loving support. I will be eternally grateful and can only hope that I can "repay" her (even if this means assisting in her research by collecting loads of fish mucus).

Aside from being an essential "behind-the-scenes" person for this project, throughout our many years together, Dawn has truly been the most wonderful, supportive, and loving companion that anyone could ask for. Her contribution to this project — and to my life — is immeasurable, and it is to her that I dedicate this book. I love you, Bee.

# The Ancient Andean Village

# **1**

# *Introduction*

## Ancient Nasca

As ONE OF THE MAJOR AREAS in the world where complex societies developed, the ancient Andes has a prehistory rich with expansive empires; spectacular crafts made by skilled artisans; resplendent cities with guilds of craftworkers, royalty, priests, and peasants alike; and great temple centers to which pilgrims from hundreds of kilometers flocked — all in one of the most varied environments in the world. The south coast of Peru is one region in the Andes that played a part in this development. Known for more than a century primarily for the colorful ceramics of the Nasca culture, the story of the development of civilization on the south coast is just beginning to unfold. This book tells the story of Nasca from the perspective of a small, rural village called Marcaya.

Nasca (ca. AD 1–750), a prehispanic society that flourished on the south coast of Peru, has gained worldwide attention for its artistically and technically spectacular polychrome pottery, its enigmatic geoglyphs (the "Nasca Lines"), and excavations at the ceremonial center Cahuachi (fig. 1.1). While the widespread distribution of finely made polychrome ceramics bearing the principal motifs of Nasca iconography was originally interpreted to mean that Nasca was an expansive state society (Rowe 1963), research has shown that the extent of Nasca society was limited to a much smaller territory comprising the Ica and Rio Grande drainages.

Archaeologists now believe that Early Nasca (ca. AD 1–450) was a pre-state "middle-range" society consisting of many rural villages located in the foothills of the Andes that shared a cultural tradition of utilizing fine polychrome pottery and participated in public rituals at the ceremonial center Cahuachi and on the Nasca Lines, but these villages all appeared to have been relatively independent of one another socio-economically. The seat of power in Early Nasca was Cahuachi, as it served as the center of a regional Nasca cult, as the focus of pilgrimage, and as a venue for sociopolitical competition where ceremonial feasts were held. Regional

FIGURE I.I
Nasca has been known
for many years because
of excavations at the
ceremonial center
Cahuachi (top; note
the sand-covered
mountain Cerro Blanco
in the distance), the
Nasca Lines (middle),
and Nasca polychrome
pottery (bottom).
This headjar is from
Marcaya, an Early
Nasca village. Photo-
graphs by Kevin
Vaughn.

compositional data of ceramics suggest that the principal bearer of religious iconography, polychrome pottery, was produced in limited contexts somewhere near the ancient ceremonial center Cahuachi, suggesting that the production of this fine craft was directly related to the power that Early Nasca elites held.

Middle Nasca (ca. AD 450–550) witnessed a major transition in Nasca society as aqueducts (called *puquios*) were built in the dry lower valleys to allow people to settle there for the first time, as construction at Cahuachi halted and as ceramic iconography shifted to include what art historians refer to as "bizarre" and "proliferous" elements. Late Nasca (ca. AD 550–750) society witnessed further upheaval as competition increased, people aggregated into large villages, and eventually the region was incorporated into the expansive Wari empire beginning ca. AD 750.

This brief reconstruction of Nasca society is based primarily on (1) the analysis of material artifacts — especially ceramics — collected from the surfaces of residential sites, excavations at ceremonial centers and tombs, and unfortunately from artifacts collected by looters; (2) excavations at the ceremonial center Cahuachi; (3) settlement survey; and (4) analysis of regional features such as prehispanic aqueducts and their relation to ancient habitations and geoglyphs (the so-called Nasca Lines). While valuable, these studies have left archaeologists with an incomplete portrait of ancient Nasca, one that has not considered the activities comprising the daily lives of people in their residential villages. Lacking data from a rural context, archaeologists are unable to evaluate this Andean society completely, least of all from the perspective of smaller social scales such as the community and the household. In this book, I offer a perspective on Nasca that has up until now been lacking, despite the fact that scientists have carried out investigations on this civilization for more than a century. What I offer here is a village perspective.

## The Research Problem

All societies are organized by a hierarchy of social units, from the individual to the household to the community to the regional political entity (Johnson and Earle 2000). Fundamental tasks of anthropology include understanding how humans are organized, how they practice their daily lives, and how this daily practice negotiates relationships at a larger scale.

Archaeologists have a privileged position in this endeavor because with the proper methodological tools, we are able not only to evaluate a variety of the social scales that make up a particular society, but also to critically examine these diachronically.

Archaeological investigations have demonstrated the importance of investigating villages in the Andes, as well as those outside the Andes. The variation seen in villages is key to understanding broader processes in regional polities. Because a village or community has its own socio-political order, economic patterns, ritual practices, and overall histori-cal trajectories — often completely different from those witnessed at other scales — investigating villages in complex societies necessarily comple-ments regional analyses. Ultimately, the analysis of villages provides fine-grained perspectives on agency, ideology, and daily practice that cannot be provided by other approaches.

This book investigates the importance of villages and rural commu-nities in the development of early Andean complex societies. In the pages that follow, I employ a "village approach" to evaluate the renowned Nasca culture from the "outside in," that is, from the perspective of a small, rural community called Marcaya. Marcaya was one of many Early Nasca vil-lages recently recorded in the region, but up until now, it is the only one to have been investigated fully. Employing methods from archaeology and drawing from a long tradition of both archaeological and art historical research, I will reconstruct Nasca subsistence and political economies, interactions between elites and commoners, and the ritual activities that were conducted in daily Nasca life. I will also offer a perspective on how one of the most celebrated art styles in the prehispanic New World was used and incorporated into the daily lives of Nasca commoners.

By taking this approach, investigations at Marcaya that I describe fo-cused on the ways in which villages in pre-state societies were integrated into regional polities. The village approach evaluates the ancient commu-nity by seeking to define domestic units, in this case households, as they are visible archaeologically (e.g., Stanish 1989; Robin 2003), and then at-tempts to understand both local and regional processes from the perspec-tive of those archaeologically defined units. In particular, I seek to con-sider three aspects of Nasca society through investigations at Marcaya employing the village approach: (1) power and inequality in the village; (2) economic organization, in particular its subsistence and political economies; and (3) ideology as seen through ritual. Specifically, is there evidence for status differences at Early Nasca villages? If so, what were the foundations of these status differences and how were these differences maintained? How were Early Nasca villages organized in terms of the production, distribution, and consumption of resources of both the subsistence and political economies? How was ritual and ceremony organized in Early Nasca villages if at all, and how did these activities relate to what took place at the great ceremonial/pilgrimage center Cahuachi? As I will explain in the pages that follow, I believe that all of these aspects of Nasca society can be addressed through the study of power and political economy.

In this book, I intend to show that employing this methodological approach results in a completely unique perspective of Nasca society. While Early Nasca power and political economy have been previously evaluated, the lack of data from a domestic context has greatly hindered a holistic understanding of Nasca and how these aspects of Nasca life were practiced on a day-to-day basis.

## The Organization of This Book

To situate this study within broader anthropological theory, my theoretical orientation is outlined in chapter 2. Generally, I draw from two perspectives to interpret the ancient village: agency and political economy. Both of these orientations have gained increasing favor in recent years of archaeological research. While there have been many recent archaeological case studies that have taken an agency perspective, each in their own way focuses on individuals as agents of change that have the capacity to transform society. Taking this perspective allows archaeologists in Nasca to go beyond rather sterile debates as to what was Nasca's societal type (i.e., chiefdom or state), and instead allows us to focus on the nature of power in Nasca society.

One way to focus on the nature of power is to evaluate the political economy and how elites establish and maintain political economies. While the locus of power in Nasca appears to have been the ceremonial center Cahuachi, it is not possible to understand the processes responsible for the emergence of that power without understanding how people in rural villages enabled and responded to these changes. Towards that end, I outline how archaeologists can evaluate local villages in the Andes and suggest methods through which villages in pre-industrial "middle-range" societies are integrated into larger processes taking place at major civic-ceremonial centers. In particular, I focus on power and inequality, subsistence and political economies, and ideology as seen through ritual activities.

First, this research focuses on evaluating status differences at residential sites. This is critical because revealed differences can shed light on the nature of leadership in early complex societies, as well as how early leadership articulates with emerging power at the ceremonial center. Second, this research focuses on the economic organization of the village to determine whether households were self-sufficient or whether villages were part of a larger political economy characteristic of early complex societies. Finally, the nature of community and household ritual is investigated. Commonly in complex societies, ritual expresses both social solidarity and social differences simultaneously — often benefiting those who sponsor the rituals. Without understanding how people integrated both corporate symbols and the rituals in which these symbols were displayed in domestic life, it is impossible to understand the purpose of ritual and ceremonies in early complex societies and whether they were successful in benefiting those who sponsored them.

In chapter 3, I provide an archaeological background for this study. I summarize the geographic and environmental context of the south coast of Peru in which Nasca developed. I also provide a summary of the prehistory of the region and outline our current understanding of Nasca society based on more than a century of both archaeological and art historical research. One aspect of Nasca archaeology that has been sorely missing is the analysis of a single village. Indeed, after a full century of research, virtually nothing is known of Nasca villages, and therefore any argument of Early Nasca political economy has been speculative and any reconstruction of Early Nasca society has remained incomplete.

In chapter 4, I present my methodology to evaluate an Early Nasca village. I refer to this methodology as a village approach and argue that employing this approach is necessary to complete our understanding of Early Nasca society. Indeed, without this approach, a large segment of the population — those individuals living in small, rural villages — is completely absent from the reconstruction of Nasca prehistory. Leaving these individuals out of the picture results in an incomplete portrait of agency, power, and political economy in Nasca.

I present investigations at Marcaya, a small, rural Early Nasca village in chapter 5. First recorded in 1989, extensive surface analysis and excavations were undertaken in 1997 and 1998 at Marcaya. This chapter describes the basic research methodology used in conducting the surface analysis and excavations. Households organized into patio groups were defined as the basic unit of analysis. Because of a lack of deposition, these could be recorded on the surface of the site. To evaluate variability in households, patio groups to be excavated were selected based on archaeological measures of status. Samples of eight patio groups, including groups of both high and low status, were excavated with three excavated fully in order to understand the nature of differences between households at the village. The surface analysis and excavations are presented with a summary of the major findings in the fieldwork, including: a summary of Early Nasca architecture as seen at Marcaya, the presentation of previously unrecorded storage features, a summary of radiocarbon dates revealing a short occupation dating to the late fourth century and early fifth century AD, and a summary of the types and distribution of artifacts and features found in excavations. A comparison of two patio groups reveals status differences at the village.

In chapter 6, I present an analysis of the most common artifact found in excavations: pottery. Following previous analyses from excavations at Cahuachi and from analysis of burial assemblages, the pottery assemblage from Marcaya was divided into fineware (painted polychrome pottery) and plainware (unpainted utilitarian pottery). I summarize the major vessel shapes of each class of pottery. Decorated bowls and vases are the most common vessel types in the village vessel assemblage. Indeed, polychrome finewares make up more than 50 percent of the entire vessel assemblage. No evidence for pottery production was found, despite the high frequency of consumption of both painted polychromes and undecorated utilitarian wares by all households investigated. A geochemical sourcing study indicates that the painted polychromes are compositionally homogeneous, and comparison with assemblages from around the southern Nasca region — as well as comparison with parallel compositional studies — indicates specialized production of polychromes in Nasca. On the basis of a clay survey in the region and increasing evidence for production-related artifacts and features at the ceremonial center, I argue that the majority of polychromes at Marcaya were produced at Cahuachi. This has profound implications for the Nasca political economy and I return to this in the final chapter of the book.

Other artifacts aside from pottery were instrumental in ancient political economies of the Andes. Thus, in chapter 7, I consider non-pottery artifacts such as spindle whorls—which relate to textile production— lithics, and faunal remains. Analysis suggests that the village was self-sufficient economically, except when it came to pottery production.

Considering the perspective outlined in this book, chapter 8 summarizes Marcaya as an Early Nasca village. Specifically, I discuss household identification and organization, status, subsistence and political economies, and evidence for ritual in the village of Marcaya. The subsistence economy is characterized as a mixed agro-pastoral economy with the use of camelids for meat and wool augmented with Andean domesticated staples. Obsidian was obtained from the highlands, perhaps through down-the-line exchange from llama caravans. I affirm that with the exception of pottery production, households were economically self-sufficient with no evidence for communal organization of storage, production, or consumption.

Evidence for an emerging political economy is seen by status differences at the site in the form of larger households, as well as restricted access to certain artifact classes—especially particular polychrome vessel types such as headjars and cup bowls. This suggests that certain members of the community, perhaps lineage heads, had access to activities taking place outside of Marcaya, most likely at the ceremonial center Cahuachi.

Household ritual is seen by the ubiquitous presence of Nasca polychrome finewares that were used for basic consumption at the site, probably in small household rituals replicating larger ceremonies that took place at Cahuachi. Leaders at Marcaya had access to restricted goods including certain vessel types, and comparison with modern indigenous Andean communities suggests that these leaders were probably representatives of the community at larger regional ceremonies, including those that took place at Cahuachi.

Following a discussion of the village and political economy of Marcaya, this book's conclusions are situated within the wider context of Early Nasca society in chapter 9. I discuss the Nasca ceremonial center Cahuachi in light of the new findings generated by this research and suggest that comparison with excavations at Marcaya show evidence for a permanent, elite residence at the ceremonial center. In the context of this interpretation of Cahuachi, I offer an interpretation of Early Nasca society and evaluate how Marcaya fits into the wider context of this Andean middle-range society.

I conclude this chapter with a discussion of the importance of the village approach to complex societies. I argue that the analysis of Nasca through the lens of a small rural community illuminates our understanding of status, economy, and ritual, giving archaeologists a far more detailed and complete picture of Early Nasca society. Furthermore, I argue that this approach is essential if Andeanists are to fully understand the ancient societies that they study.

The results presented in this book have implications not just for our understanding of Early Nasca society as they provide Andean scholars with the first glimpse into Nasca domestic life, but also for our understanding of the role that villages played in early complex societies. It was at these small, humble settlements where the majority of ancient lives were carried out, where household activities such as production, consumption, and ritual were articulated with wider societal endeavors. It is for this reason that I argue that a village approach is essential for the understanding of any complex society.

# 2

# *Agency, Power, and Villages in Middle-Range Societies*

As ARCHAEOLOGISTS ATTEMPT TO understand the development of complex societies, they have come to recognize that it is impossible to fully understand a pre-industrial society without investigating what the majority of people — those who lived in rural villages — were doing. Many archaeologists who study ancient societies focus on political capitals and ceremonial centers, with the underlying (often unintentional) assumption that these are the most important sites in early civilizations. Furthermore, the implicit assumption of research that focuses on capitals and civic/ceremonial centers is that the people who occupy these centers — elites, priests, and other individuals and groups with power — are the only people with the capacity to make decisions and to transform society. In short, they are the only people with agency.

But we know from history that the great majority of people do have the power (or, shall we say, the *capacity*) to act, not just *react*. Numerous researchers over the past several decades have shown that we can evaluate the lives of these people through the unique methods of archaeology. Here, in particular, I wish to explore one early civilization — Nasca — from the perspective of a small rural village. Before we embark on this exploration, I situate this study theoretically by discussing agency, power, and political economy in middle-range societies.

## Middle-Range Societies

Thanks to contemporary research, there is general agreement among scholars that Nasca was a ranked society, though the degree to which rank existed is still open to discussion. Most agree, however, that Nasca was probably sociopolitically organized as a chiefdom, that is, an analytical type of social formation that includes those societies "that organize centrally a regional population in the thousands . . . [and that have] some degree of heritable social ranking and economic stratification" (Earle 1991:1).

Societies labeled as chiefdoms range from relatively small-scale ones to highly complex societies with substantial degrees of ranking and inherited positions of power. The great range of variation within the social category has been the cause of much discussion (and consternation) over the past several decades of archaeological research since Elman Service (1962) used the term "chiefdom" to describe those societies that fell between "tribes" and "states" in his proposed continuum of social evolution. Since Service's publication and the subsequent adaptation of his typology by processual archaeologists, the term has been criticized, while some investigators have even flatly rejected the label. As early as the 1970s, Colin Renfrew suggested that the type encompassed at the very least two kinds of societies, which he labeled "group-oriented" and "individualizing" chiefdoms (Renfrew 1974) and which were later characterized as "corporate" and "network" modes of society by Richard Blanton et al. (1996).

Subsequently, other archaeologists criticized the evolutionary types of Service (as well as other neo-evolutionists) and the explanatory efforts of early processual archaeologists. The most important criticism was that these typologies focus on "directional development through evolutionary stages that are static societal types" (Blanton et al. 1996:1) and that by merely using the term "chiefdom," archaeologists ignore much of the variability that exists between societies labeled as such (Feinman and Neitzel 1984). Ultimately, when employing such rigid, neo-evolutionary types, it is difficult to draw from theories of human behavior that account for political competition between individuals and more generally human agency. It is this final criticism that I focus on here by turning to an agency approach to evaluate these kinds of societies. To avoid the pratfalls of neo-evolutionary typologies, I prefer the term "middle-range societies" to refer to those pre-state societies such as Nasca that are between polities organized by the independent village and bureaucratic states.

## Agency and Power in Middle-Range Societies

Following long-term trajectories in general social theory, archaeological theory of the past several decades has moved from analyzing the data of the archaeological record in terms of systems and adaptation derived from neo-evolutionary models to attempting to evaluate individual motivations and actions that serve to create and transform those systems. In general, this break is what Susan Gillespie has referred to as the move from holistic theories that "consider society as an entity that exists beyond the individuals who compose it" to individualistic theories in which "explanations of all social phenomena are based on individuals and their actions" (Gillespie 2001:73). Ultimately, these individualistic approaches rely on some concept of human agency.

Human agency has become such a fashionable subject in archaeological research that an introductory chapter in a summary volume on the issue is entitled "Agency in Archaeology: Paradigm or Platitude?" (Dobres and Robb 2000). The fact that archaeologists have embraced the concept, however, is not too surprising. Indeed, as part of the post-processual critique that has been part of the archaeological landscape of the past several decades, archaeologists have become acutely aware that in order to understand the past, we need to understand how human action and motivation can serve to transform societies. While there are a variety of theoretical approaches that fall within the rubric of "agency" approaches, such as methodological individualism (Kantner 1996), Darwinian archaeology (Maschner and Patton 1996), practice theory (Bourdieu 1977; Giddens 1984; Ortner 1984), and historical processualism (Pauketat 2000) (see, for example, Dobres and Robb 2000:table 1.1 for the variety of ways in which the concept of agency has been employed in archaeological research), I suggest that all of these approaches have the following in common:

1. They focus on the *individual* as the primary object of research.
2. They seek to evaluate the so-called "black box" (Brumfiel 1992; Dobres 2000) or "faceless blobs" (Tringham 1991) in archaeological interpretation. That is, they evaluate the actual people (sometimes referred to as *agents* or even *actors*) that are responsible for social change.
3. They focus on the idea that society and social structure are ultimately transformed because of the collective actions of individuals.

I believe that Paul Goldstein's (2005:18) definition of agency is useful; he describes it as "the sum of actions, choices, and strategies for achieving the goals of individuals or groups within a society." It is this sum of actions and choices that produces transformations in society. With new agency approaches, archaeologists have essentially rejected the redistribution-based model of chiefdoms, originally formulated by Service, in favor of a "less rigid, conflict-based model of power relations that recognizes a range of variation in the strategies used by elites to create and manipulate structures of inequality" (Stein 1998:10). In other words, this new research emphasis is one that focuses on the practices that create and maintain inequality. Since it is recognized that forms of inequality exist in all social formations (see, for example, Bender 1989; Cashdan 1980; Sassaman 2000; Wiessner 2002), the primary question for archaeologists has become: How does inequality become *institutionalized* in social formations (e.g., Price and Feinman 1995:4)? Relations of inequality, however they are structured (e.g., by social, economic, political, or ideological dimensions), are most easily understood as power relations (O'Donovan 2002; Vaughn et al. 2005). Institutions of power are already established in state-level societies; thus, the process by which power is developed and maintained in middle-range societies has become one of the primary subjects of archaeological discourse in recent years.

In a commonly cited work, Michael Mann (1986:6) describes social power as the ability to pursue and attain goals through "mastery exercised over other people." Mann defines four sources of social power: economic, political, military, and ideological. His general definition of power is not without controversy, however, despite its often uncritical use in archaeological discourse. In particular, his idea of power has been criticized as being "dyadic" and treating power as a resource that one either has or lacks, and which "counter poses" such social agents as elites vs. nonelites, leaders vs. commoners, etc. (Moore 2005:261). Furthermore, there is often an implicit (though sometimes explicit) notion in this "taxonomy of power domains" (Moore 2005:261) that agents consciously select from separate power bases (e.g., ideological, economic, and so forth) as they see fit, as if these domains are themselves separate essential types.

Instead, much work in social theory stipulates that power pervades all interactions and that all human agents have power. Daniel Miller and Christopher Tilley (1984) make a useful distinction between types of power by defining "power to" and "power over." The former refers to the *capacity* of individuals to act, and specifically the ability to *convince* others to follow demands without the requisite ability to coerce individuals. "Power over" specifically refers to having access to institutionalized mechanisms (i.e., negative sanctions) to coerce individuals to do what they might not otherwise do. "Power over" as described by Miller and Tilley is more akin to the power of which Mann speaks. The two types of power are complementary rather than in opposition (as they are often characterized). While all people have the capacity for power, it is those who have access to sanctions that can exercise power and exploit it to their own advantage.

Whether or not conditions of power (in the "power over" sense) ever existed in pre-state societies remains a question open to debate, not one that has been easily resolved (for example, see O'Donovan 2002). However, analyzing power in middle-range societies has tended to focus on the dynamics of power between different agents and the ways in which power might become institutionalized. Charles Cobb expresses this succinctly: "Inequality in nonstratified societies is promoted through a subtle form of exploitation and is as likely to occur on an individual basis as between groups or classes. Moreover, the 'power to' is highly fluid rather than restricted to interest groups, classes, or lineages; thus, power and inequality tend to be cyclical rather than stable. However, in some small-scale societies, certain individuals and groups manifest a 'power to' more consistently than others do" (Cobb 1993:51).

Thus, when concerned with power in middle-range societies, archaeologists consistently grapple with the question of why people cooperate with their own subordination in noncoercive circumstances (Stanish 2003). One useful way to approach this problem is to distinguish between what Anthony Giddens (1981) refers to as allocative vs. authoritative resources. Allocative resources are those resources that comprise the material world — food, water, and raw materials, for example — while authoritative resources comprise the social world, religious knowledge, speechmaking ability, charisma, and so forth. In societies such as those comprised of mobile hunter gatherers, in which material storage and ownership of resources is difficult, authoritative resources — those that involve the retention of knowledge — are far more important. In highly stratified state societies, of course, both kinds of resources are important. Elites and upper classes in states are in their position because they have allocative resources and they can usually justify this status through authoritative resources. For anthropological archaeologists, it is the middle-range societies that are most elusive, and at the same time most intriguing, because in these societies there is a constant negotiation between access to allocative and authoritative resources that provides the arena for social power.

The agency approach assumes that all individuals have the capacity to make decisions, so it is within a specific sociopolitical context that power is exercised. The context that agents in middle-range societies negotiate is one in which people, even incipient leaders, are tied by kinship obligations that keep a check on political ambitions (Moore 2005:263). To break out of these obligations, anthropological archaeologists have suggested that emerging leaders have several different options. In the following section, I turn to these possibilities.

## Political Economy and Power in Middle-Range Societies

One way in which to focus on the way power is exercised, manipulated, and resisted is by focusing on political economy and how it emerges and is manipulated by individuals for their own benefit. While William Roseberry (1989) generally defines political economy as the study of "social relations based on unequal access to wealth and power" (Roseberry 1989), when applied to archaeology, the term entails a more specific meaning that focuses on an analysis of the control and manipulation of an economy by emerging political figures, and the production, distribution, and exchange of wealth (Feinman and Nicholas 2004; Stanish 2003). Thus, while the study of political economy has tended to focus on more complex bureaucratic states (even the modern capitalist world system; see Ortner 1984; Wallerstein 1974), most contemporary archaeologists acknowledge that political economic strategies exist in "social formations of widely varying degrees of complexity and scale" (Blanton et al. 1996:3).

We can distill the efforts of emerging political figures to control and manipulate economies into three analytically separate but interrelated categories: exchange, production, and ideology. I explore these three variables to see how they contribute to emerging political economies in noncoercive circumstances.

A good place to begin is with the observation that archaeological and ethnographic evidence demonstrates that in middle-range societies, there is a critical tension between leaders, who wish to accumulate wealth, and their followers, who may challenge their ambitions to accumulate wealth (Cobb 1996:254). What makes the situation in middle-range societies unique when compared to stratified state societies is that commoners tend to be in advantageous positions when inequalities have yet to be institutionalized, primarily because they own the means of production in these societies (Wolf 1982). In the absence of a hierarchy wherein producers own the means of production, individuals (such as an aspiring elite) or interest groups (such as corporate groups or factions) tend to manipulate the political economy by either (1) accumulating goods through alliance networks and exchange; (2) by intensifying production (especially of craft products) through either their charisma or through kinship ties; or (3) by using some combination of these strategies.

Furthermore, archaeological and ethnographic evidence suggests that in order to be convincing, individuals and groups often turn to ideologically charged ritual in order to make the changes that occur palatable to those who give up some level of autonomy when these transformations are made. Thus, I follow Charles Stanish (2003) here to suggest that it is the interplay between exchange, the intensification of production, and the manipulation of ideology through ritual that are key to building emerging political economies in noncoercive circumstances. To use Giddens' terms, it is the interplay between allocative and authoritative resources that early leaders in middle-range societies manipulate.

*Exchange and Production in the Political Economies of Middle-Range Societies.* Political economies based on networks and exchange in middle-range societies tend to focus on "prestige" goods, items that are highly valued because of their scarcity and because of the knowledge and skills required to produce and obtain them. Prestige goods are also valued in middle-range societies because they tend to be portable and have a high value-to-weight ratio (especially when compared to staple goods; e.g., see Brumfiel and Earle 1987). Due to these intrinsic qualities, prestige goods can be directly converted to power that exceed their use-value (Goldstein 2000:335). Ironically, however, the aspiring individuals who may long for these goods have little control over their production, since their procurement tends to take place completely outside of their sphere of persuasion. Of course, it is often this distance and "exoticness" that adds to the power and allure of prestige goods (Helms 1993, 1999).

Controlling craft production is another potential ingredient in fostering the accumulation of wealth (Schortman and Urban 2004:189). While craft production can develop in middle-range societies for a variety of reasons, including creating interpersonal ties (Cross 1993) and establishing ethnic identity and alliance building (Sassaman 1998), archaeological and ethnographic evidence suggests that more commonly, craft production is intensified to establish and manipulate a political economy as part of an emerging elite's agenda to acquire prestige and wealth (Bayman 1999; Earle 1997; Hayden 2001; Mills 2000).

Cathy Costin (1996:211) specifically suggests that there are three principal reasons why elites (whether they are aspiring or established) sponsor (or attempt to sponsor) craft production, and why control over craft production is desirable for these individuals. First, craft production generates income to finance other projects and activities such as feasting, ritual, and long-distance exchange. Second, through the monopolization of key resources such as metal ores, clays, pigments, and flocks of wool-producing camelids, control over craft production promotes political and economic control. Finally, craft production is the mode through which symbols used to legitimize power are created (see Inomata 2001). I return to this final point below.

In middle-range societies, there are significant obstacles to increasing production, however, and the emergence of a political economy is problematic for would-be leaders precisely because they are tethered to other individuals by kinship obligations (Wolf 1982, 1990). There are two ways in which production has the potential to be intensified: through the labor of a leader's own kin, or through the labor of non-kin members through charismatic persuasion (Cobb 1993:48). Household modes of production, however, pose major impediments to this because people within this mode of production tend to resist intensified production.

*Feasting in Middle-Range Societies.* According to Stanish (2003, 2004), the key to the production-intensification process is the way in which the surplus is mobilized. Departing from Marshall Sahlins' (1972) statement that to achieve a surplus, one must either get people to work more or get more people to work, Stanish suggests that the key to surplus production in societies with emerging inequality (what Stanish generally refers to as the emergence of *ranked* societies) instead is convincing people to work in more efficient labor organizations (Stanish 2003:25). This is because there are significant hurdles related to the domestic mode of production that one must overcome in order to successfully mobilize a surplus.

According to this model (Stanish 2003:26), one effective way that

emerging elites can maintain more efficient labor organizations is by host-
ing group ceremonies and feasts permeated with religious significance.
Feasts, of course, are "public ritual events of communal food and drink
consumption" (Dietler 2001:69). A great deal has been written about
feasts in the last decade of archaeological discourse (see, for example,
Arnold 1999; Dietler and Hayden 2001; Jennings 2005; Jennings et al.
2005; Potter 2000; Spielmann 2002), and the bulk of this literature points
to the importance of feasts as an impetus for sociopolitical change, since
they afford opportunities for feast sponsors to display their generosity
by distributing food and wealth, thereby enhancing their social prestige and gaining political capital (see, for example, Dietler and Hayden
2001; LeCount 1999, 2001; Walker and Lucero 2000). This is accomplished through the creation of reciprocal obligations between sponsors
and guests through the gifting of food, drink, and material goods.

The importance of feasts is not just that they provide the settings for
public rituals and give feast sponsors the opportunity to display their
generosity; they also provide the very impetus to articulate regional exchange systems and they provide the mechanism for labor intensification
(Dietler 2001:69; see also Lucero 2003; Junker 2001; Spielmann 2002).
Indeed, Stanish (2003, 2004) argues that feasts are a distinct form of
exchange and as such can provide the impetus for labor intensification.
There is another aspect of feasts that are important in providing the social
and economic impetus for emerging leaders to promote a "sense of solidarity, inclusiveness and equality" (Walker and Lucero 2000:132) while
simultaneously promoting inequality by accumulating more material and
social capital. Pierre Bourdieu (1990:195; see also Walker and Lucero
2000:132) refers to this general phenomenon as *collective misrecognition*. I
argue here that it is in the social arenas provided by feasts where collective misrecognitions are promulgated, and these can provide important
stimuli for rapid social change.

There are multiple examples of feasts in the ethnographic and archaeological record that demonstrate that they are important arenas for public
rituals, provide mechanisms for labor intensification, and can provide an
impetus for exchange and promoting solidarity. For example, Laura Lee
Junker (2001:271) describes Spanish accounts of sixteenth-century feasts
in the Philippines as important features of the political economy of Philippine middle-range societies. Feasts of "ostentation, merit, or vanity," as

they were called, were associated with elite rites of passage such as birth and marriage, as well as "life-crisis events" such as illness and death. Feasts were also important prefaces to key events of the political economy such as trading expeditions, harvests, warfare and raiding, alliances, and chiefly successions.

In orchestrating feasts, a chief was able to accumulate wealth by drawing on the labor of his constituency and then redistributing that wealth in ritually charged social arenas whereby his ostensible generosity "emphasized his role as a superior kinsman and strengthened the often tenuous bonds that held together political coalitions" (Junker 2001:271). Feasts were also arenas where chiefs would give valuables such as metal gongs or porcelain bowls to elite participants, thereby securing alliances and political relationships. Indeed, though there was great variety in the way feasts were conducted, as well as their scale and complexity, for the purposes of this discussion, there were two features that were common to *all* feasts in the sixteenth-century Philippines: (1) social prestige was always conferred upon the feast's sponsor (who was almost always a chief), and (2) valuables were always exchanged among elites.

While the Philippine example is one that shows that feasts were social arenas where exchange took place and elites benefited, other examples demonstrate the importance of labor intensification. "Work-party feasts," for example, are those feasts in which a group or individual sponsors the event in exchange for the labor on a specific project. This kind of feast was common cross-culturally (see Hayden 2001), and one of the most well-known examples was in the indigenous Northwest Coast of North America (Perodie 2001). There, feasts were frequently orchestrated for the purpose of post carving and post raising, as well as house building. Labor was provided by the family of the sponsor as well as other households, and many work-party feasts were intracommunity events (Perodie 2001:195).

Another good example of a work-party feast has been described as taking place among the Samia of Kenya (Dietler and Herbich 2001; see also Bandy 2005a). Feasts were organized by aspiring leaders in order to extract iron ore to produce iron hoe blades. One measure of wealth was based on the number of wives an individual had, because women would cultivate millet and brew it into beer that could in turn be distributed at these social events (Dietler and Herbich, 2001:250). Feast hosts were responsible for providing food and drink for participants while participants worked to extract iron ore. The iron hoe blades produced from these raw materials were then used as a prestige good to purchase livestock or to serve as bridewealth to acquire additional wives. Thus, this kind of feast provided the impetus for both intensified production and exchange leading to "growth spirals" (Dietler and Herbich 2001:253).

All of these examples demonstrate that feasts provide one venue for the intensification of production (working "differently," as Stanish [2003, p. 15] puts it) and for the exchange of valuables and other kinds of goods that could potentially circulate regionally. The key point here is that the ultimate benefactor of these kinds of feasts is the feast sponsor, and that these events may be one of the critical social avenues through which aspiring leaders can actually intensify exchange and production.

Additionally, all participants in these ethnographic examples of feasts are negotiating these new structured relationships, and in large part, it is the responsibility of the feast participants to allow for this generosity and ritual knowledge to be displayed. Otherwise, in the structure of a middle-range society, leveling mechanisms would prevent an individual from gaining prestige and/or status.

*The Importance of Ideology.* While archaeologists and ethnographers have demonstrated that feasts provide the potential arena for these kinds of changes in exchange and production, a fundamental paradox remains for aspiring leaders in middle-range societies. Specifically, given the resistance to these kinds of changes, even if aspiring leaders can develop exchange networks, and if they transform existing labor organizations and get people to work more efficiently, how are they to convince other people that it is in their best interest to ultimately support these endeavors? To paraphrase the French anthropologist Maurice Godelier's important question: Why would people cooperate with their own subordination in noncoercive circumstances? While "growth spirals" can occur and are documented in certain ethnographic cases such as the Samia, other cases suggest that incipient leaders often turn to manipulating ritual closely tied to ideology (Aldenderfer 1993, 2005; Lucero 2003) in order to convince people to support their endeavors. The very fact that, ethnographically, feasts are so often the cornerstone of political, economic, *and* religious life in middle-range societies speaks to their importance in emerging political economies.

Garth Bawden (2004:119) provides a useful definition of ideology in this context as "that special formulation of social discourse that promotes the interests of its advocates in the wider community." The most important aspect of ideology here is that it creates a means to justify developing inequalities because of unequal exchange and production relationships, especially in societies where physical and economic forms of power are lacking (Earle 1997). One important means of attaining ideological power is through rituals directly tied to religious concerns (Aldenderfer 2005; Lucero 2003; Potter 2000; Schachner 2001). While ritual can be a conservative force that expresses asymmetrical relations of power, it can simultaneously serve as a dynamic force that acts to reproduce and transform relations of power (Aldenderfer 2005; Dietler 2001:71; Ortner 1984; Rick 2005). For example, Sherry Ortner (1984:154) describes early anthropological treatises of ritual as emphasizing how "norms, values and conceptual schemes get reproduced by and for actors." It was through "the enactment of rituals of various kinds that actors were seen as coming to be wedded to the norms and values of their culture, and/or to be purged, at least temporarily, of whatever dissident sentiments they might harbor" (Ortner 1984:154). More contemporary approaches of ritual suggest that by performing ritual, "actors not only continue to be shaped by the underlying organizational principles of those practices, but continually reendorse them in the world of public observation and discourse" (Ortner 1984:154).

Rituals forming the basis of ideological power are often linked to agricultural cycles in sedentary agricultural societies and can be effective means "for negotiating power relationships at all levels" (DeMarrais et al. 1996:17). While the rituals themselves are important in creating collective misrecognitions, also critical in ritual performances are the items that are produced for and used in these contexts. These items can include ritual attire, paraphernalia, as well as objects depicting important religious symbols that are enacted or displayed in rituals. By giving ideologies physical form through "a codified visual symbolism" (Bawden 2004:119), items used in ritual contexts serve as a constant reminder of one ideology's primacy over others. In an influential treatise, Elizabeth DeMarrais et al. (1996:16) call this process by which ideologies take material form the "materialization of ideology."

The materialization of ideology is a critical component of power building in societies where ideology is a significant source of power because it provides a tangible way to manipulate beliefs and "to guide social action" (Earle 1997:10). Materialization of specific ideologies are important to emerging leaders in power building because, first of all, an elite extending its ideology "through materialization promotes its objectives and legitimacy at the expense of competing groups" (DeMarrais, et al. 1996:17), and second, by materializing ideology, ideology is made a "significant element of political strategy" (DeMarrais et al. 1996:17). Most importantly, materialized ideology—whatever form it takes—provides the integration and legitimization of this new socioeconomic formation.

Materialization takes many forms, from the smallest portable objects to massive monuments, to actual events such as communal and ceremonial feasts. The forms used by individuals are critical in the efficacy of ideology as a source of social power. DeMarrais et al. (1996:17) divide these forms of materialization into four principal categories: ceremonial events, symbolic objects and icons, public monuments and landscapes, and writing systems. Each varies in terms of a person's access to resources, as well as the strategies by which it is used to materialize ideology. For example, monumental architecture and ceremonies can serve to integrate and define disparate populations, while symbolic objects and icons can be used as emblems of office or as highly portable vessels that display the principal symbolic motifs of an ideology.

The most important aspect of the argument formulated by DeMarrais et al. is that archaeologists deal with *material* things. Because of this, materialization can provide archaeologists with direct access to the strategies used by people in their efforts to materialize ideology. Of course, the flipside to the materialization of ideology as I describe it here is that materialization provides an arena for the contestation of the power upon which the ideology is based.

All in all, the mechanisms I describe for building and maintaining a political economy in middle-range societies are in sharp contrast to those of societies in which power and inequalities have been established, such as they are in highly complex, stratified state societies. That is, once "power over" becomes established, long-distance exchange, craft production, and ideology tend to act to reinforce as well as to legitimize unequal power relations. Of course, I am focusing on individuals and groups that "have power" in the Mann sense of the word. Certainly, those who do not have power (really, those who do not have access to coercive force) can resist power in various ways (see Brumfiel 1996 for a specific example of women in the Aztec empire resisting power). Our concern here, however, is political economy in middle-range societies, and I wish to turn to one way in which I argue that we can better understand political economy and agency in those middle-range societies: through the analysis of villages.

## Villages and Agency in Middle-Range Societies

The study of prehispanic Andean societies in much of the twentieth century has been characterized by an emphasis on urban sites and ceremonial centers. Katharina Schreiber (1999:162) calls this the "temples-and-tombs" approach. As she states: "This approach can be very useful: certainly much has been learned from the tomb of the Lords of Sipán about Moche rulers and their access to resources, labor, and items of prestige. Ultimately, though, this approach reveals a great deal about a rather small segment of society — those with power" (Schreiber 1999:162).

Indeed, as Schreiber indicates, this emphasis on larger, more spectacular archaeological sites came at the expense of understanding smaller, more humble settlements, which not only make up a significant proportion of a society's population, but which also, and perhaps more importantly, are where the practice of daily life transpires. Given anthropological archaeologists' interest in agency, this bias towards larger, more spectacular sites is all the more surprising. The dynamics of power and political economy should be visible to archaeologists at these smaller settlements, and it is here where we should be able to see how power is manifested, negotiated, and resisted. If archaeologists are truly concerned with agency, it is inconceivable to ignore villages.

Villages are a fundamental residential unit in sedentary complex societies. Humans have lived in villages since the Pleistocene, when people began to occupy sedentary villages in otherwise mobile foraging populations. Once people began to settle into villages, fundamental changes took place in human social, political, and economic organization. Populations became larger and social organization became much more complex; however, the importance of villages lies in more than their residential primacy. I suggest here that one of the ways in which archaeologists can understand how political economies emerged in middle-range societies may be through analysis of the village, because this is where broader regional processes would have been incorporated into daily life. If the primary processes through which emerging elites can manipulate political economies are exchange, production, and the manipulation of ideology—especially a materialized ideology—all of these should be visible at the local, village level. Therefore, it is important for archaeologists to outline a methodology by which excavations at a local village can be used to better understand the emergence of political economies and power in middle-range societies.

This is not to say that anthropological archaeologists have been unconcerned with anything but tombs and temples. Indeed, since Kent Flannery (1976) edited the volume *The Early Mesoamerican Village*, various research perspectives have been developed in the realm of archaeological theory that intersect at the analysis of a local group (as opposed to the regional group, or regional system). These research strategies, all related in that they narrow the traditional analytical focus from the region to a smaller area, have been called a variety of names such as the "local perspective" (Bermann 1994), the "community perspective" (Kolb and Snead 1997; Canuto and Yaeger 2000), and "rural archaeology" (Schwartz and Falconer 1994). The distinctions between each of these research strategies are ambiguous because they are all intertwined both in their primary assumptions and in their methodologies. What they have in common, however, is their level of analysis: All focus on single communities.

## Villages and Agency in the Andes

One could argue that since the 1980s, Andean archaeology has seen a shift in emphasis from focusing on large urban and ceremonial centers to focusing on both regional settlement patterns and communities outside of the centers of settlement systems. This trend in Andean research parallels a general movement since the 1960s in Americanist archaeology that focuses on regional settlement systems and community patterns rather than on so-called temples and tombs (e.g., Billman 1999). Other research programs complement the regional approach as well. For example, the analysis of prehispanic features across the landscape such as raised fields (Bandy 2005b; Kolata 1994) has greatly enhanced our understanding of the Lake Titicaca region in prehistory.

The focus on settlement systems, or taking a "regional approach" (Bermann 1994:3–6; Billman 1999:131), is critical in archaeological research to evaluate (1) the cultural history of a region, (2) the sociopolitical and economic organization of a prehistoric society, and (3) changes in that organization over time. The regional approach, however, is limited in its ability to evaluate fine-grained data that archaeologists have access to through excavations—especially those fine-grained data that would help us focus on agency.

Obtaining these data requires excavations where people lived and practiced their daily life. The "local perspective" (Bermann 1994, 1997) is a good example of this kind of analysis. This perspective attempts to view the relationship between a sociopolitical and urban capital and smaller sites from the perspective of these subordinate sites (Bermann 1994:11). The broader research goals of the local perspective are to evaluate evolutionary changes in society (in the specific case that Bermann evaluates, Tiwanaku society), and the emphasis on the local level of research is due to the bias in previous research at Tiwanaku, where researchers have conducted decades of what Bermann refers to as the "capital-centric perspective" (Bermann 1994:10). A major assumption of the local perspective is that smaller communities are not passive or simply reactive to larger, regional processes. Indeed, they have their own "developmental trajectories" (Bermann 1994:13), and these trajectories are key to understanding broader societal patterns.

In order to evaluate this segment of society, like all social scientists archaeologists must employ a variety of interpretive scales to build satisfactory models. I refer to the approach taken here as the "village approach" to focus on single communities. While the village approach does not ignore patterns of change at a regional level, it assumes that analyzing smaller settlements is a valuable medium to evaluate human societies. Because a village or community has its own sociopolitical order, economic patterns, and historical trajectories, often very different from those witnessed at other scales, the village approach necessarily complements regional analyses. The village approach provides relatively fine-grained perspectives on social and economic organization, as well as a perspective on agency and the dynamics of power that regional approaches simply cannot provide. Furthermore, a village approach enables the archaeologist to evaluate the ways in which emerging political economies are articulated at a local level.

## Households

Regardless of the name of the approach, archaeologists who focus on smaller scales of analysis than the region must have a primary unit of analysis. Although some approaches have employed entire communities as a single unit of analysis (e.g., Kolb and Snead 1997; Canuto and Yaeger 2000; Kantner and Mahoney 2000), households are more frequently employed. "Household" as an anthropological concept distinct from "family" was first evaluated by anthropologists, who distinguished the two by the fact that one concept resulted from proximity and one from kinship. That is, while the term "household" refers to a "local or spatial group, marked by propinquity," "family" refers to a "kinship group marked by kinship relationships" (Bohannan 1963:78).

Households as analytical units have been used at least implicitly in archaeological research since settlement pattern analysis. In the larger research agenda of settlement archaeology, individual sites were considered a reflection of communities, while individual structures were considered the remains of families — and therefore direct correlates of family organization. Other past attempts to define the household have been more detailed, suggesting different activity areas within households and determining variability between households (Flannery and Winter 1976).

Richard Wilk and William Rathje (1982) first operationalized the concept of households for archaeological research. They defined the household as "the most common social component of subsistence, the smallest and most abundant activity group" and suggested that households are at the scale where individual social groups "articulate directly with economic and ecological processes" (Wilk and Rathje 1982:618). Demonstrating an archaeological perspective, the definition of household by Wilk and Rathje comprises three distinct components: social, material and behavioral. The social component consists of "the demographic unit," which is roughly equivalent to the term "family," while the material component consists of the material goods that accompany and sustain the household, such as the dwelling itself, material possessions, and the material byproducts of daily activities. Finally, the behavioral component of the household coincides with Barbara Bender's "domestic functions" and is simply the activities performed by the household.

Archaeologically, the term "household" was somewhat problematic, however. For example, Bender and others (e.g., Goody 1972) demonstrated that households are not necessarily "housed" under a single roof, and groups that live under one roof do not necessarily cooperate in economic activities. Thus, Wilk and Rathje asserted, archaeologists do not excavate households, but instead they excavate the material remains of individual *dwellings* (Wilk and Rathje 1982:620), an important distinction. This caveat did not limit productive archaeological analysis, however, and ultimately we could define five "categories of function" encompassing the activities that engage households cross-culturally: production, distribution, transmission, reproduction, and consumption.

Of course, all of this assumes that households are essentialist units that allow societies to adapt to their environment, not surprising since most of this early theoretical work was undertaken as part of the techno-functional requirements of a processual archaeology program. Households are more than this, however, as many anthropologists and archaeologists have shown. They are not just the locus of passive, domestic activities performed by females used to perpetuate a domestic group juxtaposed with an arena of active, political activities performed by males (Robin 2003:312). Indeed, archaeologists have shown that many households were the locus of ritual performances and political meetings and they were critical locations for extra-household production in many societies (Robin 2003:312). Because of this, they are an ideal focal point for evaluating agency in middle-range societies.

The shift in theoretical orientation commonly taken when analyzing the household has resulted in a variety of anthropological problems being addressed by the household approach, including the evaluation of ethnicity (Aldenderfer and Stanish 1993; Reycraft 2005), community organization (Bawden 1982), power and the organization of craft activities (Janusek 1999, 2003), local evidence of status and the maintenance of power relations (Hirth 1993; Robin 2003:320), social complexity in the rural context (Iannone and Connell 2003), and migration and factional competition (Van Gijseghem 2006). Here, using households as an analytical unit, I look to a single village to evaluate agency and the political economy in Nasca society.

In the Andes, the household archaeology approach has been, and continues to be, very influential as archaeologists directing major research programs have embraced its tenets (e.g., Stanish 1992; Bermann 1994;

Janusek 1999; Bawden 1982; Moore 1985; Van Gijseghem 2001, 2004).
Ethnographic and ethnohistoric evidence demonstrates that nuclear family households are the fundamental economic units in Andean societies
(Allen 1988; Isbell 1977; Mayer 2002; Spalding 1984). They are the primary productive, consumptive, and exchange units in ethnographic examples of Andean society. As the principal economic unit in traditional Andean society, the household is an essential unit for the archaeologist to use
in evaluating economic and political relationships within archaeological
settlements (Stanish 1989:7).

Because the ethnographic household is difficult to recover with archaeological data, archaeologists have modified the ethnological concept
of household to one that is appropriate for archaeological analysis: the
"archaeological household" (see, for example, Stanish 1992). In sum,
there are three components essential to the concept of the household: coresidence, domestic functions, and familial relations (Stanish 1989:8).
Archaeologists have access to evidence of at least two of these three components: co-residentiality and domestic functions. Thus, we can define the
archaeological household as the minimum co-residential domestic group
(Stanish 1989:11), and in order for this domestic group to be visible
archaeologically, it should meet the following criteria:

1. There should be spatial segregation of individual structures or
   structure groups at a particular site.
2. These structures or structure groups should contain material correlates of domestic activities such as storage and food preparation.
3. These basic structure groups and material correlates should be repeated within a community.

Once we define archaeological households, I suggest that through the
analysis of archaeological households at a single village we can evaluate
agency, power, and political economy in middle-range societies. If we
assume that all individuals have the capacity to make decisions and that
the emergence of institutionalized inequality is due to the sum of actions
and choices of individuals, then the best place to evaluate this emergence
is at the village, where daily life is practiced. Below I outline how archaeologists can identify emerging political economies from the perspective of
a village. Specifically, I show how status, political economy, and feasting

and ritual can be seen at the village level and what implications this has for emerging power in middle-range societies.

## Power in the Village

One method to identify power in villages is by measuring status differences among households. High status is directly correlated to power over other individuals, whether status is related to authoritative or allocative resources. Specifically, archaeologists have outlined various criteria to identify status among households. In comparing households, first it should be noted that there may be some structures within a community that are larger than others. Ethnographically and ethnohistorically, individuals of higher status tend to have larger households than those of lower status (Coupland and Banning 1996); a larger household size results in much larger physical structures. Second, there may be structures that contain a variety of specialized architectural features, are subdivided into public and private space, or have had a greater labor investment in their construction (Abrams 1989). And finally, there may be structures whose associated artifact assemblage contains goods of higher value and more items overall, since higher-status households can potentially consume more while producing less than lower-status households (Hirth 1993). These valuable goods can be in the form of "exotics," or goods that are produced within the community with higher labor investments. All three of these expectations can serve as indicators of higher status not only for households, but also for individuals and families.

## Subsistence and Political Economy

Measures of status also have implications for the emergence of political economies. In middle-range societies, goods and services can be mobilized to support ephemeral classes of high-status individuals or families establishing an incipient political economy. On the other hand, the economic system can lack the features of a true political economy and form a subsistence economy that is organized to meet the basic needs of a household in terms of a domestic mode of production.

Because the subsistence economy is organized to meet the basic needs of the household, at its simplest, it is organized in terms of a "domestic mode of production" (Sahlins 1972). In this mode of production, households are essentially self-sufficient, as they are a "microcosm" of the larger economy in terms of gender and age groups and therefore do not require production interdependency between households. If households were economically independent of one another in a prehistoric community, we would expect the following archaeological correlates: (1) Each defined household would have the necessities to sustain a single domestic unit, including storage facilities, food processing and cooking tools, and the necessary sustenance procurement technology. (2) There should be no communal storage facilities or locations of communal food processing and/or cooking equipment.

If, on the other hand, households were economically *interdependent*, we would instead expect that first of all, not all defined households would have the necessary artifacts and features to sustain a single domestic unit; second, there would be communal storage, food processing, and/or cooking facilities or production areas. Moreover, communal facilities would be larger than typical residential units since they would need to accommodate more people than a typical household.

If goods and services were mobilized to establish an emerging political economy, we would expect various archaeological signatures. A high quantity of nonlocal goods may be present if exchange was a means through which emerging leaders gained status. These nonlocal goods should be concentrated in households of high-status individuals. If production were an avenue towards an emerging political economy, then we might see evidence for efforts to monopolize the production of goods.

## Feasting and Ritual

Feasting and group-oriented ritual are instruments of change and arenas for the emergence, contestation, and maintenance of power. Therefore, the analysis of feasting and ritual at the village level is imperative. Given the above discussion, we would expect there to be heightened concerns for religiously charged ritual in the formation and institutionalization of inequality.

Archaeological evidence for feasting and ritual may be in the form of open or carefully defined spaces, distinct architectural features, special structures, or ritual and ceremonial paraphernalia (Aldenderfer 1991). Furthermore, if group-oriented ceremony transpired with the entire community participating, we would expect architectural features and structures dedicated to this activity to be prominent, perhaps centrally located, and fairly distinct. If these ceremonial activities were instead restricted to select individuals or households, we would expect structures and architectural features reserved for these activities to also be distinct, but to be located near the residences of the people who had access to them. If distinct architectural features or structures are not identified within the community, then one could argue that ritual activities were confined to other loci.

Additionally, vessel assemblages may be indicative of feasting and ritual. High quantities of serving, storing, and cooking vessels were likely to have supported participants in feasts, and different kinds of vessels may have been exclusive to feasting activities.

## Summary

I have argued thus far that the emergence of the political economy in middle-range societies may rest on several interrelated factors: exchange, craft production, and ideologically charged feasting and ritual. In middle-range societies, we would expect that emerging political economies would be visible at residential villages and I have argued that the analytical unit at villages is the archaeological household. In the following chapter, I will turn to the archaeological context of the region and outline our current understanding of Nasca based on more than a century of archaeological and art historical research. One salient point that will become readily apparent is that a village approach is sorely lacking in Nasca studies.

# 3

# *Ancient Nasca*

## THE ARCHAEOLOGICAL CONTEXT

THE CENTRAL ANDES COMPRISE "extreme" topography that includes the Pacific desert coast, the world's second-tallest mountain range
after the Himalayas, and the far western edge of the largest rainforest in
the western hemisphere. This tremendous diversity is condensed into a
wildly undulating and steep terrain that encompasses no more than three
hundred kilometers from ocean to jungle as the condor flies. The natural
setting provided by the Andes mountains and its surrounding regions has
had profound influence on the nature of human settlement there from the
beginning of prehistory to the modern era.

It was within this context that ancient Nasca developed. Here, I intro-
duce the Nasca region and the archaeological and historical context of this
study. First, I summarize the local environmental context. Following that,
I provide an analysis of our contemporary understanding of Nasca society
based on recent research.

## The Nasca Region

Ancient Nasca flourished along the south coast of Peru, usually defined as
that area comprising the modern Department of Ica and including the
Acarí Valley in the Department of Arequipa (Silverman 1996). The south
coast, although not a locus of autonomous state emergence, was the setting for the independent development of several complex societies, most
notably Paracas in the Early Horizon, Nasca in the Early Intermediate
Period, and the Tiza polity in the Late Intermediate Period (fig. 3.1). The
Wari and Inca empires also occupied this area of what is now Peru during
their respective dominance of the central Andes.

The heartland of Nasca society, or the "Nasca Region," is situated in
the Ica and Río Grande de Nasca drainages. The latter is the southernmost

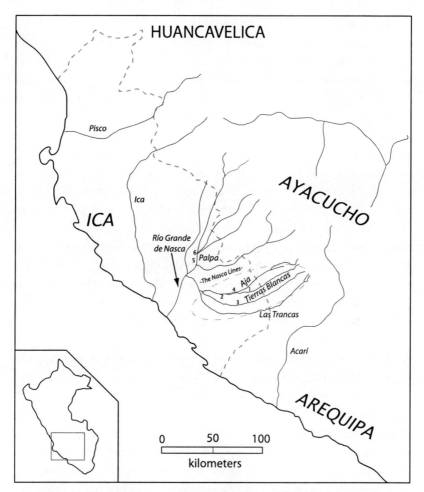

FIGURE 3.1 The south coast of Peru is encompassed by the modern Department of Ica (dotted line) and the Acarí Valley. Early in research, the Nasca
polity was presumed to reign over this territory. It is now known that the
Nasca heartland was limited to the Río Grande de Nasca and Ica drainages,
including their tributaries. The focus of this book is the encircled Southern
Nasca Region (SNR). 1 = Marcaya, 2 = Cahuachi, 3 = Pajonal Alto, 4 =
La Tiza, 5 = Los Molinos, 6 = La Muña.

of these two drainages and is comprised of a number of smaller rivers that flow together to form the principal drainage, which subsequently flows into the Pacific Ocean. For convenience, researchers divide the Grande drainage into northern and southern groups of tributaries (Schreiber and Lancho Rojas 2003). The southern group is composed of the Aja and Tierras Blancas rivers, which together join to form the Nasca, the Taruga, and the Las Trancas rivers. I refer to this region as the Southern Nasca Region (or SNR), and this area comprises the principal focus of this book.

Historically, the Nasca region has been described by various authors as a transition zone between the Pacific coast and the highlands (Kosok 1965:50). It is essentially desert intersected by riverbeds, which are in places completely lacking in water (Schreiber and Lancho Rojas 2003). The Oficina Nacional de Evaluación de Recursos Naturales (ONERN) of Peru classifies the Rio Grande de Nasca drainage below two thousand meters as a "pre-montane desert formation." The climate of the region in general is warm, with an average annual temperature of 21.3 degrees Centigrade, and as a whole, the region is very dry. Precipitation is scarce and increases as one moves east up the Andes, ranging from just a few millimeters in the lower elevations to 125 millimeters annually in the upper reaches of the region.

The area's rivers originate high in the Andes and the water flow of the coastal valleys is entirely dependent on rainfall in the highlands. Thus, the rivers in the Nasca region are ephemeral, only intermittently flowing. The Aja River has the greatest volume of the four rivers that comprise the SNR, with 30 million cubic meters of water per year. By comparison, the Río Grande has an annual flow of 198 million cubic meters (see Schreiber and Lancho Rojas 2003 for a summary). Comparing this water regime to rivers on the north coast, such as the Chicama, with its annual flow of more than 800 million cubic meters, one appreciates the limitations ancient people faced in the region.

Technically, the rivers in the SNR are "influent" streams because of the transmission loss in river volume as the water flows into the lower foothills due to deep valley alluvium (Schreiber and Lancho Rojas 2003). This causes the rivers to flow partially above the surface of the ground; at the base of the foothills where the alluvium is deep, the rivers are reduced to a trickle until they seem to disappear below the surface. Based on the presence of surface water, the region's valleys are divided into four sections:

the *upper valley*, where water is always available; the *zone of infiltration*, where water is often available but in years of prolonged drought may not be; the dry *middle valley*, which never has surface water except during seasonal flooding; and the *lower valley*, where water re-emerges (Schreiber and Lancho Rojas 2003).

For a time, the overall lack of arable land was seen by scholars as a major hindrance to the development of large complex societies in this region of the Andes. Paul Kosok (1965:58–59) even suggested that the smaller valleys of the Río Grande de Nasca were so sporadically watered that "conditions never arose whereby a secular state could appear." But although the environment appears inhospitable, Nasca society developed — indeed flourished — in this dry context, and as we will see, the challenges of a marginal environment became an important part of Nasca ideology.

## Ancient Nasca—A Brief Reconstruction of Prehistory

Early settlement of the south coast of Peru is poorly understood, though humans must have been here shortly after small groups of foragers entered the South American continent sometime during the late Pleistocene. There was a clear Archaic occupation in the Nasca region, at least on the coast, comprised of small temporary encampments focusing on marine resources and having ties to the highlands with the exchange of highland obsidian. Inland, the Archaic occupation of the south coast is poorly understood, though several sites have been recorded with dates as early as 4400 BC at La Esmeralda (Isla Cuadrado 1990) and 2475–2135 BC (calibrated 2Σ) at Upanca (Vaughn and Linares Grados 2006; table 3.1). Whereas elsewhere in Peru, large coastal monuments were being erected (Shady Solis et al. 2001), the settlement of this region of the Andes appears to have been limited to temporary encampments.

The Initial Period (1800–800 BC) is poorly understood in the Nasca region. Throughout the Andes, this period was momentous in the development of complex societies (Moseley 2001). Large-scale irrigation, the use of pottery, and monumental constructions were intensified throughout the Andean coast during the Initial Period. At sites such as Sechín Alto and El Paraiso, ancient residents constructed monumental and ceremonial architecture, indeed some of the largest buildings in the New World at the time (at Sechín Alto). Most of this activity occurred on the north coast and in the southern highlands.

The south coast did not experience similar developments, and there is a dearth of sites found from during this time. Settlement is known, especially in the Acarí drainage, where a small settlement called Hacha has been recorded (Riddel and Valdez Cardenas 1987), and at Erizo, located in the Ica Valley. The Initial Period coincides with a long drought (see Eitel et al. 2005) and this increasing desiccation may have prevented long-term, permanent settlement in the region.

The Early Horizon (ca. 800–100 BC) represents the first extra-regional integration of the Andes in prehistory. This integration came in the form of what is thought to be a religious cult based in the northern highlands, known as Chavín. Because the Peruvian chronology was reconstructed from ceramic styles from the master sequence in Ica, the Early Horizon technically begins when the artistic influence of Chavín first appears in the ceramics of the Ica Valley, although Chavín's influence likely began earlier in areas closer to Chavín itself. Specifically, this influence begins with the appearance of resin-painted pottery in the Ica Valley sequence.

The south coast manifestation of the Chavín phenomenon is known as the Paracas culture. Excavations by Julio C. Tello on the Paracas Peninsula made this culture famous by revealing elaborate textiles known as Paracas Necropolis and Cavernas traditions. While these were originally thought to be successive temporal phases, they have now been reclassified as separate cultures that are roughly contemporaneous. The complexity of the textiles is an indication of increased craft specialization during this time (Paul 1991). Towards the latter part of the Early Horizon, there is a substantial increase in settlements in the north (Cook 1999; DeLeonardis 1997) and the SNR appears to have witnessed an increase in population as well. Hendrik Van Gijseghem (2006) interprets this dramatic increase in population as the result of a migration from the north. The migrants established new settlements throughout the SNR.

The Early Intermediate Period (or "EIP," ca. 100 BC–AD 750) is a time in which the ideological integration of Chavín seems to have dissipated, and independent, regional development of local polities takes its place. This pattern is most pronounced on the north coast of Peru, where Gallinazo-Moche civilization reached its apex, as well as on the south coast, where despite presumed limiting environmental factors, Nasca culture emerged as a distinct polity, became fully developed, and subsequently declined. The development of Nasca society during this time period also coincides with an apparent regional desiccation (Eitel et al. 2005). Indeed, the EIP and Middle Horizon have been defined as the driest periods in the region during the Holocene with the exception of the modern era.

The Nasca sequence is generally divided into three Nasca "cultures," each corresponding to major changes in local settlement patterns and ceramic iconography (Schreiber and Lancho Rojas 2003). Archaeologists divide Nasca culture history into phases 2–7 and group these phases into the Early (phases 2–4), Middle (phase 5) and Late (phases 6–7) Nasca cultures (see Schreiber 1999). Lawrence Dawson originally seriated Nasca ceramics into nine phases (see Rowe 1960), but recent research has revealed that phase 1 is culturally associated with the earlier Paracas tradition (see Van Gijseghem 2004, 2006), and phases 8 and 9 are associated with the Middle Horizon (Schreiber 1998). Early, Middle, and Late Nasca are labeled "cultures" because the phases included in each correspond to major changes in local settlement patterns and ceramic iconography (Schreiber and Lancho Rojas 2003).

Based on settlement patterns in the SNR during Early Nasca, the majority of people lived in small villages located in the upper valleys of the SNR that relied on seasonal flooding from highland rainfall (Schreiber and Lancho Rojas 2003). This system nourished crops on an annual basis, and during the period there emerged a loose alliance of multi-village polities (chiefdoms) with a mixed agro-pastoral economy focusing on maize, the exploitation of marine resources, and camelid herding (Vaughn 2005). Villages were integrated into a larger cultural system through pilgrimages to Cahuachi, Nasca's ceremonial center.

The hallmark of Nasca society is its polychrome pottery (Proulx 2006). Nasca pottery is rightly famous for the highly refined technique used in its construction, as vessel walls are very thin (usually around four millimeters), and Nasca artisans used a palette of fifteen distinct mineral-based pigments (some pots can have up to thirteen on a single vessel) to paint natural and supernatural motifs on a wide range of vessel shapes. All iconographers agree that the pottery was Nasca's principal medium through which ideology was displayed and disseminated. Using the terminology presented in chapter 2, one might say Nasca pottery appears to be "materialized ideology." However, while the pottery was very finely made, everyone appears to have access to this particular artifact type, since polychrome pottery is found in large quantities on the surfaces of ordinary domestic sites. This high quantity suggests that polychrome pottery may have been an integral part of Nasca domestic life, a point that I will return to later in this chapter.

Three major transitions occurred in Middle Nasca (phase 5). First, artisans added innovations to ceramic iconography that included a greater emphasis on abstract rather than depictive motifs (Roark 1965). Second, monumental construction ceased at Cahuachi (Silverman 1993), though populations continued to use the site for ceremonial purposes and for burying the dead (Ogburn 1993). Third, *puquios*, aqueducts that tapped subsurface water, were constructed in the middle valleys, allowing people to move into this area for the first time (Schreiber and Lancho Rojas 2003). Finally, the health of populations decreased, as is evidenced by greater frequencies of enamel hypoplasia and dental caries that indicate an increasing reliance on cariogenic foods such as maize (Kellner 2002:107). During Late Nasca, the SNR witnessed an increase in conflict and a reorganization as populations aggregated into a few large villages in each valley (Schreiber 1998:263). This increase in conflict is also seen through a higher frequency of cranial trauma in skeletal populations (Kellner 2002:108).

The Wari empire expanded into the Nasca region during the beginning of the Middle Horizon at approximately AD 750 (Schreiber 2005). With this expansion, Nasca society underwent a massive cultural upheaval that resulted in major shifts in political structure throughout the region (Conlee 2005). Wari established two colonies in the SNR, one at Pacheco and one at Pataraya (Schreiber 2005), the former a political and ritual capital, and the latter a colony established for economic intensification. Local populations apparently resisted this encounter (Conlee and Schreiber 2006; Isla Cuadrado 2001) and ultimately, when Wari collapsed, these centers were deserted.

The collapse of the Wari empire generated yet another reorganization in the SNR (Conlee 2003). In contrast to the EIP and Middle Horizon, during the Late Intermediate Period (or "LIP"), focus shifted away from elaborate ceramics and textiles with complex iconography that materialized ideology. Tiza, the local polity of the SNR during the LIP, comprised the large urban center La Tiza with smaller villages such as Pajonal Alto composed of local elites (Conlee 2003, 2005). Long-distance exchange was brisk and included many goods such as ceramics, obsidian from the highlands, and *Spondylus*. These goods were exchanged for imported fine-ware ceramics (mostly from Ica to the north), marine resources, and dyed camelid fiber.

Following the LIP, the Inca empire entered the south coast in AD 1476 (Menzel 1959), met little resistance in the region, and established two centers: one at Caxamarca, which is today referred to as Paredones, and one at La Legua in the Ingenio Valley. While originally thought to be an administrative center, Paredones is now considered to be the private re-treat of an Inca emperor (Schreiber and Lancho Rojas 2003). It is thought that there were few changes made to the region politically and econom-ically by the Inca. Indeed, apparently local elites rather than Inca admin-istrators were responsible for administration of the region (Conlee 2005; Schreiber and Lancho Rojas 2003).

As can be seen in this brief overview of Nasca prehistory, much has been learned in the past several decades of archaeological research. My primary focus in this book is Early Nasca (phases 2–4). There are two reasons for this. First, this is the "culture that comes to mind when most people hear the word 'Nasca'" (Schreiber and Lancho Rojas 2003:14). More importantly, this is the time period for which we have the most evidence for an emerging political economy and power. As such I now turn to our current understanding of Early Nasca based on the results of the last several decades of research. In particular, I focus on the issues described in the previous chapter: political economy and power.

## Early Nasca Society

The extent of Nasca society was originally defined by the distribution of fine polychrome ceramics of the Nasca style throughout the south coast of Peru from the Pisco Valley in the north to the Acarí valley in the south (e.g., Rowe 1963; Sawyer 1961). Despite this widespread distribution, recent research demonstrates that Nasca cultural development was pri-marily limited to the Ica and Rio Grande drainages.

Nasca is perhaps most famous to the general public and even to profes-sionals for its geoglyphs, or "Nasca Lines," giant figures made on the dry desert pampa by removing rocks with a reddish-brown "desert varnish" to expose light sediment below. The monumental lines were constructed in the shape of birds (e.g., hummingbirds [see fig. 1.1], condors), insects (such as spiders), and marine and terrestrial mammals (such as killer whales and monkeys), geometric figures, as well as straight lines and trapezoids (Aveni 2000; see fig. 1.1). The most famous of the lines are located on the raised pampa between the Nasca and Ingenio drainages, with the majority of these figures constructed in Early Nasca (Clarkson 1990), though hundreds of additional geoglyphs have recently been recorded in the Palpa, Viscas, and Grande drainages (Isla Cuadrado and Reindel 2005; Lambers 2006).

An enormous literature ranging from the scholarly to the ridiculous has focused on the function and meaning of the lines. Absurd suggestions include the infamous "theory" by Erich von Daniken that the lines were used as extraterrestrial runways. Some of the more serious but unlikely suggestions include that they were astronomical calendars (Reiche 1968) and that the trapezoids pointed to underground water sources (Johnson et al. 2002). Neither of these two hypotheses have held up to close scrutiny, however (Aveni 2000; Schreiber and Lancho Rojas 2006:92).

Though the lines were probably used for myriad purposes (Isla Cuadrado and Reindel 2005:66; Lambers 2006), based on ethnographic analogy and extensive contextual analysis, the most robust anthropological interpretation of the Nasca Lines is that they were ritual pathways used for the worship of mountain gods who controlled rain in traditional Andean belief systems. Johan Reinhard argues that the lines were most likely manifestations of the worship of mountain gods, or *apus*, who controlled rain, clouds, lightning, and other important weather-related phenomena in traditional Andean belief systems (Reinhard 1988:365). Drawing from Andean ethnography and ethnohistory, Reinhard argues that the geoglyphs were ritual pathways related to religious practices enacted to ensure that water would be provisioned for people and their crops (Reinhard 1988). Johny Isla Cuadrado and Markus Reindel (2005:66), departing from other researchers, believe that the lines represent a form of "specialization" organized by a centralized government.

The Nasca Lines were not the only manifestation of the fundamental concern with agricultural fertility and water in Nasca society. For example, while "trophy" heads offer material evidence of apparent violence, they

also seem to be symbolically related to agricultural fertility. Early interpretations suggested that they were trophies taken in battle, much like those
taken by the ethnographic Jivaro, located in the tropical forests of Ecuador
(Proulx 1971). However, several recent studies suggest that many known
trophy heads came from women and children, not just young males (Kellner 2002; Williams et al. 2001). This implies, at least, that heads were not
taken in full-scale battle, but perhaps in small-scale raids. For example, an
analysis of trophy heads from cemeteries in the Las Trancas Valley collected by Julio C. Tello revealed many females and children in the samples,
suggesting that most trophy heads in Early Nasca were actually not related
to organized warfare (Kellner 2002). Similarly, additional analyses of trophy heads collected by Alfred Kroeber during the Marshall Field Expedition to Peru provide little evidence for organized warfare in Early Nasca
(Williams, et al. 2001; Forgey 2006).

No matter how they were obtained, trophy heads, at least in Early
Nasca, appear to have been symbolically linked to fertility (Carmichael
1992; DeLeonardis 2000). Trophy heads are conceptualized by archaeologists as part of what Patrick Carmichael (1992) refers to as the "life to
death continuum," where blood from decapitated heads was seen as essential for human and plant fertility. Iconographically, clear links exist between trophy heads and the growth of important crops. For example,
numerous symbols in the "sprouting head" motif are found on painted
ceramics on which Nasca artisans depicted plants growing directly out of
trophy heads (Carmichael 1994). Trophy heads were integral to certain
rituals, given archaeological evidence for caches of heads found throughout the Nasca region (Browne, et al. 1993). With little evidence for warfare in Early Nasca, trophy heads are generally seen as fertility symbols
connected to beliefs about ancestors and fertility (see Silverman and
Proulx 2002:149; c.f., Proulx 2001).

Also well known, of course, is polychrome pottery. Ceramic iconography is well known because of many studies of museum specimens by
archaeologists and art historians. Common motifs on the pottery include
agricultural products such as beans, chili peppers (ají), and maize. Also
common are fauna that are associated with water in Andean belief systems. For example, fish, killer whales, and other creatures from the ocean
are often depicted on Nasca polychromes. Birds such as the swallow are
another common motif. Swallows are associated with water because they

appear in the region during the wet season, when the waters from rains in the highlands flow down the mountains.

Other motifs, including geometric figures and supernatural creatures with provocative names such as the "anthropomorphic mythical being," the "horrible bird," and the "serpentine creature" (see Proulx 1968, 2006), appear frequently on the polychrome pottery as well. Contextual analysis of polychromes with these natural and supernatural motifs demonstrates that "almost the entire corpus of Nasca iconography is a sacred, inter-related visual system with its referents tied to the dominating themes of water and propagation" (Carmichael 1998:224). As such, Nasca poly-chromes are well known as the "principal vehicle for Nasca ideology" (Carmichael 1998).

While polychrome pottery appears to have played this role in Nasca society and its manufacture involved a high degree of technical skill, the pottery was not simply reserved for ceremonial contexts and burials, nor was it merely an elite good. In fact, pottery deposited as grave goods shows use prior to being interred in tombs (Carmichael 1988). Research-ers have noted the presence of a large amount of polychromes on the surface of habitation sites when compared to smaller quantities of utili-tarian vessels (Carmichael 1994:231, 1998:216; Silverman 1993:339). Some have suggested that Nasca polychromes were part of an "open, shared system to which all members of society had access" (Carmichael 1995:171, 1998).

*But Where Are the People?*

Nasca has been known to the Western world in art historical, archaeologi-cal, and even lay circles for more than one hundred years as a result of its geoglyphs, finely made polychrome pottery, and other features such as trophy heads — but very little was known about the people who made the lines and pottery until relatively recently. Settlement survey over the past decade has recorded literally thousands of sites dating from 4000 BC all the way to the colonial period in the sixteenth century. Surveys have been undertaken in all major river valleys in the south coast, and here I focus on the SNR where a University of California, Santa Barbara team of archae-ologists, led by Katharina Schreiber, has been undertaking a full-coverage survey for about two decades (see summary in Schreiber and Lancho Rojas 2003).

During Early Nasca (from AD 1–450, ceramic phases 2–4), settlement in the SNR is characterized by small villages (usually covering less than a few hectares) dotting the foothills of the Andes as they made their way up into the highlands. Settlements were strongly tied to the valleys, where water was available, and the region was dominated by the large ceremonial center of Cahuachi, located in the lower Nasca valley dozens of kilometers from the primary settlements.

Excavations over the past few decades have revealed that Cahuachi, with its dozens of platform mounds and pyramids, served as the ceremonial center of Nasca. At close to 250 hectares in size, the site itself is immense and is composed of large temple mounds, including the "Great Pyramid" and the "Great Temple" plazas, as well as other architectural features that have slowly been covered by valley alluvium over time by strong prevailing winds.

Several researchers—most notably William Duncan Strong in the 1950s, Helaine Silverman in the 1980s, and Giuseppe Orefici from the 1980s to the present—have undertaken excavations at the site. Despite early suggestions that Cahuachi was the capital of the Nasca state (Rowe 1963), excavations have demonstrated that the center was not an urban metropolis with thousands and thousands of residents. Instead, Silverman (1993) has made a case that Cahuachi was a sparsely populated pilgrimage center and that religious ceremonies were regularly held there. Basing her argument on a comparison with a long tradition of pilgrimage centers in the Andes beginning about five thousand years ago, she maintains that people from around the south coast made pilgrimages to the site, participated in feasting and ceremonies, and eventually returned to their residences scattered throughout the region.

The emergence of Cahuachi as a sacred place is not surprising given its location. Today, the site is known by locals as a place " '*donde aflora el agua*,' where the water comes to the surface" (Silverman 1993:305). The direct association of the most important site in the Nasca landscape with water and hence the agricultural cycle is not insignificant. Katharina Schreiber and Josué Lancho Rojas (1995:249) state that "it is no surprise to us that the region was sacred to the prehistoric inhabitants; the emergence of the river . . . in the midst of some of the driest territory on the coast of Peru, must have had great religious significance."

There is little disagreement among archaeologists that Cahuachi was a sacred, ceremonial space. The numerous temple mounds, plazas, and other structures at Cahuachi clearly point to a ceremonial and sacred function. Other lines of evidence also clearly demonstrate that Cahuachi was a pilgrimage and ceremonial center: (1) the evidence for feasting at the site, (2) the nonfunerary ceremonial caches that have been found in excavations there, (3) the number of burials that are found in this region when compared to other locales in the SNR, and (4) the fact that the site seems to have been a locus of polychrome pottery production.

*Feasting at Cahuachi.* One of the primary activities that took place at Cahuachi was ceremonial feasting. If we turn to ceramic iconography, there is evidence that suggests that large ceremonies involving feasting were a key aspect of Nasca ceremonial life. For example, Richard Townsend (1985:125, fig. 7) reports a bowl that depicts some kind of agricultural ceremony. According to Townsend, the ceramic artisan "intended to represent a costumed figure such as those who appeared in the public plazas, and perhaps also in agricultural fields, to celebrate the great annual feasts of the Nazca region" (Townsend 1985:125). In another example, Patrick Carmichael (1998:224, fig. 13) describes a particular double-spout bottle depicting a scene with an individual holding a panpipe surrounded by ceramic containers and people playing musical instruments. Carmichael interprets this scene as a festival.

Archaeological evidence supports this type of interpretation of Nasca iconography and demonstrates that large ceremonial feasts took place at Cahuachi. In some of the earliest scientific excavations at Cahuachi, William Duncan Strong reported finding "broken panpipes, llama remains, bird plumage, and other apparently feasting and sacrificial materials" (Strong 1957:31). More recently, Lidio Valdez Cardenas (1994) reported on excavations carried out at Cahuachi under the direction of Orefici in 1986. The excavations, located near Strong's Cut 9 from excavations earlier in the century, revealed a small circular structure with abundant food remains, including maize (*Zea mays*), beans (*Phaseolus lunatus*, *Phaseolus vulgaris*), and camelid bones from all parts of the animal — all suggestive of a brief feasting episode (Valdez Cardenas 1994). Finally, Silverman

(1993; also see Silverman and Proulx 2002) interprets most of the material remains at Cahuachi as relating to periodic pilgrimage and feasting.

Large public spaces appropriate for feasting are abundant at Cahuachi. For example, the "Great Temple" (designated "Unit 2" by Silverman and "Y5" by Orefici) is flanked at the bottom by a plaza measuring forty-five by seventy-five meters. These kinds of public spaces are not present on Early Nasca habitations (Van Gijseghem and Vaughn 2006) and seem to be exclusive to this ceremonial center.

*Ceremonial Caches at Cahuachi.* Other evidence of Cahuachi's sacred and ceremonial nature lies in the number of ceremonial caches that have been found in excavations there. Again, Strong's excavations in the 1950s revealed an enormous textile woven from a single cloth that was approximately sixty meters long and eighteen meters wide buried in sterile soil to the west of the "Great Temple" (Strong 1957:14). Elena Phipps estimates that more than 1700 miles of yarn would have been needed to weave this cloth, requiring an estimated 44,000 hours of spinning, or roughly five years of labor (Phipps 1997:114).

Orefici in his excavations at Cahuachi found two large deposits in the early 1990s. In 1991, his team found a cache that contained sixty-four camelids, all buried with necks bent backwards and oriented towards the east (Orefici and Drusini 2003). In 1994, the excavations of the project found a cache of twenty-seven large panpipes measuring between seventy and eighty-seven centimeters.

In her excavations of the Unit 19 mound at Cahuachi, Silverman encountered a cache of twenty-three guinea pigs (called cuy). The preserved cuy were decapitated and had long slits up their abdomens. Their inner organs were removed, leading Silverman to suggest that "the feature is strongly reminiscent of modern-day divining and curing practices in the Andes, which suggests that the guinea pigs were used in a magical / religious rite" (Silverman 1993:168). Also found in excavations at Cahuachi were other caches containing maize, huarango seeds and pods, as well as trophy heads (Silverman 1993:172, 187, and 220).

Finally, Mary Frame (2004) has recently reported a cache of Early Nasca dresses and shawls from Cahuachi excavated by Orefici in 1998. The cache, found in the temple mound designated "Y16" by Orefici's excavations, contained forty complete and fragmentary remains of women's

dresses, eight shawls, container cloths, and a bundle containing unfin-
ished textiles. The garments within the cache are clearly associated with
death, fertility, abundance, and water. For example, some appear to have
been stained with libations, and some were filled with charred black beans
(*Phaseolus vulgaris*). Black beans replaced a corpse within a bundle of
Nasca textiles at a burial at Wari Kayan on the Paracas Peninsula (Tello
and Mejia 1979). "In the symbolic code of ritual burial at the Necropolis
site, the substitution of beans for a human body suggests that the buried
corpses within the mummy bundles were conceptually likened to seeds
that would regenerate" (Frame 2004:37). Ultimately, Frame concludes
that the cache is evidence of a ritual domain that was centered on women.

The caches at Cahuachi are more than just another line of evidence for
Cahuachi's ceremonial nature. They are material evidence for an ideology obsessed with agriculture and fertility. As Frame (2004:14) states,
"[m]any caches, particularly those involving bloodletting and botanical foodstuffs, appear to propitiate for agricultural abundance, perhaps
through the metaphoric associations between heads/seeds and blood/
water."

*Cemeteries at Cahuachi.* A third piece of evidence that demonstrates Cahuachi's sacred/ceremonial nature is the number of burials located there.
Extensive cemeteries are situated both up and down valley from Cahuachi
to a distance of almost ten kilometers each way (Schreiber and Lancho
Rojas 2003:15).

While Silverman and Orefici emphasize the fact that Cahuachi was
primarily used during Early Nasca because this is when the major construction events of the site took place, there is clear evidence for use of
the site after Early Nasca. This can be found in occupations such as the
"Room of the Posts" (Silverman 1993), as well as the quantity of later
materials that Orefici's excavations are recovering (e.g., Orefici and Drusini 2003: fig. 43 e–h). Furthermore, the cemeteries surrounding the site
date to all time periods.

*Pottery Production at Cahuachi.* Finally, my own work has revealed that
Cahuachi was a locus of an excess of polychrome pottery production
during at least the Early Nasca phases. I, along with colleagues, undertook
a survey of potting clays in the region and compared their chemical com-

position to ceramics found on the surface of residential sites (Vaughn and Neff 2004; Vaughn et al. 2006). We found that a clay within four kilometers of Cahuachi matched the chemical signature of these polychromes. Four kilometers is within the ethnographic upper limit of clay transport (see Arnold 1985), and we concluded that given the nature of materials found at Cahuachi — including paintbrushes, caches of pigments and unfired clay, small kilns, and other pottery-making materials (Orefici and Drusini 2003:144) — Cahuachi was a source of this production. The production of the "principal purveyor of ideology" at the location in the region with all the trappings of power is not insignificant, a point that I will return to later.

## Elite Residence at Cahuachi?

It is clear that Cahuachi was a sacred, ceremonial place. But was it merely that? A growing body of evidence suggests that it was actually the elites of Nasca society themselves who lived at Cahuachi. In fact, Silverman — who was the champion of the empty ceremonial center model — originally suggested that there may have been elites living at Cahuachi. She likens Cahuachi to Pachacamac (Silverman 1993:311–312), the paramount Andean pilgrimage center first constructed in the Early Intermediate Period and later utilized extensively by the Inca empire (Shimada 1991). Silverman argues that certain buildings at Cahuachi may have functioned as elite residences and could have been the settings for "dramatic rituals, administrative hubs, and the places where visiting dignitaries were received, leaders installed, tribute presented, and captives displayed and dispensed" (Silverman 1993:312).

A growing cadre of archaeologists who work on the south coast have suggested that Cahuachi was indeed an elite residence (Isla Cuadrado and Reindel 2006; Reindel and Isla Cuadrado 2006; Schreiber and Lancho Rojas 2003). This would certainly fit well with the model of Early Nasca as a middle-range society with a central ceremonial center and autonomous villages coming together on occasion for the sake of pilgrimage and group-oriented ceremony. It also fits well with John Rowe's (1963) original discussion of the nature of Andean ceremonial centers, which he described as "a grouping of public buildings housing common facilities, such as shrines, meeting places, markets, and law courts, which is used

TABLE 3.1 Andean and regional chronology. Environmental data from a recent study by Eitler et al. (2005) are included to contextualize major environmental changes in the region.

| Horizons and Intermediate Periods | Local Period | Culture | Phases | Paleoclimate (Eitler et al. 2005) | Approximate Dates |
|---|---|---|---|---|---|
| Late Horizon | -Inca- | Inca | n/a | arid (n < 50 mm) | AD 1476–1532 |
| Late Intermediate Period | -Tiza- | Tiza | n/a | semi-arid (n = 150–200 mm) | AD 1000–1476 |
| Middle Horizon | -Loro- | Loro, Wari | Nasca 8, MH 1-2 | arid (n < 100 mm) | AD 750–1000 |
| Early Intermediate Period | -Nasca- | Late Nasca | Nasca 6-7 | arid (n < 100 mm) | AD 550–750 |
|  |  | Middle Nasca | Nasca 5 |  | AD 450–550 |
|  |  | Early Nasca | Nasca 2-4 |  | AD 1–450 |
| Early Horizon | -Formative- | Proto Nasca Paracas | Nasca 1 | arid (n < 150 mm) | 100 BC–AD 1 |
|  |  |  | — |  | 800–100 BC |
| Initial Period | -Initial Period- | Initial Period | — | semi-arid (n < 250 mm) | 1800–800 BC |
| Archaic | -Archaic- | Late Archaic | — |  | 3000–1800 BC |
|  |  | Middle Archaic | — | semi-arid (n < 250 mm) | 6000–3000 BC |
|  |  | Early Archaic | — |  | 10000–6000 BC |

seasonally or at prescribed intervals by the population of a considerable surrounding area. Between the occasions when a ceremonial center is used it is either closed and empty or houses only a small permanent population of caretaker personnel. The general population which makes use of the center may be entirely dispersed in the surrounding countryside, or it may be clustered in urban centers" (Rowe 1963:296).

Even so, the issue of elite residence at Cahuachi is one that is testable, and I will return to this matter in the final chapter of this book. The important point here is that Nasca had all the trappings of a middle-range society: a large, central ceremonial center; elaborate crafts (probably of specialized manufacture); and modest villages located in the upper valleys of the region, all integrated through a ceremonial complex involving feasting and an ideology centered on fertility at Cahuachi. The question remains: What was the nature of power in Nasca, and how was this related to the political economy?

## Power and Political Economy in Nasca

While it has been established that Nasca was a middle-range society, it is unclear whether or not individuals or groups in Nasca had "power over." One thing is clear: The ancient Nasca found themselves in an inhospitably marginal environment, and it was more inhospitable during the Early Intermediate Period than it had ever been in the previous eight thousand years (see table 3.1). Cultural features of Nasca all point to a constant concern for agricultural fertility, water, and propagation. This is seen in everything from trophy heads to the Nasca Lines to Nasca iconography to the very locations of the settlements in which Nasca residents lived. Additionally, widespread desiccation (Eitel et al. 2005) and a lack of evidence for health-related problems (Kellner 2002), usually indicating a lack of access to resources, make it highly improbable that anyone or any group had control over agricultural resources.

For example, at least during Early Nasca, agriculture appears to have been limited to floodwater farming, as no large irrigation features were constructed (puquios were most likely constructed during phase 5; see Schreiber and Lancho Rojas 2003). Furthermore, with neither full-coverage regional survey nor excavations at Cahuachi revealing large-scale storage features for subsistence goods, there is very little evidence that anyone had a monopoly on food or water.

When evaluating all of the evidence, physical coercion appears to have been somewhat limited in Nasca society (at least in Early Nasca — indeed, we do find that conflict and warfare seems to increase in the Late Nasca phases; see Kellner 2002). While trophy heads have been argued to be evidence for warfare, they appear to be at most related to small-scale raiding, given the demography of the trophy heads themselves (that is, their age and sex as far as that can be determined). Furthermore, contextual analysis suggests that no matter how the heads might have been obtained, they were subsequently used in the context of fertility and propagation.

With evidence for neither monopolization of scarce economic resources nor a substantial degree of coercive force, it follows that the power Early Nasca elites attained must have been fairly limited. Of course, this is expected in nonstratified societies, where power tends to be cyclical and ephemeral (Cobb 1993:51). When coercive force and monopolizaton of resources are lacking, ideology tends to provide a basis from which to gain access to social power, and one conduit to social power is through rituals directly tied to religious concerns. In other words, to use Anthony Giddens' terminology, power can focus on authoritative rather than allocative resources.

Indeed, power and ideology seem to have been closely linked in Nasca. The elites of Nasca have been described as "ritual specialists" who gained their status through their access to ritual and knowledge (Silverman 1993:338; Silverman and Proulx 2002). Status for these elites was probably very flexible, involving political acts and display at civic-ceremonial centers such as Cahuachi (Silverman and Proulx 2002:247). These political acts were integrally related to the association that aspiring leaders had with agricultural fertility, and this ideology was communicated in major group ceremonies and feasting events. While these events may have taken place around the Nasca region, clearly the most important of affairs took place at Cahuachi.

Elites also probably gained status through esoteric knowledge that was intimately related to agricultural fertility and to the importance of water. This fact is clear through an analysis of iconography on polychrome pottery. Indeed, most cultural features of Nasca society tend to revolve around the central issues of water and agricultural fertility. As Silverman (1993:323) states: "Nasca religion appears to have sought to control, through ritual, such . . . factors as the life-giving power of water, the growth potential of seeds, and the productivity of plants."

Indeed, esoteric knowledge was clearly an important authoritative resource in Nasca. Those who had access to the supernatural world and who appeared to have the ability to control such vital resources as water and agricultural fertility could have easily attracted a following. It is not difficult to imagine that those individuals who sponsored feasts and ceremonies tied to agricultural cycles, and who associated themselves directly with places on the landscape related to fertility and water, would have gained much status as intermediaries between the natural and supernatural worlds. Since it was a middle-range society, high status in Nasca must have been a transient, cyclical "office" held by virtue of the elite's ability to attract followers at a given time based on their personal prominence and their access to esoteric knowledge.

If ceremonies tied to agricultural cycles were the critical events in which political acts were carried out, the materialization of the elite's ideology would have made it possible for an elite group sponsoring these feasts to not only establish and reinforce their power (see for example, DeMarrais et al. 1996:17), but also to help them broaden the scope of their power. That is, ideological materialization would assist in establishing power over more and more people over time. The monuments at Cahuachi and the ceremonial feasts were important forms of materialization; however, another important means—one that was highly portable and could serve to remind people on a daily basis of elite-serving ideologies—was polychrome pottery.

Ultimately, though, we will never fully understand how important Nasca polychromes were—let alone the nature of power in Nasca—without understanding village life. How did local villages fit into the picture of Nasca society? How was the domestic economy organized? Is there evidence of rank or status within villages? How did villages fit into the broader context of Nasca society? Were they economically independent? Did they operate under the auspices of a broader regional economy to which they were inextricably linked? Clearly, excavations at a village context can provide data critical to our ability to address these questions, and, more generally, to broaden our understanding of Nasca society. In the following chapter, I will discuss the primary research questions that arise when investigating Nasca through focusing on a single village.

# 4

# The Village Approach
to Nasca Society

BY THE END OF THE TWENTIETH CENTURY, what archaeologists understood about Nasca was a product of the kind of research that had been undertaken in the region. The study of Nasca had included regional studies, site-specific studies, and studies focused on artifacts. Regional survey during the last twenty years has been a major research emphasis, as most valleys of the south coast of Peru have been surveyed. Regional studies also include analyses of region-wide features such as *puquios* and the Nasca Lines. Sites that have been evaluated include cemeteries, the ceremonial center Cahuachi, and secondary ceremonial centers such as Los Molinos. Artifacts from the ancient south coast, especially ceramics and textiles, have been the focus of research for much of the century.

All of these analyses have contributed much to our understanding of Nasca. What we lack, though, is analysis of a single village to further illuminate how the people of ancient Nasca were integrated into this middle-range society. Without taking this village approach, a large segment of the population — those living in rural villages — are absent from the reconstruction of Nasca prehistory, and we have an incomplete picture of agency, power, and political economy in the region (fig. 4.1). In this chapter, I situate the present study by posing research questions about what we might expect at a rural village in Nasca. Given our understanding of power, inequality, and political economy in this ancient society, how might these transpire and be manifested at the local level?

## Power and Inequality

As we have seen, Nasca was what anthropological archaeologists would call a middle-range society. This kind of society is typically characterized by unequal social relations and forms of inequality. While Nasca appears

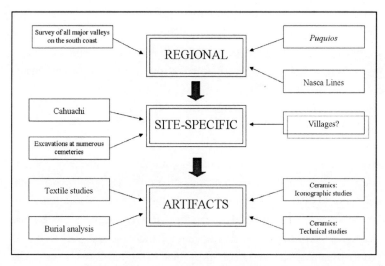

FIGURE 4.1  While archaeological research in Nasca has focused on regional survey, artifact analysis, and excavations at large sites such as Cahuachi, up until now, we have lacked research at a village.

to have lacked institutionalized inequalities in the form of stratification, inequalities in the form of rank were clearly present. These inequalities were manifested in differential burials, suggesting that certain members of Nasca society were ranked above others; however, this degree of differentiation, which Patrick Carmichael refers to as a "status continuum" (1995:175) has not been demonstrated in local communities.

Markus Reindel and Johny Isla Cuadrado (2001) have excavated several sites in the Palpa Valley that would suggest that there were institutionalized inequalities in Nasca, but these are limited to sites that postdate Early Nasca. For example, at La Muña, a Nasca 5 center, Reindel and Isla Cuadrado recorded and excavated a large site with civic-ceremonial architecture, as well as a large mortuary complex with elite burials (Isla Cuadrado and Reindel 2006). One heavily looted tomb was clearly the burial site of a very important individual. The tomb itself was impressive at thirteen meters deep. Though looted, remains in excavations included gold, fine ceramics, and textiles. No tombs of equivalent scale, however, have been found dating to the Early Nasca period.

Evidence of Early Nasca settlements in the SNR demonstrates a clear pattern of a central ceremonial center, Cahuachi, located in the lower valleys, with a series of small rural villages located in the upper valleys. This settlement pattern is a classic manifestation of a middle-range society. Other valleys exhibit a similar pattern. For example, in Palpa, settlement is characterized by numerous habitations in addition to the civic-ceremonial center Los Molinos.

Given our expectations for middle-range societies, we would anticipate that power and agency would be negotiated at all levels of society, including the level of small communities. From survey, we do know that the majority of people in the SNR lived in the foothills of the Andes in small, relatively undifferentiated habitations. Indeed, in the SNR, Katharina Schreiber (summary in Schreiber and Lancho Rojas 2003) has located more than five hundred habitation sites through full-coverage settlement survey, approximately fifty of which date to the Early Nasca period. Early Nasca habitation sites are located in the foothills just above the dry coastal plain. The sites are located on the hillsides flanking the valley floor, as prehispanic occupants of the area utilized the valley bottoms for agriculture. The sites are small, generally less than three hectares in size, and from surface analysis they do not appear to have evidence of monumental or ceremonial architecture (Schreiber 1999).

Despite the recording of dozens of habitations, we know very little about them. Specifically, if Early Nasca communities were the locus of inequalities and exhibited signs of social rank, we would expect to find one or more of the following at these sites:

1. Structures within these communities that are larger than others.
2. Structures that contain a variety of specialized architectural features, are subdivided into public and private space, or show a greater labor investment in their construction.
3. Structures whose associated artifact assemblages contain goods of higher value than those of others — such as exotic goods or goods produced within the community through higher labor investments — as well as more items overall.

These three expectations serve as indicators of individuals, families, or households of higher status as outlined previously. On the other hand, if none of these expectations are met in prehistoric communities, then perhaps there was a lack of significant social inequality at the community level.

Documented villages in the Nasca region seem to lack many of the features that would indicate higher-status households. For example, Schreiber describes these sites as "being composed of round stone buildings. These are typically located on artificially leveled areas on hillsides. They range from round to ovoid in plan, are four to nine meters in interior diameter, and are generally made of angular broken stone set in mud mortar" (Schreiber 1988:71). She does not indicate that any buildings have dramatically larger structures on them that would indicate drastic local status differences.

Helaine Silverman has recorded a number of sites in the Ingenio Valley, many of which date to the Early Intermediate Period (phases 1–5; Silverman 2002). Silverman describes Early Nasca habitation sites recorded in Ingenio as "more or less large, with almost rectangular structures." Furthermore, "these structures are found on terraces made of fieldstone that follow the topography of the hills upon which they are situated" (1993:112, my translation). In short, based on previous descriptions, there seems to be little in the way of monumental architecture, special structures, or special architectural features that would indicate people or households of higher status at these sites (Browne 1992:79; Schreiber and Lancho Rojas 2003). The exception to this may be in Palpa at Los Molinos, where Reindel and Isla Cuadrado (1999) have recorded a civic ceremonial center dating to Nasca 3 comprised of elite adobe architecture consisting of platform mounds, elite residences, and ceremonial ramps. Aside from the special situation at Los Molinos, however, there does not appear to be differentiation at sites outside of Cahuachi.

Because no excavations have been undertaken at Early Nasca villages, the differences in artifact assemblages at these sites are unclear. One significant point is that there appears to be a high quantity of polychromes present on the surfaces of residential sites of the Ica-Grande region (Carmichael 1998; Reindel and Isla Cuadrado 2001; Schreiber 1999; Silverman 2002). Because excavations have been limited, however, it is unknown whether these surface ceramics correlate with domestic occupations. Outside the Ica-Grande heartland, Nasca polychromes are present at sites, though these appear to be trade pieces and elite goods (Carmichael 1992; Valdez Cardenas 1998).

## Subsistence Economy

A village approach to the study of complex societies will reveal much about the organization of the subsistence economy of local communities. The subsistence economy is organized to meet the basic needs of the household in a domestic mode of production. In this mode of production, households are self-sufficient, not requiring production interdependency between households.Indeed, there is some argument that the goal in traditional Andean communities was to strive for household independence (Johnson and Earle 2000:319).

What we do know about the subsistence economy in Nasca comes through excavations at Cahuachi, through isotopic analysis of skeletal populations, and, indirectly, through excavations of a village dating to the Late Intermediate Period called Pajonal Alto. The subsistence economy of Nasca appears to have been heavily reliant on maize (*Zea mays*), as shown by an isotopic study by Brenda Kennedy and Patrick Carmichael (1991) as well as a more recent study by Corina Kellner and Margaret Schoeninger (n.d.). In addition to maize, the Nasca diet was composed of peanuts (*Arachis hypogaea*), beans (*Phaseolus vulgaris*, *Phaseolus lunatus*), squash (*Cucurbita moschata*, *Cucurbita maxima*), achira (*Canna edulis*), manioc (*Manihot esculenta*), sweet potato (*Ipomoea batatas*), potato (*Solanum* spp.), jicama (*Pachyrhizus erosus*), *ají* (chili pepper; *Capsicum* spp.), lucuma (*Lucuma bifera*), guava (*Psidium guajava*), and avocado (*Persea* spp.). The pod of the huarango (*Prosopis chilensis*) also provided sustenance (Towle 1961; Orefici and Drusini 2003: 106). Excavations at the Late Intermediate Period site Pajonal Alto revealed that the three most important subsistence crops during this time period (based on the order of abundance) were *Prosopis* spp., *Zea mays*, *Phaseolus lunatus*, *Capsicum annum*, and *Inga feuillei* (called *pacae*) (Conlee 2000:240).

If other coastal Andean societies are any indication, agricultural resources would have been augmented with domesticated animals, including the cuy or guinea pig, llama, alpaca, and probably the muscovy duck. Indeed, camelids were also an important component of the Nasca subsistence economy. Llamas were found at Cahuachi (Silverman 1993) and Usaca, a ceremonial complex in the lower valley (Isla Cuadrado 1992:150). Silverman (2002:151) speculates that guanaco must have been hunted as well, given their depiction in iconography. In addition to camelids, guinea pigs were consumed (Silverman 1993:168). While shellfish remains are found on the surface of Nasca habitations and marine life is depicted on ceramic iconography, marine resources apparently were not consumed in great quantities (Kennedy and Carmichael 1991).

## Political Economy

The archaeological correlates of status differences in households also have implications for political economy. Goods and services can be mobilized to support an ephemeral class of high-status individuals or families establishing a political economy. The variability of artifact assemblages, subsistence remains, and storage facilities of houses within a community should reveal patterns of a political economy if one existed. At the community level, variability in subsistence remains and artifact assemblages across households should be present, with higher-quality foods and more valued artifacts associated with higher-status individuals or families. Two of the most important ways that aspiring elites can differentiate themselves in middle-range societies is through exchange and production.

### Exchange

Evidence for exchange and production in Nasca is limited. Exchange for goods from outside the region appears to have been limited to obsidian and, far less frequently, *Spondylus*. Obsidian has been recovered widely in the region through excavation (Isla Cuadrado 1990; Strong 1957) and survey (Schreiber and Lancho 2003; Silverman 2002). While some of this obsidian was used for special, ritually related artifacts (see Silverman 1993:285), the majority of it was used to make functional tools. Researchers have assumed that this obsidian is from the Quispisisa source (e.g., Isla Cuadrado 1990) and some obsidian from the region has been chemically analyzed confirming this assumption (Burger and Asaro 1979). *Spondylus* is found much more rarely in the region. Survey revealed fragments in the Ingenio Valley (Silverman 2002), and some *Spondylus* has been re-covered in excavations at Cahuachi (Orefici and Drusini 2003:111; Silver-man 1993).

Exchange of polychrome ceramics can be seen outside of the immediate Nasca region. Indeed, outside the Ica and Grande drainages, Nasca poly-chromes were exchanged as part of a system of elite interaction. For exam-ple, in the Pisco and Acarí Valleys (Silverman 1997; Valdez Cardenas 1998), a small quantity of Nasca polychromes are found in limited elite contexts, while local styles (specifically, the Estrella and Huarato styles) seem to be imitations of the Nasca styles. Even as far away as the Moquegua Valley, more than five hundred kilometers to the southeast, limited quanti-ties of Nasca ceramics appear in elite contexts (Goldstein 2000). This has been interpreted to be a part of long-distance interaction that local chiefs engaged in as part of their prestige-building efforts. Other evidence for exchange includes exotic animals such as monkeys from the selva that are frequently depicted on Nasca ceramics. But despite evidence for exchange, the frequency and intensity of trade in prehistory is unknown.

## Production

The processes involved in the production of most goods in Nasca are unknown; however, several models have been proposed to understand the production, distribution, and consumption of Nasca pottery. While pot-tery was the "principal purveyor of ideology" in Nasca society and its manufacture involved a high degree of technical skill, the pottery was not simply reserved for ceremonial contexts and burials, nor was it merely an elite good. Instead, pottery deposited as grave goods shows use prior to being interred in tombs (Carmichael 1988); pieces were not solely re-served for burials. Other researchers have noted the presence of a large amount of polychromes on the surface of habitation sites when compared to smaller quantities of utilitarian vessels (Carmichael 1998:216; Silver-man 1993:339). Some have suggested that Nasca polychromes were part of an "open, shared system to which all members of society had access" (Carmichael 1995: 171, 1998).

The art historical research focus on Nasca pottery throughout the last century has largely been a consequence of the availability of pottery in collections and museums. Most examples of pottery in collections are either without provenience or were obtained from excavations that concentrated almost entirely on burials. Carmichael (1998) has attempted to evaluate the social context of Nasca pottery production and the technology of Nasca ceramics as well. He proposes that Nasca pottery was manufactured by part-time producers operating in family or household units to satisfy domestic or lineage (*ayllu*) needs, though this scale of production could have been augmented with exchange between communities. Part-time Nasca potters probably operated seasonally between the planting season (January) and harvest (March), when there was not only free time between agricultural activities, but the dry climate was most favorable for pottery manufacture.

Carmichael's model is largely based on the absence of pottery workshops in excavations and in extensive survey of the entire Ica-Grande region. Indeed, modern potters report adequate clay sources as widely available in the region, so the production of pottery in geographically disperse locations was certainly feasible. Carmichael also argues that, despite the high degree of technical skill and "artistic virtuosity" in Nasca pottery, by no means would this level of skill imply full-time specialists (Carmichael 1998: 215); part-time potters working between agricultural tasks could have easily produced the pottery (Carmichael 1998:215).

Concerned specifically with the production of Nasca pottery, Carmichael did not explore in detail its distribution and exchange. He does state, however, that household production may have been accompanied by exchange, and that pottery did play an integral role in festivals and ceremonial activities (1998:224). From the perspective of the ceremonial center Cahuachi, Silverman (1993:302–304) postulates a scenario for the distribution and exchange of polychromes. She speculates that polychromes were manufactured by different groups from around the region and brought in pilgrimage to the ceremonial center, where they would have been redistributed and exchanged, with some being ritually broken. Following the ritual exchange and redistribution, intact vessels would have been taken back to residential sites. Thus, vessel assemblages at domestic sites would comprise various styles of Nasca fineware, including nonlocal styles (Silverman 1993:302).

Because data from a domestic context were unavailable, Carmichael's propositions of household pottery production and Silverman's model of pottery exchange remained speculative. Moreover, the lack of data from a habitation was lamented as a major barrier to fully understanding the nature of not only Nasca pottery production, but Nasca society as well (Carmichael 1994: 230).

Carmichael's and Silverman's models of pottery production are in sharp contrast to my own model, which is based on a political economy and agency perspective. Because polychromes appear to have been the "principal purveyor of ideology," we might expect that they would have been important ritual paraphernalia (in DeMarrais et al.'s terms). That is, could the polychrome pottery have provided individuals with a materialized ideology? If so, we would expect a completely different scenario of production, exchange, and consumption of polychromes than that proposed by either Carmichael or Silverman. Instead of household production, we would expect that the production of polychromes would be monopolized by elites in their prestige-building efforts. The location at which this most likely would have taken place would have been Cahuachi. This model is consistent with recent data that I have collected suggesting that a production source of the majority of polychrome pottery can be traced to near the ceremonial center (Vaughn and Neff 2004; Vaughn et al. 2006), a point that I will return to later.

What remains to be seen is how polychrome pottery was actually used in the domestic context. In the Nasca scenario, if polychrome pottery was a vehicle for ideology, and if materialization extends ideology "to communicate the power of a central authority to a broader population" (DeMarrais et al. 1996:16), the variability of polychrome consumption at residential sites should provide an indication of whether people not directly responsible for this ideology accepted it and incorporated it into their daily lives. Additionally, since consumers at residential sites also engage in power relations (Goldstein 2000:336), we may see differences in the ways in which this was incorporated. That is, individuals of high status may have had greater access to elite ideology, and materials that manifested this ideology might have been used as political currency to further individual and group political ambitions (LeCount 1999).

## Ritual Activities

Present understanding of Early Nasca society suggests that it was organized partially in terms of an integrating religious system centered at Ca-

huachi. It has been established that Cahuachi functioned as a ceremonial/
pilgrimage center where group-oriented ceremony took place. Was there
an equal concern for group-oriented ceremony at local communities?

One aspect of ritual that has been noted among Andean ethnographers
is the differences between communal festivals and household ritual. For
example, in Sonqo, Catharine Allen (1988:201) describes the different
kinds of rituals that take place among communities in public venues, as
well as in private within the household. "In communal festivals, it is not
the household but the *ayllu* (community) as a whole that commands
ritual attention." These communal festivals for the entire ayllu often took
the form of processions and pilgrimages. In contrast, certain small-scale
rituals such as the *despacho*, in which the earth and sacred places are nourished with offerings of coca, food, and alcohol, occurred within the house
and were led by the head of the household (Allen 1988:153).

Allen also illustrates that "power objects" in Sonqo called *enqa* and
*istrilla* are important in understanding the ritual lives of modern indigenous Andean groups (Allen 1988:201). These power objects were
brought out on special ceremonial occasions from their holding places.
They are said to be *kawsaqkuna*, or "living ones," and "they are the source
of the health and fertility of the livestock, the crops, and the family members themselves" (Allen 1988:59). Furthermore, they "store vitality and
well-being by forging a connection between the household and the Sacred
Places" in Sonqo (Allen 1988:201).

If these ceremonial activities did take place within communities and
away from Cahuachi, we would expect to find archaeological evidence for
this at a single community. Evidence for group-oriented ceremony may be
in the form of open or carefully defined spaces, distinct architectural features, special structures, as well as ritual and ceremonial paraphernalia.
Furthermore, if group-oriented ceremony transpired with the entire community participating, we would expect architectural features and structures dedicated to this activity to be prominent, perhaps centrally located,
and fairly distinct. If these ceremonial activities were instead restricted to
select individuals or households, we would expect structures and architectural features reserved for these activities to also be distinct, but to be
located near the residences of the people who had access to them.

If distinct architectural features or structures are not identified within
the community, then the argument that group-oriented ceremonial ac-

tivities during Early Nasca times were confined to Cahuachi would be supported.

While we may see an increase in exchange and production with the advent of Early Nasca due to political competition and emerging elite efforts, one of the ways in which this actually transpired was through feasting. The evidence for feasting in Nasca comes from two sources: excavations at Cahuachi and ceramic iconography. Certainly, feasting took place at Cahuachi as discussed in the previous chapter, and everything that we know suggests that this feasting was orchestrated by sociopolitical elites at Cahuachi as part of their larger ceremonial/political efforts.

If these kinds of activities took place locally as well, we may find special architectural features and spaces near households identified as high status. Furthermore, we can look at special pottery-firing features, storage features, and vessel assemblages that suggest extra household consumption (Blitz 1993; Jennings 2005; Potter 2000).

## Summary

Clearly, in order to address power, political economy, and agency in ancient Nasca, excavations at a single village are required. Investigations at a single village allow for an evaluation of power and inequality, subsistence and political economies (including exchange, production, and feasting), and ritual activities. We would expect all of these in middle-range societies, but the degree to which we will find these at a village is completely unknown. In the next chapter, I will turn to investigations at Marcaya, an Early Nasca village.

# 5

# Investigations at Marcaya

ALTHOUGH SOME ATTEMPTS HAVE BEEN MADE to conduct analysis of domestic remains in the Nasca region, none have been fully successful for reasons having to do with local formation processes and the nature of habitation at excavated sites in the region. For example, one of Helaine Silverman's (1993:110–111) original intentions in excavating at Cahuachi was to test the "urban hypothesis" by excavating domestic contexts. The excavation results suggested to her that there was not a permanent occupation at Cahuachi, thus she rejected the urban hypothesis. Domestic remains were excavated at the Late Nasca site Taruga as well (Schreiber 1994). Taruga, however, was severely water damaged and the lack of deposition rendered local preservation less than ideal (Schreiber 1998).

The sites in the upper valleys in the Nasca region differ from these, however. The lack of significant deposition in the upper valleys along the hillsides prevents the burial of architectural foundations (as in the lower valleys), and since these foundations were constructed of fieldstone, they still remain on the surface today. Although deflation does occur, severe wind and water erosion have not "blown out" a significant amount of material as they have in the middle valley, where Taruga is located. In fact, much of the Proyecto Nasca Sur survey proceeded by first consulting Peruvian Air Force air photos to locate sites in the field, since those in the upper valleys are visible on these photos (e.g., Schreiber and Isla Cuadrado 1996). For these reasons, the potential for analyzing single communities in the upper valleys of Nasca is great. Architectural foundations still exist on the surface such that individual structures and the groups of structures they compose are visible from surface analysis alone.

## Marcaya

Marcaya is a one-hectare village site located in the foothills of the Andes in the Yunga zone, just as the foothills begin to make their steep ascent into

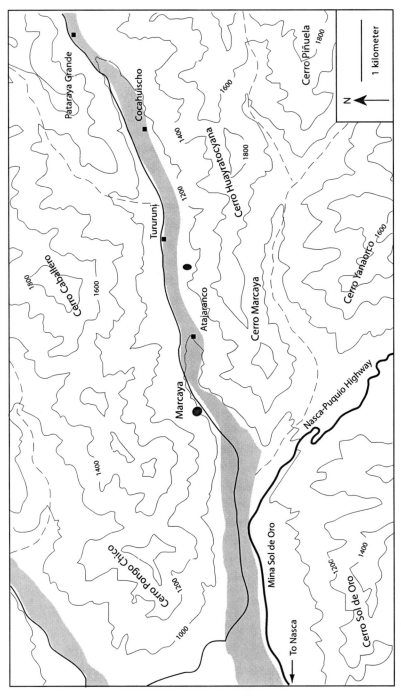

FIGURE 5.1  Marcaya is located in the Tierras Blancas river valley, 16 kilometers east of the modern town of Nasca at an elevation of 1000 meters above sea level.

the highlands. Lying sixteen kilometers upstream of the modern town of Nasca, at an elevation of one thousand meters above sea level, the site is situated on the northern hillside of the Tierras Blancas River Valley on a gently sloping colluvial fan just southeast of Cerro Pongo Chico (fig. 5.1).

Marcaya was recorded in 1989 by Katharina Schreiber as a single-component Early Nasca domestic site based on the diagnostic ceramics located on its surface (the site was originally recorded as Site #89–20). According to field notes and photographs from 1989, and according to Schreiber, the site was very well preserved, as structure walls remained and the surface showed few signs of damage from erosion or from looting. In 1996, I joined Schreiber in the last season of the Proyecto Nasca Sur in order to visit the site. Schreiber's observations were confirmed in the field, and Marcaya's potential for being the focus of excavation and analysis of an Early Nasca village was noted. That season, a few more ceramics were collected from the surface, further confirming the site's status as a single-component Early Nasca site. Brief fieldwork also consisted of some preliminary mapping and photographing, as well as the sketching of plan views and architecture.

## Tierras Blancas Yunga Environment

The valley in which Marcaya is located is fairly narrow and widens considerably as the river (when flowing) flows west towards the modern town of Nasca. The alluvial deposits in the river valley are amenable to a wide range of both indigenous and non-indigenous crops, and modern residents use the section of the valley directly below the site to plant modest crops of maize, wheat, and beans. Water—when it flows—is channeled from the river into a small *cocha*, or basin. The water stored here is enough to sustain the fields for the entire growing season. Prehispanic agricultural activities have since been obscured by modern agriculture, though I assume that this part of the valley was used for agriculture in the past as well.

Aside from the small amount of modern cultivation, the valley bottom is characterized by scattered forest of huarango (*Prosopis julifora*) and "espinos" (*Acacia macracantha*). Modern residents of the valley rely on a mixed economy of agricultural products grown locally and livestock (mostly goats) that they herd and graze on the scarce vegetation of the

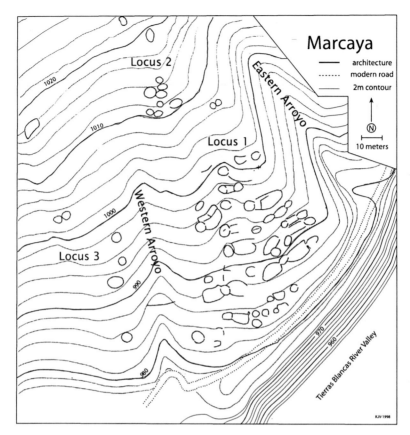

FIGURE 5.2  Topographic map of Marcaya.

hillsides and the more abundant vegetation of the valley bottoms. The majority of products grown or raised by the valley residents are sold in the market in Nasca.

In the hydrogeographic scheme proposed by Katharina Schreiber and Josué Lancho Rojas (2003), Marcaya is located at the juncture between the upper valley and the zone of infiltration. During fieldwork, prior to the El Niño flooding of 1998, water infiltrated into the valley alluvium approximately fifty meters east (upvalley) of the site. Local informants revealed that seasonal flooding generally occurred every year, but the river remained flowing for only a week or two during a normal year and up to several months during a particularly wet year. The summer of 1997–1998 was one such wet year, and once the river began to flow past the site at the end of December 1997, it remained flowing until the end of March 1998.

## Site Boundaries and Context

Dense agglutination of architectural features exists in at least three spatially separate loci at Marcaya (fig. 5.2) Loci 1 and 2 comprise the main part of the site and are defined by arroyos flanking both its western and eastern sides. Locus 3 consists of isolated structures and is located to the west of the Western Arroyo. A modern road leading from the Nasca-Puquio highway to the Ronquillo hot springs upvalley cuts through the lower portion of the site (Locus 1) and it appears that several structures were probably destroyed in the construction of the road. Just below this road, the hillslope becomes a steep cliff, which falls about twenty meters to the valley bottom below. The valley is about one hundred meters wide in this location and is dry for most of the year, as the permanent trickle of water in the river bed infiltrates below the surface. The opposite side of the valley rises sharply to Cerro Marcaya, the site's namesake. Due to the pitch of the terrain, the southern slope of the valley is uninhabitable and has no evidence of prehispanic occupation.

From Marcaya itself there is a good view of Cerro Blanco (fig. 5.3), the large, sand-covered mountain that was ethnohistorically integral to the sacred geography of Nasca (Reinhard 1988). Besides offering an unobstructed view of Cerro Blanco, the location of Marcaya facilitates an expansive view downstream and upstream as well. With the undulating terrain of the region, Marcaya is the only habitable place in the valley within one kilometer east or west that affords such a commanding view in either direction.

## Architectural Layout of Marcaya

Because there is little soil formation in this environment, architectural foundations are exposed on the surface, making it easy to document the spatial layout of the site. The architecture at Marcaya can best be described as "opportunistic" and "organic" rather than "planned" or "geometrical" (Williams León 1980:477). Structure walls are curvilinear and do not conform to a rigid architectural canon of construction. Structures were

FIGURE 5.3  The sand-covered mountain Cerro Blanco as seen from Marcaya.

completed on the hillside in low-relief areas using fieldstone available on the hillside itself. Initial surface inspection at Marcaya suggested a dichotomy in basic structure types (fig. 5.4) Based on their spatial organization, as well as comparison with other architectural styles in the region (for example, see Williams León 1980), the two types of structures were thought to be houses and associated patios.

Houses are round, measure three to five meters in diameter, and are constructed of broken fieldstone from the colluvial fan that makes up the hillside. Houses were constructed by digging into the hillside to create a relatively flat space, and then building walls using mud mortar and fieldstone to a height of 1 to 1.5 meters. Many houses have well-defined interior wall faces. In some, field stones were partially dressed to make a flat surface, creating a clearly delineated interior space. Doors in houses were generally found in the east-northeast wall of the structure (fig. 5.5). This is probably due to a prevailing southwesterly wind that blows up valley every day. Doors in houses were generally bounded by doorframes composed of two dressed stones placed vertically on either side, and they were seventy centimeters to one meter wide.

Rows of fallen rock measuring up to one meter were recorded in the

FIGURE 5.4 Two patio groups at Marcaya. Photo taken from above (facing south). Both patio groups consist of a house and a patio, while the patio of Patio Group XII is internally divided. Compare to Figure 5.6.

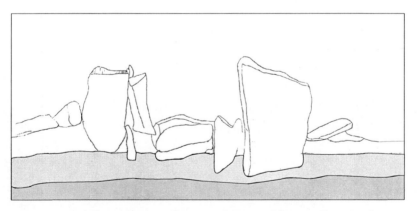

FIGURE 5.5 A door between a house and patio at Marcaya. Drawing by Dawn Vaughn.

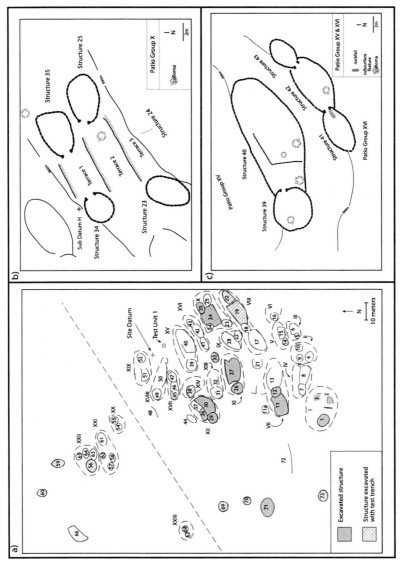

FIGURE 5.6 (a) Patio groups and structures at Marcaya. Patio groups are labeled with roman numerals, while structures are labeled with Arabic numerals. (b) Planview of Patio Group X. (c) Planview of patio groups XV and XVI. Note the internal architectural features in patio groups X and XV and the lack of these features in Patio Group XVI.

interiors of some of the houses and appeared to have fallen from the original structure walls. These rows of rocks appear to have originated from the doorframes and also from opposite sides of structures, suggesting that their placement may have served to hold up a roof above the relatively short walls. A simple roof consisting of no more than brush and branches from the river valley below could have been laid over these short columns of rocks. Even more simply, when these columns of rocks were not found, roofs could have been supported by the wall foundations to provide rudimentary protection from the elements. Roofs of a similar nature exist on modern dwellings located in the river valley downstream. The roofs at Marcaya have probably since been taken away by people over the years, since brush, branches, and wood are valuable commodities in this dry valley.

Doors in patios were also in the east-northeast wall of the structure and generally led to the exterior of the site. When there was a substantial wall, doors in patios were similar to the doors in houses. When patios lacked substantial walls, however, a line of rocks forming a pathway served as an entry and exit to patios. No evidence for roofs was found in patios. It is unlikely that there were roofs on patios since their walls were not substantial. Instead, patios were open, artificially defined spaces constructed adjacent to houses.

Of course, there are some deviations from this basic pattern. The most common deviation is not in form but in the structure's spatial relationship to other structures at the site. For example, thirteen structures at the site have the same basic form as a house or patio, but they appear to have had a different function. Each exists in isolation and none are conjoined with other structures. Good examples of these are the structures in Locus 3, west of the Western Arroyo, as well as isolated structures in the upper portion of the site. Because their functions could not be determined through surface analysis alone, these unique structures were explored with excavations.

*Patio Groups.* Clusters of structures at Marcaya comprise associated houses and patios. Although there are exceptions, clusters are typically formed by one or more houses adjoining one or more patios. There are twenty-three clusters that can be distinguished on the surface of Marcaya. In addition to these structure clusters, there are thirteen structures that do not appear to be associated with groups (fig. 5.6).

Based on the methods of defining archaeological households outlined previously, Marcaya's structure groups appear to fulfill two of the three requirements for an archaeological household. That is, they are spatially segregated (i.e., these groups are distinct), and the groups are repeated within the community. Without excavations, it was not possible to verify whether they have the material correlates of domestic activities, the final criterion for defining households.

From this assessment, it appeared that the structure groups were the loci of residential groups. I refer to them as "patio groups." While this term is often used in the context of multiple dwellings surrounding a single patio, or activity area, as the term is often used in Mesoamerica or in the Andean region, here it denotes a single hypothesized household whose dwellings included a house and one or more patios or activity areas. From the surface analysis, the working hypothesis was that each patio group formed the loci for an archaeological household. The goal of the excavations was to test this proposition and to evaluate differences between patio groups.

*Households at Marcaya.* If the patio groups were households, there are several testable propositions that can be made about their organization. First, there appears to be variability in the way that these households were organized. While the majority of patio groups included a single house and a single patio, there are several patio groups with more than one defined house sharing a single patio, more than one patio attached to a single house, and some houses without associated patios. From the surface, it is unclear whether this variability is indicative of differences in activities or of differences in status. Excavations, however, would elucidate these distinctions further.

Second, from surface analysis, it appears that most activities were organized at the household level. Community-organized activities would be expected to be centrally located, architecturally distinct, and larger than the loci for residential units, but evidence for these simply does not exist on the surface of Marcaya. There are no obvious loci for community-oriented activities such as communal organization of subsistence production, subsistence processing, or the use of storage facilities, and there are no obvious spaces in which ceremonial activity might have taken place.

*Patio Group Size and Architectural Quality.* A surface analysis was undertaken to determine the variability in household size and labor investment present at Marcaya. We recorded the size of patio groups, the quality of architecture, and the presence of internal architectural features in the analysis. The size of patio groups at Marcaya measured in square meters varies considerably (table 5.1). This is due not only to the size of individual structures, but also to the number of structures per patio group. Sizes of the patio groups range from the very small Patio Group III ($16.4 \text{ m}^2$) to the very large Patio Group VIII ($145.5 \text{ m}^2$). Based on overall dimensions, patio groups were defined as either small or large, with patio groups more than ninety square meters defined as large.

The variability in architectural quality was also recorded. At first glance, the construction techniques used at Marcaya seem fairly uniform: fieldstone and mud mortar were used to build simple, round houses. Patios are simply defined by rows of field stones surrounding an open space. There are qualitative differences, however, in the techniques used to construct houses at Marcaya, and I propose that these are indicative of differential investment in labor in the construction of structures. While in most houses, walls were constructed using simple fieldstone and mud mortar, in some houses, an effort was made to delineate well-defined interior spaces by using partially dressed field stones with smooth, flat sides. The effort to partially dress fieldstone to create well-defined interior spaces is a factor that distinguishes many houses from others throughout the site. Walls constructed of worked fieldstone are present in about half of the patio groups at Marcaya. Architectural differences were also manifested in the construction of house doors. Doors were either made by leaving a gap in the wall construction or by being framed by two dressed stones placed vertically on either side of the gap.

Finally, we also recorded any internal features and architectural spaces visible on the surface. Internally defined spaces within houses and patios were very rare, however, and were found in only three patio groups (see figs. 5.6 and 5.11) In short, in regard to surface evidence of status differences, there were four criteria that differentiated households: (1) size of the patio group; (2) presence of internal architectural features; (3) presence of worked stone in wall architecture; and (4) presence of worked stone in the doors of houses. Only three patio groups at Marcaya—X, XII, and XV—met all four of these criteria, and based

TABLE 5.1 Status indicators in households at Marcaya. Based on surface analysis, only three patio groups had all the components of high-status households.

| | | Area (m²) | Size | Worked Stone Walls | Worked Stone Door | Internal Architecture | Status Based on Surface Analysis |
|---|---|---|---|---|---|---|---|
| Patio Groups | I | ? | ? | y | y | n | low |
| | II | 34.5 | small | n | y | n | low |
| | III | 16.4 | small | n | n | n | low |
| | IV | 54.6 | small | y | y | n | low |
| | V | 128.0 | large | y | y | n | low |
| | VI | 30.9 | small | n | n | n | low |
| | VII | ? | ? | n | y | n | low |
| | VIII | 145.5 | large | y | y | n | low |
| | IX | 57.6 | small | n | y | n | low |
| | X | 126.9 | large | y | y | y | high |
| | XI | 91.8 | large | n | n | n | low |
| | XII | 95.9 | large | y | y | y | high |
| | XIII | 63.7 | small | y | y | n | low |
| | XIV | ? | ? | y | y | n | low |
| | XV | 112.0 | large | y | y | y | high |
| | XVI | 54.0 | small | y | y | n | low |
| | XVII | 44.2 | small | y | y | n | low |
| | XVIII | 66.6 | small | y | y | n | low |
| | XIX | 32.2 | small | n | y | n | low |
| | XX | 26.8 | small | n | n | n | low |
| | XXI | 57.0 | small | n | y | n | low |
| | XXII | 71.5 | small | n | y | n | low |
| | XXIII | 25.8 | small | n | n | n | low |
| Isolated Structures | 21 | 23.8 | | n | n | n | n/a |
| | 33 | 7.1 | | n | n | n | n/a |
| | 44 | 10.0 | | n | n | n | n/a |
| | 48 | 15.9 | | n | n | n | n/a |
| | 59 | 21 | | n | n | n | n/a |
| | 60 | 19.63 | | n | n | n | n/a |
| | 66 | 47 | | y | n | n | n/a |
| | 69 | 16 | | n | y | n | n/a |
| | 70 | 9.6 | | n | y | n | n/a |
| | 71 | 32 | | n | n | n | n/a |
| | 72 | 73.72 | | n | n | n | n/a |
| | 73 | 16.6 | | n | n | n | n/a |

on these surface differences, they were defined as high-status households (table 5.1).

## Excavations

Sponsored by the Instituto Nacional de Cultura (INC) of Peru, excavations at Marcaya were undertaken in 1997. The proximate goal of excavations was to sample houses and patios to verify the distinctions between
them and to clarify their respective functions. The ultimate goal of the
excavation was threefold: (1) to test the proposition that the defined
patio groups were indeed households; (2) to obtain information on the
nature of activities that took place in the patio groups; and (3) to obtain information on the variability in artifact assemblages between patio
groups. Thus, the strategy was to excavate a sample of houses and patios in
a wide variety of patio groups.

Excavations began with a test unit (labeled "Test Unit 1") outside of a
house (see fig. 5.6, panel "a"). No cultural material was found in this
test unit and subsequent excavations focused within patio groups. Excavations proceeded by levels of natural stratigraphy and were conducted
until sterile soil was reached. All materials were dry-sieved through a one-
fourth-inch screen in the field. Column samples were taken in each unit
and a one-liter sample of sediment from features was collected for dry
sieving through a finer screen. Soil stratigraphy varied slightly from structure to structure, but a general stratigraphic sequence was apparent in
most excavations. Depending on wind deposits, deflation, slope, and degree of modern disturbances such as floral- and faunalturbation, the depth
of these deposits varied from structure to structure (fig. 5.7).

Stratum 1 is characterized by a very thin layer of loose aeolian deposits
and disturbances of pedoturbation, especially floralturbation and faunalturbation (see Schiffer 1987). The sediment is a very pale brown
(10YR7/3), loose, silty sand with frequent pebbles. This stratum was
found mostly within structures, and if it was present outside of structures,
it was extremely shallow.

Stratum 2 is the main cultural stratum at Marcaya and is defined by a
darkish compacted silt (10YR6/3) with small to large pebbles and dispersed with frequent ash and organic mottling. Stratum 2 is the most
variable of the strata defined in this site stratigraphy. For example, in some
locations, Stratum 2 has been deflated to an extremely thin layer. In other

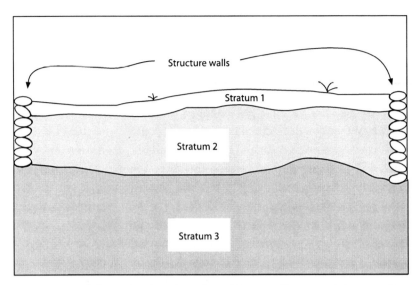

FIGURE 5.7 Schematic of stratigraphy at Marcaya. Stratum 1 is loose, eolian silt, 10YR7/3. Stratum 2 is the principal occupational stratum at Marcaya and is composed of compacted silt with frequent ash mottling and organic matter, 10YR6/3. Stratum 3 is the sterile stratum (eroding bedrock) and is composed of very rocky, sandy silt, 10YR7/6.

locations, there are several levels within the stratum that were divided because of slight changes in soil composition and color. In no cases, however, were these levels found to be temporally distinct, as conjoining sherds were found in sequential layers and sherds from earlier in the stylistic sequence were found above those from later in the sequence. Levels within Stratum 2 were most likely the result of floralturbation, as roots of the local flora were found decomposing in *situ*.

Stratum 3 is the sterile stratum at Marcaya and is composed of eroding bedrock. Sterile soil was a very rocky, sandy silt with a Munsell color of yellow, and a Munsell number of 10YR7/6. This soil type was determined after excavating fifty centimeters below what was thought to be a sterile level in Structure 27 Unit I, and by excavating a test unit in the exterior of the site (Test Unit 1—see below). No cultural materials were found in either of these, and it was confirmed that the levels were sterile. A sterile level of this soil composition was reached in all excavations of all structures and exteriors. In addition, this stratum is exposed on the surface of much of the exterior of Marcaya where significant deflation has occurred.

Generally, subsurface preservation was good, although there was some pedoturbation, mainly floralturbation. Aside from a few cacti, the most common flora at the site is a woody shrub that appears to be a type of manzanita locally referred to as *pati pati*. Due to the dry climate, the root system of this particular species is quite extensive, and when present, it frequently disturbed Stratum 2.

In all, twenty-three structures were excavated, including ten houses, five patios, and eight undefined structures. Excavations included a total of 206 square meters and are summarized by structure in table 5.2. A judgmental sampling strategy was chosen to attain excavation data that would permit evaluation of the differences between high- and low-status households. Excavations were conducted within eight different patio groups (as well as ten isolated structures), of which two were high status and six were low status.

The most common features encountered in excavations were those related to food processing, preparation, and storage. Each of the patio groups excavated contained artifacts and features related to these activities, though the identified features and quantity of material recovered varied from one patio group to another. Hearths delineated by field-stone were found in numerous structures, including both houses and patios, and large *batanes* (grinding stones) and *chungas* (rockers) were also recovered.

Excavation and surface analysis — many structures were exposed on the surface — revealed stone-lined pits in virtually every structure (fig. 5.8). Stone-lined pits similar to those found at Marcaya have been recorded at sites throughout the south coast. For example, Alfred Kroeber (1944:137) recorded subsurface, rock-lined pits at Huaca Santa Rosa. They were recorded as tombs and there is no further mention of them in the publication. Dwight Wallace (1971) reanalyzed the features at the site and maintained that although they were probably reutilized as tombs by later populations, their contents and placement suggested that they were originally storage pits. Sarah Massey (1986:315) concurs with this view, as she has observed similar features at Animas Altas in the upper Ica Valley (Massey 1983). In addition, Silverman (1993:341) has noted that there are storage pits alongside houses in the upper Ingenio Valley, although these storage pits are not described in detail.

Along with colleague Johny Isla Cuadrado, I visited the highland hamlet of Chuquimaran, located approximately 2500 meters above sea level in

TABLE 5.2 Summary of excavations at Marcaya. The amount of material recovered is expressed as an index (grams/cubic meters; for spindle whorls, the index is count/cubic meters).

| | | Area (m²) | Meters³ Excavated | Obsidian | Other Lithics | Spindle Whorls | Fineware | Plainware | Panpipes | Fauna | Shellfish |
|---|---|---|---|---|---|---|---|---|---|---|---|
| Patio Groups | I | ? | 10.5 | 0.92 | 5.14 | 0.1 | 36.67 | 472.86 | 0 | 0.76 | 2 |
| | V | 128.0 | 16.7 | 3.02 | 69.76 | 0.54 | 32.16 | 293.53 | 0 | 12.87 | 5.99 |
| | VIII | 145.5 | 1.5 | 1.33 | 16 | 0 | 33.33 | 344 | 0 | 0 | 3.33 |
| | X | 126.9 | 8.0 | 0.25 | 4.75 | 0.5 | 143.88 | 1381.13 | 0.75 | 1.13 | 3.88 |
| | XI | 91.8 | 26.7 | 1.1 | 6.93 | 0.86 | 97.57 | 843.18 | 0.19 | 17.28 | 5.73 |
| | XII | 95.9 | 22.2 | 0.43 | 15.63 | 0.23 | 130.7 | 968.4 | 0.68 | 1.85 | 6.58 |
| | XIV | ? | 0.5 | 2 | 0 | 0 | 128 | 1248 | 1 | 10 | 18 |
| | XXII | 71.5 | 0.9 | 0 | 0 | 0 | 32.22 | 163.33 | 0 | 0 | 1.11 |
| Isolated Structures | 59 | 21 | 0.3 | 0 | 0 | 0 | 27 | 361 | 0 | 0 | 0 |
| | 60 | 19.63 | 0.3 | 0 | 0 | 0 | 0 | 81 | 0 | 0 | 0 |
| | 69 | 16 | 0.3 | 0 | 0 | 0 | 0 | 0 | 0 | 0 | 0 |
| | 70 | 9.6 | 0.2 | 0 | 0 | 0 | 0 | 0 | 0 | 0 | 0 |
| | 71 | 32 | 4.8 | 0 | 0 | 0 | 22 | 13 | 0 | 0 | 0 |
| | 73 | 16.6 | 0.3 | 0 | 0 | 0 | 0 | 0 | 0 | 0 | 0 |

FIGURE 5.8 *Collomas* found in Patio Group XI.

the Chuquimaran valley.[1] The town was hit hard by the 1996 earthquake that devastated many populated areas of the south coast, including Nasca. However, many modern and historic structures and their associated structural features were still standing in Chuquimaran with little visible damage when we visited. Among the ruins of the devastated town, we found historic features similar to the stone-lined pits at Marcaya. Although they have been replaced in recent years by plastic and metal containers, an elder in the village informed us that these features — called *collomas* — were once used for domestic storage. Based on their similarity in appearance to modern-day features, I adopted the term *colloma* to refer to the stone-lined pits at Marcaya.

Structurally, the collomas at Marcaya are similar to the modern features found at Chuquimaran and to the stone-lined pits found in prehistoric sites throughout the south coast. Their analogy to modern features, as well as their similarity to other prehistoric stone-lined pits on the south coast — argued by other authors to be used primarily for storage — strengthens the hypothesis that the collomas found at Marcaya were likely used for domestic storage, probably food storage. Due to a combination of a lack of soil formation and extensive wind erosion in this location, some collomas are visible on the surface today, while others were encountered only during excavations. Buried collomas were found in many of the patio groups excavated including I, V, XI, and XII, whereas within other patio groups, collomas were exposed on the surface.

Many collomas were found empty or filled with sterile sand, while others contained domestic garbage consisting of ceramic sherds, bone, shell, broken spindle whorls — flyweights used on spindles for spinning fibers — and food remains. Although few food remains were found in primary context at Marcaya in part due to poor preservation, the location of collomas inside patio groups strongly suggests that they were used for domestic storage. Agricultural products could have been stored within collomas for individual household use.

The distribution of collomas encountered through both surface analysis and excavations indicate that there is at least one, sometimes more, in most defined patio groups. Another notable pattern of colloma distribution at Marcaya is that they are found in both patios and houses, and with only two exceptions,[2] they are found within structures. This pattern suggests that domestic storage was a household rather than a community endeavor. There is no apparent morphological difference between collomas located in houses and collomas located in patios. Furthermore, based on excavations, there is no apparent functional difference between collomas located in patios versus those found in houses, since in both cases they were found filled with secondary domestic refuse rather than primary deposits.

It is possible that house collomas and patio collomas were used to store different goods. For example, collomas located in patios, where it appears that many domestic activities such as food processing and preparation took place, may have been reserved for the storage of comestibles consumed in daily activities. Collomas in houses, on the other hand, may have been reserved for more valued items such as polychrome pottery and panpipes.

### Radiocarbon Dates

Multiple samples of excavated charcoal were reserved for radiocarbon dating. Three samples were exported to the United States, where they were submitted to Beta Analytic for analysis. Sample 1 was a large chunk of charcoal taken from a charcoal dump associated with Feature 13 in Structure 29 (AD 240–420 calibrated 2Σ). Sample 2 was also a large piece of charcoal taken from a charcoal dump associated with Feature 20, a colloma in Structure 27 (AD 370–540 calibrated 2Σ). Sample 3 was a large piece of charcoal found in the Feature 6 hearth recorded in Structure 11 (AD 130–420 calibrated 2Σ). Although the three samples are statistically indistinguishable, they overlap from AD 370 to AD 420, suggesting that this is the primary time period during which the site was occupied.

### Excavations in Two Patio Groups

By way of comparison, here I summarize the findings of excavations in two patio groups, XI and XII (descriptions of additional excavations can be found in Vaughn [2000]). The excavations in these patio groups are representative of the excavations undertaken in the remainder of the site. They are suitable for comparison also because Patio Group XI was

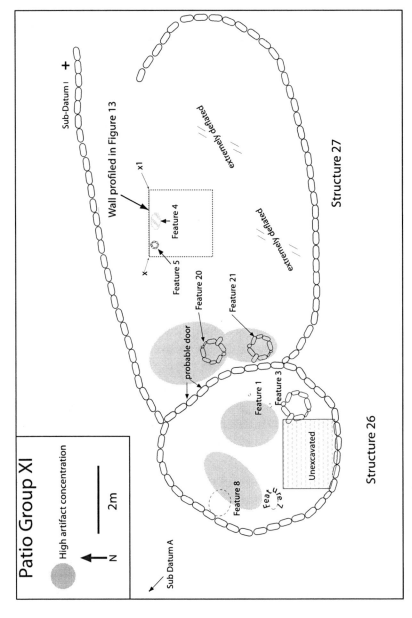

FIGURE 5.9 Excavations in Patio Group XI.

designated a low-status household based on surface analysis, while Patio Group XII was designated a high-status household.

*Patio Group XI.* Patio Group XI is a simple patio group consisting of a house, Structure 26, attached to a patio, Structure 27 (fig. 5.9). Structure 26 is a fairly large house that, on the surface, has very poorly defined walls. The original walls, which are difficult to delineate, are surrounded by substantial wall fall. The subsurface deposit of this structure appeared to be fairly deep. No surface artifacts or features were recorded on the surface. Structure 27 is a large patio abutting Structure 26, though a door between them is not visible. An opening within the northeast wall of Structure 27 leads to the exterior of Marcaya. Instead of a door, the opening is a pathway bounded on both sides by a two-meter row of rocks that extends from the foundation of the structure. The surface of Structure 27 was devoid of features, but a few polychrome sherds were noted.

Excavations in Structure 26 revealed a shallow surface layer (Stratum 1) with few artifacts and consisting of aeolian sediment, a relatively deep cultural deposit with an average depth of about fifty centimeters, and a sterile stratum (3) of rocky silt (fig. 5.10). Features included a small whole bottle (Feature 1)[3], a possible posthole (Feature 2), a colloma (Feature 3), an ash dump (Feature 7), and a possible hearth (Feature 8).

Upon removing the wall fall, original structure walls were revealed and were found to be poorly constructed without dressed fieldstone lining the interior of the structure. Furthermore, despite efforts to reveal one, a door was never found. Given the poor construction of the walls, the significant amount of wall fall may have completely obscured any possible door.

Excavations in Structure 27 revealed a deep cultural deposit in the western half of the structure, and a very shallow and deflated deposit in the eastern half. Features included two collomas (20 and 21), a small pit (5), and two ash dumps (4 and 6).

Results of the excavations conducted within Patio Group XI appear to confirm the third requirement for archaeological households. That is, the patio group contains material correlates of domestic activities, including artifacts related to cooking and serving food, lithic production, and textile production. In addition, features relating to the cooking and storing of food, such as a possible hearth (Feature 8), and storage pits (features 3,

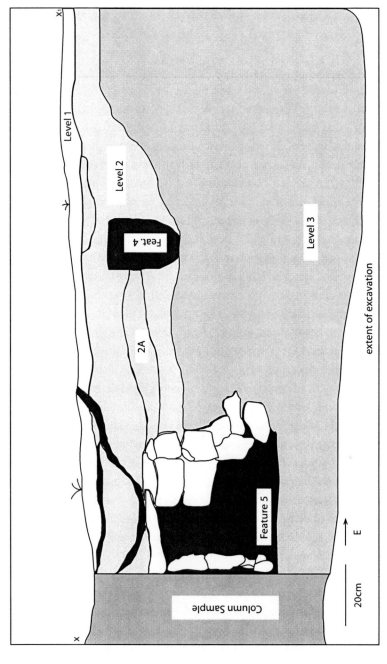

FIGURE 5.10  Profile of excavations in Patio Group XI, 27I, north wall. Level 2a is slightly more compacted than Level 2, though its constituents are basically the same. Feature 5 matrix is composed of compacted, pebbly silt.

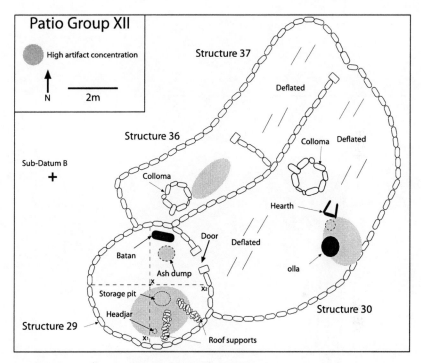

FIGURE 5.11  Excavations in Patio Group XII.

20, and 21) were recorded. In short, the activities needed to sustain a single domestic unit were found in the excavations of this patio group.

*Patio Group XII.* Patio Group XII was one of the largest patio groups at Marcaya and consisted of a house (Structure 29) and a large patio subdivided into three internal rooms (called structures 30, 36, and 37) (figs. 5.11 and 5.12). This patio exhibits one of the few examples of internal architecture at Marcaya. Structure 29 is a well-constructed round house with clear walls and a very well-defined door. The walls of Structure 29 are some of best examples of wall construction at Marcaya as they are large, flat, and placed in a systematic, circular fashion. A seventy-centimeter-wide door in the eastern end of the structure leads directly to Structure 30, the attached patio.

The patio is large, abuts the house, and is subdivided into three rooms, which were originally designated "structures" 30, 36, and 37 in the field. Structure 30 is large, with a well-defined foundation. The eastern half of

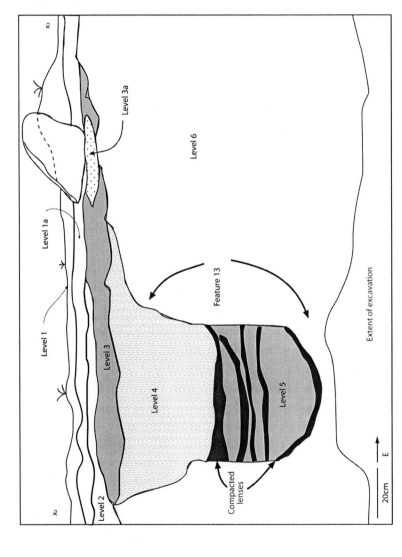

FIGURE 5.12  Profile of excavations in Patio Group XII, Structure 29.

the structure does not have walls, however, and instead is delineated by foundations more typical of other structures at Marcaya. Its long axis is oriented towards the northeast, and there is a small clearing between it and Structure 37 in its far northeast corner. The surface of this structure was littered with utilitarian ceramics, but no other artifacts were present. A large colloma just to the north of the center of the structure was recorded on the surface as well. Structure 36 is a small, ovoid room. A well-constructed door connecting Structure 36 to Structure 37 is in the north-eastern corner of the structure. No artifacts or features were recorded on its surface. Structure 37 is similar to 36. Surface artifacts were limited to ceramics, and no surface features were recorded.

In summary, Structure 29 excavations contained a great deal of domestic refuse including ceramic sherds, a headjar, spindle whorls, faunal remains, shellfish remains, and ash deposits. Artifacts also included what would normally be considered distinct from domestic refuse, such as a high quantity of fineware, as well as fragments of panpipes. Features included a pit apparently used for disposing domestic garbage, a *batán* or grinding stone, and what was first thought to be a prepared clay surface, but on closer inspection was determined to be natural.

Structure 36 was found to contain material correlates of domestic activities with pottery, lithics, shellfish remains, and faunal material recovered in excavations. Features included a relatively large colloma with a few material remains including pottery, faunal material, a piece of obsidian, fragments of other lithics, and some shell.

Excavations in Structure 30 revealed a fairly shallow cultural deposit, but there were several significant features related to the processing and storage of food, including a large colloma in the center of the structure and a hearth and a large cookpot (*olla*). The distribution of the hearth, the stone-lined pit, and the in situ olla indicate that the primary activity conducted within this patio related to the preparation and storage of food.

Like the excavations in Patio Group XI, excavations conducted within Patio Group XII confirmed the proposition that this patio group represented a single archaeological household. The patio group contains a variety of artifacts relating to domestic activities, including lithic and textile production. In addition, features relating to the cooking and storing of food, such as a hearth (Feature 15), a cooking olla (Feature 16), and two collomas were recorded. In short, activities needed to sustain a single domestic unit were also found in excavations of this patio group.

*Patio Group Differences.* The contrasts between patio groups XI and XII revealed a basic dichotomy between patio groups excavated. Table 5.2 is a summary of the differences between architecture and artifacts of patio groups at Marcaya. This table summarizes the size of each patio group and the amount of material recovered per cubic meter excavated as expressed by an index. The index used in this calculation is simply the number of artifacts (count for spindle whorls; weight for all other artifacts) divided by the cubic meters excavated per structure. This results in an index that allows for a relative comparison of each structure in terms of the quantity of artifacts per cubic meter excavated.

The artifact quantity indices can be correlated with architectural features observed on the surface and from further excavations. When this is done, several patterns are apparent. The most salient of these patterns is the quantity of material excavated in patio groups X and XII. Both of these patio groups have high fineware indices (143.88 and 130.70, respectively) when compared to other patio groups. While two other patio groups had higher fineware indices (Patio Group XI = 97.57 and Patio Group XIV = 128.00, see below), patio groups X and XII also had very high panpipe indices (.75 and .68, respectively) compared to other structures.

The high indices of panpipes and fineware in these patio groups are also accompanied by finely worked walls and well-defined doors—some of the finest examples of architecture at Marcaya. Patio groups X and XII clearly stand out when compared to other patio groups at the site. Patio Group XI, on the other hand, has a relatively high fineware index (97.57), but a very small quantity of panpipes (.19). Furthermore, the patio group has poorly constructed architecture, with unworked house walls and no obvious door between structures 26 and 27. The only comparable patio group to patio groups X and XII in excavations was Patio Group XIV, which showed very high fineware and panpipe indices (128.0 and 1.0, respectively). Structure 38, the house associated with that patio group, had very well-defined walls and a door, both with well-worked fieldstone as well. Unfortunately, Structure 38 had been looted in the recent past and the patio of this patio group is not well defined on the surface. Thus, the only excavation in this patio group was a single test trench in Structure 38.

The artifact assemblages with high indices of fineware and panpipes, coupled with the high quality of architecture in patio groups X and XII, suggest that they are distinct from other patio groups at Marcaya. These differences suggest differences in status — a point that I will return to in chapter 8.

## Summary of Excavations

Economic activities at Marcaya appear to have been predominantly organized by the household. Archaeological correlates for economic activities found in each patio group suggest that households were the primary economic unit at Marcaya and that each was economically independent, as each patio group was functionally redundant and had the components to sustain a domestic unit. All households contained evidence for food storage and processing, cooking, and consumption. Collomas, the only known storage facilities at Marcaya, were found without exception, either within the confines of patios and houses or in closely associated patio groups. No evidence for communal storage, food processing, or other activities were revealed.

An exception to the self-sufficiency of households was that none appeared to produce pottery. Indeed, firing loci, caches of clay, wasters, and other manufacturing evidence were not found in fieldwork. Additionally, spindle whorls were made by the rather laborious process of modifying broken wall sherds from large storage vessels, providing evidence, albeit indirect, that ceramics were not made at the site.

The primary intention of excavating within patio groups was to test the proposition that they were archaeological households. The excavations described above clearly demonstrate that patio groups were the loci for a variety of domestic activities including food storage, processing, and preparation; lithic production; textile production; and, perhaps, household ritual. The full range of activities are characteristic of each patio group, indicating that most if not all socio-economic activities conducted within the community were probably organized at the household — not the community — level.

While there are some notable differences between the archaeological households at Marcaya in terms of the composition of their artifactual assemblages and the quality of the architecture that composes their structures, these have yet to be evaluated. As outlined previously, these differences are expected in middle-range societies. I will explore the significance of these results in chapter 8. For now, I will turn to a detailed discussion of artifacts recovered in excavations.

# 6

# *Pottery at Marcaya*

POTTERY HAS BEEN THE MOST frequent research topic in Nasca studies since the early 1900s. Indeed, finely crafted pottery was the principal reason that western scholars became interested in Nasca society. With a few recent exceptions, the analysis of Nasca pottery attempted to either resolve chronological problems through seriation or focused on particular iconographic issues. As a result of these studies, the Nasca ceramic sequence is well known, providing archaeologists working in the region with a solid chronological framework. Moreover, Nasca iconography is now understood as a means by which the ancient people of Nasca expressed "death and fertility symbolism" (Carmichael 1994), with the larger corpus of images relating to agricultural fertility and renewal.

Despite this focus on Nasca pottery, many of its details remain poorly understood. For example, the residential context of Nasca pottery consumption is totally unknown, a fact lamented in previous publications: "[T]he domestic context of Nasca remains absolutely unexplored. Meager excavations in habitational areas constitute a major barrier to a greater understanding of Nasca culture and its ceramic production" (Carmichael 1994:230, my translation). This has left many questions unanswered. For example, what is the composition of a domestic vessel assemblage? Are domestic assemblages similar to excavated assemblages from Cahuachi? Are particular vessels exclusive to domestic sites, and if so, have these remained unevaluated — since Nasca research has historically focused on graves and their associated goods? How did Nasca polychromes fit into the domestic assemblage, and if present, what was their function? Where was Nasca pottery produced? Finally, if Nasca polychromes acted as materialized ideology, how effectively was this ideology incorporated into residential life?

In this chapter, I address these questions by considering the Marcaya vessel assemblage. I evaluate forms present in the vessel assemblage and functional differences between pottery assemblages in patio groups at Marcaya. Because no evidence for pottery production was found at Marcaya, I evaluate Nasca pottery production indirectly by employing compositional analysis. Analysis of samples from Marcaya and a broader regional sample strongly suggests regional specialization in Nasca pottery production, and analysis of clay resources in the region suggests that Cahuachi was a locus of pottery production. These results have profound implications for our understanding of the Nasca political economy.

## Pottery at Marcaya

Pottery is the most ubiquitous artifact recovered in excavations at Marcaya, amounting to 71 percent of the artifacts collected by weight. Following Patrick Carmichael (1988) and Helaine Silverman (1993), pottery recovered at Marcaya was divided into two major categories: fineware (decorated polychrome pottery) and plainware (utilitarian, or undecorated pottery). Fineware pottery, the famous Nasca polychrome ceramics that have received so much attention in the past, is characterized by "decorative polychrome painting" (Carmichael 1988:211) and burnished surfaces. The fabric of fineware pottery is very homogeneous, consisting of fine paste with very few to no inclusions. In contrast, plainware pottery has a coarse fabric, unslipped surfaces, and thick vessel walls (thicker than six millimeters). A few plainware vessels from Marcaya are crudely decorated with simple paint splatters. Only one type of pottery is not consistent with these two broad categories: painted jars or *cantaros*, which are unslipped, polychrome painted vessels bearing thick walls and coarse fabric.

Nasca shape classifications are well known from analysis by several key researchers (Carmichael 1988; Kroeber 1956; Proulx 1968; Silverman 1993). Until recently, Lawrence Dawson's seriation of Nasca pottery had not been published, though his seriation is the classification scheme most often used by Nasca scholars today (Carmichael 1998:20). Very recently, Donald Proulx (2006) published the bulk of this seriation, though the work focuses on iconography. Proulx's earlier work (Proulx 1968) elaborated on the Dawson seriation in his study of Nasca 3 and Nasca 4 pottery in Ica and Nasca, and his published work provides the basis for this analysis.

Following Silverman (1993), all pottery was classified according to broad shape categories created by Silverman and previous researchers. Most vessel designations were made based upon relatively small diagnostic sherds, which prevented precise determination of vessel types, especially if diagnostic parts of the vessel were missing (e.g., a base). As a result, the vessel assemblage described has been necessarily biased towards easily identifiable sherds, and certain shape classes that depend on rare vessel parts (such as conical-based bowls) have certainly been underrepresented. A full 96 percent of the vessel assemblage can be placed into one of four fineware categories or one of three plainware categories of vessel types (fig. 6.1).

Only vessel types found at Marcaya are included in this classification scheme and other well-known Nasca vessels are absent. The most notable absence is the Nasca double-spout and bridge bottle, which was not found in excavations. The lack of one of the most conspicuous Nasca pottery types is significant, as it has been regarded as the "most prestigious vessel form" in Nasca (Proulx 1968:13). All double-spout bottles of known provenience, however, have been recovered from burial contexts. As no graves were found at Marcaya, the absence of double-spout and bridge bottles in the vessel assemblage strongly suggests that they were probably reserved for graves.

### Chronology

Based on the ceramics recorded on its surface in 1989 and later in 1996, Marcaya was thought to date to the Early Nasca phases of the Nasca sequence (Schreiber 1989). Excavations confirmed this initial assessment. Analysis of ceramics revealed that Marcaya indeed dates to the early Nasca phases; however, the phases are limited to Nasca 3 and Nasca 4 (fig. 6.2). Nasca 2 ceramics were not found. Three vessels recovered in excavations date to earlier phases (see below). Since these represent less than 1 percent of the entire vessel assemblage, I conclude that they are either heirlooms or trade pieces and not representative of the occupation.

### Fineware: Vessel Shapes

Following Proulx (1968) and Silverman (1993), I classified fineware into one of several different shapes: bowls, dishes, vases, and jars, with an

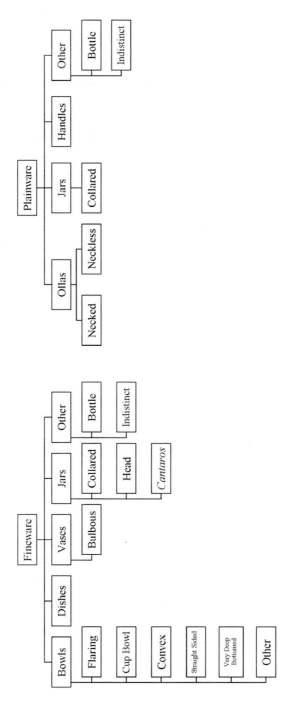

FIGURE 6.1 Vessel shapes recorded in the excavated assemblage at Marcaya. Handles are obviously not a vessel shape; however, they were found with some frequency and so are included in this schematic.

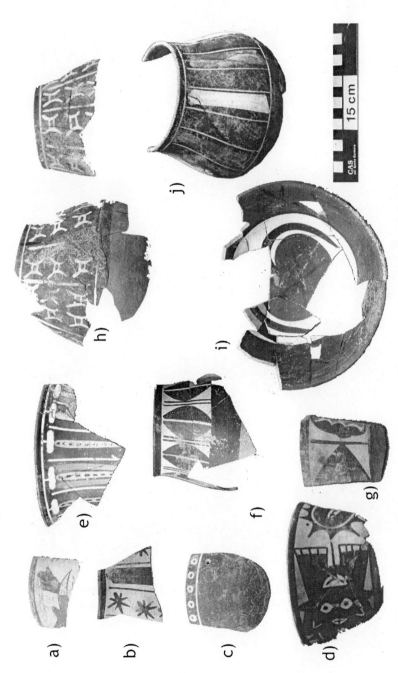

FIGURE 6.2 Composite photo of polychrome pottery from Marcaya. a) Nasca 4 (Type 2) flaring bowl, Structure 3; b) Nasca 4 bulbous vase, Structure 26; c) Nasca 4 convex bowl, Structure 26; d) Nasca 3 (Type 2) flaring bowl, Structure 27; e) Nasca 4 cup bowl, Structure 29; f) Nasca 3 bulbous vase, Structure 29; g) Nasca 4 (Type 1) flaring bowl, Structure 29; h) Nasca 4 bulbous vase, Structure 35; i) Nasca 4 dish, Structure 29; j) Nasca 4 bulbous vase, Structure 35.

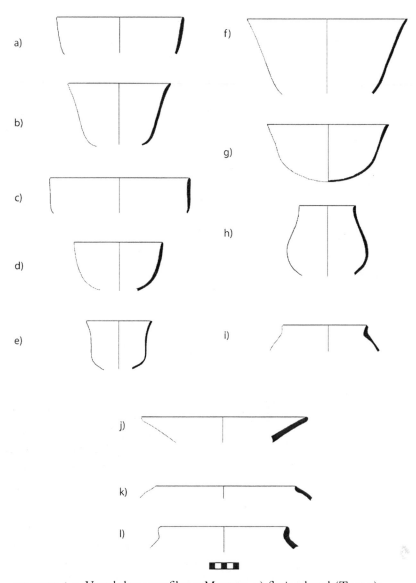

FIGURE 6.3 Vessel shape profiles at Marcaya. a) flaring bowl (Type 1);
b) flaring bowl (Type 2); c) straight bowl; d) convex bowl; e) cup bowl;
f) very deep-bottomed bowl; g) dish; h) bulbous vase; i) collared jar;
j) necked olla; k) neckless olla; l) collared jar (plain).

additional category of "other" (fig. 6.1). Because these shapes have never been described in a domestic context, I provide brief descriptions of each type below (more detailed information can be found in Vaughn [2000]).

*Bowls.* Bowls are unrestricted vessels with rounded to conical bases and walls that are either flaring, straight, or incurving. Bowls are slipped and painted on the exterior and sometimes slipped on the interior as well. All bowls recovered at Marcaya are painted, thus all are classified as fineware. In Dawson's classification scheme, bowls are subdivided into a number of subclasses, which account for the degree of flaring in the wall, curvature of the base, and depth of the vessel. These subclasses are: flaring bowls, cup bowls, round-bottom bowls, conical-bottom bowls, and very deep-bottom bowls.

Two types of flaring bowls are identified by Proulx in his refinement of the Dawson scheme. The first (Type 1) is a "vertically sided bowl with little flare" and the second (Type 2) is a "concave sided vessel with a relatively flaring wall" (Proulx 1968:12). Both types are present in the assemblage at Marcaya, though Type 1 is more common (fig. 6.3). Cup bowls are "bell-shaped vessels with a distinctive flaring rim" (Proulx 1968:12). They appear to have been derived from a high-sided variety of the Type 2 flaring bowl, though they have a much higher degree of flare.

The remaining three subclasses in Proulx's analysis are defined more by their bases than their walls (see discussion in Proulx 1968:12–13). Because the assemblage at Marcaya consisted mostly of body sherds and bases were rarely present, subclasses derived from wall form were created. Convex bowls are bowls with convex walls (without flare), while straight-sided bowls have straight, vertical walls with no curvature. A single very deep-bottomed bowl was recovered in excavations as well. Additionally, bowls were found in excavations of a form that dates to the proto-Nasca phase. This bowl form is typical of proto-Nasca (also referred to as Nasca 1; see chapter 2) and is depicted in various publications (for example, see Van Gijseghem 2006). Bowls appear to be the most common decorated vessel shape in Nasca (table 6.1). The assemblage at Marcaya is no exception.

*Dishes.* From Early Nasca after Phase 2, dishes are essentially bowl-shaped fineware vessels that are slipped on both the interior and exterior, and whose primary design is painted on the interior rather than the exterior of

TABLE 6.1 Vessel assemblage at Marcaya by shape category compared to Proulx's (1968) study, and Silverman's (1993:Table 16.7) excavations at Cahuachi. The Proulx assemblage was calculated by Silverman (1993:Table 16.7), and I use those calculations for comparison to the Marcaya assemblage.

| | Proulx | Cahuachi Fineware Assemblage | Marcaya % Total Assemblage | Marcaya % Fineware Assemblage |
|---|---|---|---|---|
| Fineware | | | | |
| Bowls | 48% | 68% | 30% | 55% |
| Dishes | 10% | 9% | 5% | 9% |
| Vases | 11% | 6% | 15% | 27% |
| Headjars | 3% | 0% | 2% | 3% |
| Collared Jars | 3% | 0% | 1% | 3% |
| Modeled Vessels | 1% | 9% | 1% | 0% |
| Double Spout Bottles | 9% | 3% | 0% | 0% |
| Other | 15% | 4% | 2% | 3% |
| | 100% | 99% | 56% | 100% |
| Plainware | | | | |
| Ollas | 2% | no data | 23% | n/a |
| Collared Jars | no data | no data | 11% | n/a |
| Cantaros | no data | no data | 6% | n/a |
| Other | no data | no data | 1% | n/a |

the vessel. Dishes are the second most common type of pottery recorded in published Nasca assemblages, but the third most common at Marcaya.

*Vases.* The only known vase form in Early Nasca is the bulbous vase. Variability in vase form occurs in later time periods, beginning in Nasca 5, when a variety of new forms emerge (see Carmichael 1988:table 6). Technically, the bulbous vase is a form of jar, and according to Proulx (1968:13), "bulbous vases are tall cylinder-shaped jars whose height is greater than the mouth diameter; on early forms there is a bulge in the wall of the vessel, usually in the lower one third of the side." Though they are more akin to jars than vases, I use the term "bulbous vase," since it has a long tradition in Nasca studies. Bulbous vases are slipped and painted on the exterior and sometimes slipped on the interior as well. All bulbous vases found at Marcaya are categorized as fineware, since they are all painted. Bulbous vases were easily distinguishable from other vessel forms, as both body and rim sherds from bulbous vases indicated a concave vessel form.

Another vase form is present in the assemblage from Marcaya, but the vessel dates to the Early Horizon (see below). This vase is globular with a truncated, inverted rim, and is decorated with negative painting. The decoration and vessel shape identified from the sherds is similar to Paracas-Cavernas type pottery depicted by Kroeber (1944:Plate16.a), and it is clearly not an Early Nasca vessel form or decoration technique. Vases are less common in known vessel assemblages than are bowls and dishes, but they usually comprise the third most frequent form. At Marcaya, the bulbous vase was the second most common fineware form found.

*Jars.* Jars are defined as any vessel with a restricted orifice and a height greater than its maximum diameter (Rice 1987:216). There are several types of jars in the assemblage at Marcaya, including both fineware and plainware. As such, jars comprise the only major category of pottery that includes decorated and undecorated vessels. One form of jar at Marcaya is the collared jar. Collared jars are generally spherical in shape with a small everted rim, or "collar" (Proulx 1968:14). In Proulx's sample, collared jars are mostly decorated fineware vessels (see Proulx 1968:65 and 78). Though fineware collared jars are rare, there are several examples of them at Marcaya.

*Headjars.* A form that appears to have developed from the bulbous vase is the so-called "headjar." Proulx defines headjars as "modeled jars in the form of a human head" (Proulx 1968:14). Proulx also includes in this category, however, "several smaller 'open mouth' jars having modeled faces" (ibid.). This latter type is the only type found in excavations at Marcaya, as true modeled headjars were not found.

Headjars were made beginning in Nasca 3, and the vessels depict distinct males with elaborate headdresses, facial markings, and usually facial hair. They are either depicted with open eyes, signifying that the individual is alive, or as "disembodied heads" (trophy heads) with upward-facing eyes and spines through the lips (DeLeonardis 2000:380). Anatomical accuracy was accomplished by placing modeled features on the heads, including ears and a nose. Though Silverman (1993:226, Note 4) has reported a headjar found in the fill in Passageway 1 of Unit 19 at Cahuachi, most headjars have been recovered in mortuary contexts. A headjar has been found deliberately replacing the head of a decapitated individual in at least one tomb, Grave 7 of Kroeber and Collier's (1998:118, fig. 154) sample, and some have argued that headjars depicting live individuals were used to replace the heads of headless bodies in tombs (Blasco and Ramos 1980). Carmichael (1988:314) reported that this practice did not occur with regularity, though Christina Conlee (2007) has recently found an example of this practice at La Tiza dating to Nasca 5. Regardless, few headjars have been found outside of mortuary contexts (DeLeonardis 2001). Headjars are rare in Proulx's sample and even more rare in Silverman's sample, as she recovered only one headjar sherd in her excavations. At Marcaya, headjars are more common than elsewhere.

*Cantaros.*  A final category of jars is what has been referred to as *cantaros.* These are unslipped vessels with a relatively simple decoration of thick, wavy, dark red lines on a white or tan background with black outline. William Duncan Strong (1957:fig. 12) originally referred to this design as "Cahuachi Broad Line Red, White and Black." Silverman (1993:fig. 13.6) found a similar design on a sherd in her excavations at the "Room of the Posts" at Cahuachi. Published literature reveals that this design is only present on a particular vessel form, a form that Kroeber refers to as "Three-Handled Jars (shape TTT)" (Kroeber 1944:Plate 28, fig. I; Kroeber and Collier 1998:figs. 90, 128, 155, and 187). Proulx refers to a single vessel from Gravelot CB in Ocucaje as a three-handled jar as well (1970:64 and Plate 12E). Johny Isla Cuadrado (personal communication) has also identified this design on jars in his fieldwork throughout the south coast, as has Katharina Schreiber (personal communication). The jars have the shape of a globular vase suitable for storing liquids and are typically painted with this design. Other jars of this shape feature different designs, such as concentric circles, though these are less well known and remain unpublished. Isla Cuadrado (personal communication) refers to these jars as "cantaros," or canteens, because of their presumed function of storing liquids. I follow his lead here and refer to the jars as cantaros as well. The two designs described above were frequently found on unslipped sherds with a coarse paste at Marcaya. When sherds with these motifs were found, the precise vessel form could usually not be determined, though their slight curvature indicated that the vessel was globular. Though their type cannot be verified without further excavations, these sherds were classified as three-handled jars, or cantaros. Silverman (1993a) found several fragments of these in excavations at Cahuachi. Proulx (1968) does not mention this vessel type at all; however, more than 6 percent of the Marcaya assemblage was comprised of cantaros.

*Other.* Four additional fineware vessel types were found in excavations, including an Early Horizon vase, a small fineware bottle, and a modeled vessel of a terrestrial animal.

## Plainware: Vessel Shapes

While fineware pottery in Nasca is well known, plainware pottery has received relatively little attention. Silverman (1993) has published the most useful analysis of Early Nasca plainware pottery, and I draw from her classification.

*Ollas.* The most common plainware vessel recovered at Marcaya is the *olla,* or cookpot. Silverman (1993:245–247) defines ollas as large, globular cooking vessels that either have an everted rim or are completely collarless. Ollas that have a rim, or collar, are "necked ollas," while those lacking a collar are "neckless ollas." Whole ollas generally have strap handles as well (see Silverman 1993:247 and Proulx 1968:fig. 17). At Marcaya, with few exceptions, handles were found separately without rims; thus, it was difficult to assess whether they were from ollas or other plainware vessels such as those discussed below.

Because Proulx's assemblage consisted of grave goods, the frequency of ollas was fairly small, making up slightly more than 2 percent of the total assemblage. Silverman (1993), however, recovered them much more frequently. Though an exact percentage of ollas in the vessel assemblage from Cahuachi is not published, Silverman (1993:table 16.4) documented 140 vessels in her excavations, the majority of which were necked ollas. At Marcaya, necked ollas comprise almost 19 percent of the total vessel assemblage, while neckless ollas make up only slightly more than 1 percent.

*Jars.* The second most common plainware vessel recovered at Marcaya was the collared jar. Silverman defines collared jars as vessels with a globular shape with short collars, slightly inverted to straight. Collared jars at Marcaya are generally wiped, not burnished, and undecorated. The Marcaya vessel assemblage consists of 11 percent collared jars. Collared jars are not considered a separate category in Proulx's scheme.

Ambiguities between collared jars and necked ollas sometimes arose when only a rim sherd was used for their classification. The main difference is that ollas have long, everted rims, while jars have short rims that are straight to inverted. Lisa DeLeonardis (1997:229–230) encountered a similar problem when evaluating the vessel assemblage in the Ica Valley. She found that plainware ollas and jars were very difficult to distinguish from each other in sherd form. To resolve this, DeLeonardis classified all plainware jars and ollas using the single comprehensive category of collared vessels. If Silverman's assemblage is any indication, jars and ollas are distinct enough in Nasca to be able to distinguish between the two based upon a small fragment, though it is recognized that some inaccuracies may result with this classification scheme.

There were three plainware vessels that could not be accounted for in one of the categories outlined above. These included three small bottles and a small jar (Feature 1), the latter of which is similar to a plainware vessel excavated by Silverman at Cahuachi (Silverman 1993:fig. 13.32).

*Vessel Assemblage at Marcaya*

The pottery at Marcaya was classified into the three basic functional categories of cooking, serving, and storage. When function could not be determined, vessels were assigned to an additional category of "other." This functional classification reveals that all serving vessels are polychrome finewares, including bowls, dishes, and vases, while all vessels relating to the storage and preparation of food are utilitarian wares, including undecorated jars, cantaros, and unpainted ollas (table 6.2). With the exception of several very small plainware bottles (n = 3), plainware vessel shapes that would have functioned as serving vessels were not found at Marcaya. This fact is consistent with Silverman's (1993) previous excavations at Cahuachi, as she found that the only utilitarian vessels used for serving were plainware bowls, restricted to the earlier Nasca 1 occupation of the site (Silverman 1993:fig. 16.34).

These data confirm Carmichael's (1995) observation that Nasca

TABLE 6.2 Vessel assemblage at Marcaya by function.

| Function | Vessel Shape | Total | %Total | %Category |
|---|---|---|---|---|
| Serving | Bowl | 128 | 30.12 | 56.64 |
|  | Dish | 20 | 4.71 | 8.85 |
|  | Vase | 62 | 14.59 | 27.43 |
|  | Headjar | 7 | 1.65 | 3.10 |
|  | Decorated Jar | 6 | 1.41 | 2.65 |
|  | Plainware Bottle | 3 | 0.71 | 1.33 |
|  | Total | 226 | 53.18 | 100.00 |
| Storage | Painted Jar | 27 | 6.35 | 41.54 |
|  | Collared Jar | 38 | 8.94 | 58.46 |
|  | Total | 65 | 15.29 | 100.00 |
| Cooking | Olla | 96 | 22.59 | 100.00 |
|  | Total | 96 | 22.59 | 100.00 |
| Other/ | Handle | 29 | 6.82 | 76.32 |
| Unknown | Other fineware | 9 | 2.12 | 23.68 |
|  | Total | 38 | 8.94 | 100.00 |
|  | TOTAL | 425 | 100.00 |  |

polychromes appear to have been used in daily life. Indeed, polychromes were used for daily consumption and serviced as vessels for serving and consuming food and drink. Vessel shapes used for serving and consumption include bowls, dishes, bulbous vases, and jars. Despite the variety of vessel shapes, the majority of polychromes at Marcaya consisted of flaring bowls and bulbous vases, found with regularity in all households.

When taken as a whole, the vessel assemblage at Marcaya includes a very high proportion of polychrome fineware. Indeed, both utilitarian vessels and finewares were found in all excavated contexts. The assemblage was evaluated using non-conjoining rim sherds as a proxy measure for entire vessels and measured as a "minimum number of individuals" (MNI). When the MNI indicator is used, the proportion of fineware vessels at Marcaya amounts to 56 percent of the total vessel assemblage (table 6.3). This is a very high percentage, even when compared to the extraordinarily high percentages found at Cahuachi.

TABLE 6.3 Comparison of vessel assemblages at Marcaya and Cahuachi (Silverman 1993:228).

|  | Marcaya | | Cahuachi | |
| --- | --- | --- | --- | --- |
|  | # Rims | % | # Rims | % |
| Plainware | 170 | 44 | 140 | 29 |
| Fineware | 217 | 56 | 339 | 71 |

When faced with the results of the MNI from excavations at Cahuachi, Silverman (1993:301) concluded that the high proportion of fineware in the vessel assemblage could not have been the result of domestic activities. Silverman suggested that if Cahuachi had functioned as a permanent habitation, the expected ratio of fineware to plainware would have been the reverse. That is, fineware would have comprised only 30 percent of the assemblage and plainware would have made up about 70 percent of the total. This was not an unreasonable assumption, as fineware make up even smaller proportions of assemblages at other habitation sites in the Andes. Differences between the ceramic assemblages at Marcaya and Cahuachi are notable. However, the difference between the Marcaya assemblage and Silverman's hypothetical domestic assemblage (30 percent fineware and 70 percent plainware) are also significant. In fact, when comparing all three, the Marcaya assemblage is more similar to Cahuachi than it is to Silverman's hypothetical domestic assemblage.

Marcaya's ceramic vessel assemblage suggests that domestic sites in Nasca do not have the low proportions of fineware that Silverman predicted. These results have implications for our understanding of not only the pottery assemblages in Nasca domestic sites, but also how we may interpret the ceramic assemblage at Cahuachi. Both of these points will be addressed further in the final chapter.

## Spatial Distribution of Pottery

Since we determined that patio groups were residential units, we expected functional categories of pottery to be distributed relatively equally across them. That is, each patio group should have yielded the necessary pottery to sustain a small household. Indeed, each patio group excavated had vessels for *preparing* food (ollas), *storing* food and drink (undecorated jars, painted jars), and *serving* food and drink (bowls, dishes, vases, jars). The most significant find, however, was that *all households had access to fineware polychromes*. I will explore status differences in pottery consumption in chapter 8.

## Design Themes of Marcaya Fineware

While there are various typologies of Nasca iconography (e.g., Blasco Bosqued and Ramos Gómez 1980; Proulx 1968, 2006), Silverman (1993:242–243) produced a modified typology based on the excavated assemblage at Cahuachi. The results of this typology provide a useful benchmark to compare the design themes present on Marcaya pottery.

Silverman uses a tripartite division of iconographic themes depicted on Nasca pottery: (1) mythical (supernatural); (2) natural (representational, referential); and (3) geometric (abstract) (Silverman 1993:243). Mythical motifs on Early Nasca pottery include the Anthropomorphic Mythical Being, the Spotted Cat, the Horrible Bird, the Killer Whale, the Serpentine Creature, the Harpy, and the Head Taster (Proulx 2006; Silverman 1993:243). Natural themes include various species of birds (swallows, hummingbirds, herons, condors, water birds, and ducks), human figures, plants, insects, fish, reptiles, other animals, weapons, and agricultural products (Silverman 1993:243). Geometric designs include step-frets, circles, triangles, diamonds, wavy lines, etc. (Silverman 1993:243).

All fineware sherds with identifiable designs were categorized into one of Silverman's three categories. The Marcaya assemblage was then compared with the Cahuachi assemblage, and table 6.4 presents these results as well as the vessels used in Proulx's analysis. Clearly, most of the design themes of the assemblage at Marcaya are centered around naturalistic and geometric motifs. Most of the naturalistic elements depicted are agricultural products such as *ají*, lucuma, etc. When compared to both the Cahuachi assemblage and the vessels used by Proulx in his analysis, the assemblage from Marcaya has far fewer pottery fragments depicting mythical, or supernatural, motifs.

TABLE 6.4 Design themes on fineware pottery from Marcaya compared to Cahuachi (Silverman 1993:Table 16.8) and Proulx's (1968) sample as reported by Silverman (1993:Table 16.8). Many decorated fineware sherds had unidentifiable designs, accounting for the relatively low number in the Marcaya sample. The geometric theme includes cantaros in the Marcaya sample.

| Motifs | Marcaya | | Cahuachi | | Proulx | |
|---|---|---|---|---|---|---|
| | # | % | # | % | # | % |
| Mythical | 7 | 5 | 75 | 22 | 112 | 19 |
| Naturalistic | 68 | 46 | 133 | 39 | 284 | 47 |
| Geometric | 72 | 49 | 132 | 39 | 205 | 34 |
| Total | 147 | 100 | 340 | 100 | 601 | 100 |

## Pottery Production

Excavations at Marcaya did not yield any evidence of pottery production activities. The only evidence, indirect at best, for pottery production at Marcaya was the presence of several polishing stones. Because many features remain exposed, a systematic survey of the entire surface of Marcaya was conducted. But despite this survey and the extensive excavations, no locus for firing pottery was found, nor were specific artifacts relating to pottery production—such as wasters, caches of unfired clay, pigments, or brushes—located on the site. Numerous steps and carefully controlled contexts for firing pottery at high temperatures in a completely oxidizing environment were required to produce Nasca fineware (Carmichael 1998:222), so I expected that material evidence would be present if fineware production did, in fact, occur at Marcaya. Although plainware required fewer steps to produce, I expected some material correlate to its manufacture as well. None was found, even though pottery is the most ubiquitous artifact recovered in excavations at Marcaya. Where was pottery being manufactured? Off-site but near the community? Or perhaps somewhere else entirely?

Knowing where and in what contexts polychromes were produced would provide archaeologists with valuable clues to their importance in Nasca society. While some have suggested that polychromes were the products of multiple households throughout the Nasca region (Carmichael 1998; Silverman 1993), the evidence at Marcaya does not support this hypothesis. Indeed, if polychromes were important to elite power—as it appears they were, as the principal medium of ideology—we would expect that their production would have been centralized and associated with the elites themselves.

In addressing the question of production, the composition of Marcaya ceramics provided some clues (e.g., Orton et al. 1993:145). Compositional analysis is generally employed by archaeologists to "[characterize] artifacts with sources or source zones where raw materials used in their manufacture originated" (Neff et al. 1996:390). The primary assumption in compositional analysis is that pottery produced in certain areas will bear a specific chemical fingerprint (Perlman and Asaro 1971:182). A compositional analysis entails comparing sherds whose origin is not known and finding groups in these materials "that *may* reflect source(s), or simply to determine whether a series of samples may or may not belong to the same group" (Orton et al. 1993:145, emphasis in original).

## Compositional Analysis

Towards this end, a pilot compositional analysis utilizing instrumental neutron activation analysis (INAA) was conducted to determine whether the ceramic assemblage recovered at Marcaya exhibited compositional variability. The explicit objective was to determine compositional groups in the sherds, if they existed, and in future research to match those groups (and, by extension, the sherds) with specific sources of raw material.

An initial exploratory analysis of paste and temper was conducted on a sample of diagnostic sherds recovered in excavations at Marcaya to determine whether the ceramics could be categorized according to distinct, macroscopic paste groups (e.g., Sinopoli 1991:57). All diagnostic sherds from three excavated patio groups (I, XI, and XII) were analyzed. Observations with a 10x hand lens were made on a fresh break of each diagnostic sherd in the sample. The low magnification limited identification of specific mineral inclusions; however, it was sufficient to place the sherds into three paste groups based on color and type and frequency of inclusions.

Paste Type A is a reddish brown to yellowish brown paste (5YR4/4-4/6) with coarse (1/2–1 mm), poorly sorted inclusions consisting of primarily quartz, mica, undifferentiated pebbles, and sometimes pyrite.

All but one sherd of Paste Type A are from crudely made plainware ollas and jars. The exception is a sherd from a negative-painted globular vase that dates to the Early Horizon. Though the group includes one painted sherd, for convenience, this paste type will be referred to as the "brown utilitarian paste."

Paste Type B is a coarse, pinkish gray (7.5YR6/2) paste with poorly sorted inclusions. The inclusions of Type B are similar to Type A and are composed of volcanic pebbles, quartz, and mica with the largest granules of these being very coarse (1–2 mm). One notable difference is that pyrite is rarely present in this paste type. Most sherds within this paste group are from thick, undecorated ollas and jars, but some of the sherds are from cantaros as well. Although they are painted, all sherds falling in this paste type are from thick, unslipped vessels and for convenience, the paste type will be referred to as the "pink utilitarian paste."

Paste Type C is a very fine paste that is light red (2.5YR6/8) to orange (5YR6/8) in color. Inclusions are scarce to absent and when present are very well sorted and composed of mostly quartz, but also occasionally feldspar and mica. All but one sherd in this paste group are from painted Nasca fineware. One specimen is a proto-Nasca bowl, one of two sherds from this phase at Marcaya. In addition to fineware pottery, panpipes recovered in excavations were also of this paste type, which is consistent with other descriptions of the paste of Nasca polychrome fineware (Carmichael 1998:217; Proulx 1968:23). Though there have been some slight differences noted in the pastes of vessels from the Nasca and Ica Valleys (Proulx 1968:23), for convenience this paste type will be referred to as the "Nasca fineware paste."

## Results of INAA

The immediate goal of the INAA study was to determine if macroscopic variability in paste composition corresponded to chemically distinct compositional groups. To achieve that end, an equal number of sherds of the three paste types was selected randomly from the sample and augmented with a judgmental selection of sherds from several nearly complete, excavated fineware vessels (all of which were composed of Paste Type C) and two samples of panpipes (also Type C). Samples underwent standard procedures for INAA at the University of Missouri Research Reactor (MURR) (Glascock 1992).

The statistical analysis produced three groups of chemically distinct pottery ("INAA groups 1, 2, and 3") and fourteen unassigned specimens ("Unassigned"). Of the one hundred specimens submitted, the majority (n = 67) of the ceramics are in INAA Group 1. This group contains almost all of the specimens from Paste Type C (40/45 = 89 percent). In addition to the samples from type C, INAA Group 1 included twenty sherds from Type B. The second-largest group of chemically similar ceramics, INAA Group 2, is composed entirely of Paste Type A, or the "brown utilitarian paste." The third group resulting from the analysis, INAA Group 3, is comprised of only four sherds from Paste Type A. Specimens that fell out of the 1-percent probability of each of these groups were not assigned to a paste group and were labeled "unassigned." The unassigned specimens included eight sherds from group A, one from group B, and five from group C. The five sherds from Paste Type C that were unassigned, however, just slightly exceed the 1-percent probability level assigned for the analysis (fig. 6.4).

If the paste groups resulting from the analysis are evaluated in terms of decoration (slip or paint), all assigned decorated specimens fall into INAA Group 1, while five decorated sherds remain unassigned. While the initial paste analysis produced some similarities between paste groups B and C (primarily in color), there were great macroscopic differences between them as well. Type B pastes, as discussed above, were coarser and contained far more inclusions than Type C pastes. As the compositional analysis demonstrates, however, the pastes are virtually identical chemically and the macroscopic distinction may have resulted simply from greater preparation in the Group C pastes. This inference is supported by the rare earth element (REE) plot (see fig. 6.4), which shows that Group B sherds fall toward the low end of INAA Group I. This pattern suggests that their pastes are more diluted with non-plastics such as temper.

While the sample is small, the results of the study were intriguing. The principal finding was that with the exception of a few statistical outliers and a single Early Horizon sherd, all painted vessels and panpipes from Marcaya are chemically homogeneous and form a single compositional

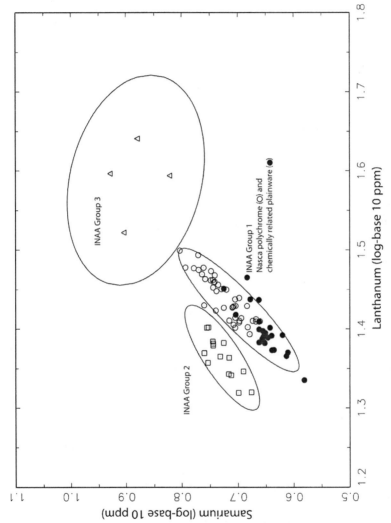

FIGURE 6.4 Bivariate projection of compositional data from Marcaya (not including unassigned specimens) with 90 percent confidence intervals. Note that specimens from paste types A and B fall toward the low end of INAA Group 1, indicating a higher proportion of nonplastic temper in the coarser paste type.

group. These data are strongly suggestive of a centralized zone of production of polychromes. In contrast, plainware ceramics from the site
are compositionally heterogeneous, strongly suggesting that multiple resource zones may have been used for plain pottery. With an absence of
evidence for pottery production at Marcaya, it would seem that this class
of artifacts was being produced elsewhere — but where?

## Further Compositional Studies

This initial pilot study has been expanded in recent years. First, the INAA
study of ceramics from Marcaya initiated a follow-up INAA study. Specifically, the goals of this endeavor were to broaden the geographic sample of
the original Marcaya study and to determine whether there was further
compositional variability in ceramics from sites throughout the region. In
order to reach these goals, the previous study was augmented by taking
samples from surface collections throughout the SNR collected by Schreiber during settlement survey between 1984 and 1996, with the intent of
evaluating settlement patterns in the SNR over time (Schreiber 1999).
Fourteen surveyed sites with a major Early Nasca component were selected to provide additional samples for this study (see Vaughn et al.
2006). Each of the fourteen sites were similar to Marcaya in that they
appeared to be primarily residential. Our analysis demonstrated that the
majority (81 percent) of polychromes from this sample fell into a single
compositional group (INAA Group 1), additional specimens were added
to INAA groups 2 and 3, and we defined one additional group (INAA
Group 4) (fig. 6.5).

A parallel compositional study has involved undertaking an analysis of
pigments on polychrome pottery. In particular, we have analyzed black
pigments on a sample of polychromes from the region. We were successful
in characterizing pigments on the surfaces of polychromes, and our results
suggested that there were uniform recipes used for the black paint found
on Nasca polychromes as well (Vaughn et al. 2005).

Thus, there are three independent compositional studies that indicated
centralized production of polychrome pottery. These analyses reveal that
ancient Nasca potters used ceramic resources from compositionally distinct resource zones, but their explanatory potential was greatly limited
without a sample of ceramic raw materials that were available to ancient

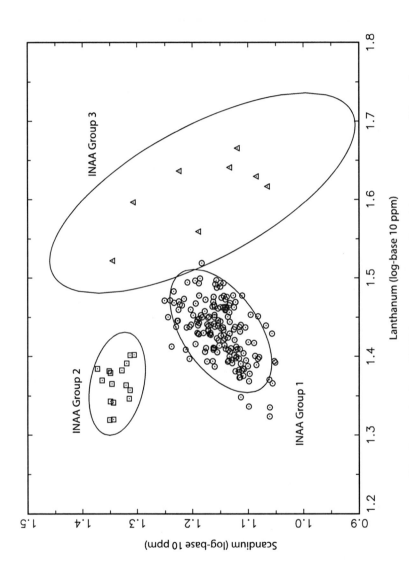

FIGURE 6.5 Bivariate projection of INAA groups 1, 2, and 3 with 90 percent confidence intervals. INAA Group 1 is the principal polychrome group, INAA Group 2 is a group of utilitarian
pottery principally from Marcaya, and INAA Group 3 is a highly variable group comprised mainly
of undecorated utilitarian pottery. INAA group 4 is not depicted.

potters. In other words, the groups that were identified in the analysis cannot be matched to resource zones because of a lack of knowledge about the locations and distribution of clays throughout the region (e.g., Arnold et al. 1991).

To remedy this, I have directed a survey of clays and pigments that were suitable to be used in the production of pottery. The survey of clays has been particularly informative as we have found that (1) clays are widely available in the SNR, (2) clays are compositionally variable, and (3) the clay that most closely matches INAA Group 1 (the polychrome group) was a small brick adobe collected near Cahuachi at the site Estaquería (Vaughn and Neff 2004). These results suggest that although clays were highly variable, ancient Nasca potters selected specific clays in the region and the clays that they selected were located somewhere near Cahuachi. Since the adobe brick in question was collected within the ethnographic upper limit of clay transport — according to Arnold's (1985) work — and because cross-culturally heavy, utilitarian items (including adobe clays) were rarely transported long distances (Trigger 1990), the study strongly suggests that Cahuachi was a likely source of an excess of Early Nasca polychrome pottery production in the region.

These results are not surprising given the recent evidence for production at the site. Orefici and Drusini (2003:144) report evidence for production at Cahuachi consisting of kilns, production-related materials such as paint brushes, as well as caches of pigments and unfired clay. The high winds at Cahuachi, the availability of good potting clays, and a resident population of elites who may have controlled the production of pottery all suggest that this was an activity that may have taken place there.

Of course, other workshops throughout the region must have existed as well, especially for the production of utilitarian pottery and perhaps for the production of copies of Nasca polychromes. These other workshops were most likely responsible for the other compositional groups and unassigned specimens that have been found in recent analyses (Vaughn et al. 2006).

Given the results of these parallel compositional studies, as well as the clay survey, we can state with confidence that (1) early Nasca ceramics were produced in limited (concentrated) contexts, (2) one of those contexts was Cahuachi, and (3) this was the production locus of the majority of polychromes that are found at Marcaya.

Indeed, Cahuachi appears to have been the source of a high percentage of polychrome pottery found at residential sites in the SNR given recent excavations at other village sites (see, for example, Vaughn 2005; Vaughn and Linares 2006). These studies have profound implications for how we view the Early Nasca political economy, and I will return to this point in the final chapter of the book.

## Summary

The analysis of pottery at Marcaya reveals that each household there had all the functional requirements to sustain domestic activities, including cooking, serving, and storage. Furthermore, analysis demonstrated that fineware polychromes made up a high percentage of the vessel assemblage and that all households had access to these polychromes. This confirms previous studies of museum specimens and the impressions of field archaeologists undertaking regional settlement survey.

Pottery, however, is but one artifact class that allows archaeologists to understand Marcaya and its wider implications. Therefore, in the next chapter I will address other artifacts found in excavations.

# Non-Pottery Artifacts at Marcaya

IN THE ANDES, material culture other than pottery, such as metal artifacts, textiles, and the shell of *Spondylus*, played a vital role in the political economy of ancient societies. Thus, while pottery is by far the most common artifact found at Marcaya, it is not the only artifact that provides insight into the political economy in Nasca. In this chapter, I turn to other artifacts found in excavations that reveal the economy of an ancient community—in particular, spindle whorls, panpipes, lithics, and faunal and shellfish remains.

## Textiles

Next to ceramics, textiles are the most studied artifact class in the Andes. While textile manufacture is a time-consuming, multi-staged process requiring a diverse toolkit of both perishable and nonperishable items, neither textiles nor the looms used in their manufacture preserve well in archaeological sites. However, the spindle whorls used to spin raw fiber into yarn for textile production are durable and commonly found in excavations. Spindle whorls recovered from archaeological contexts therefore afford the archaeologist an opportunity to explore ancient textile production (Costin 1993; Keith 1998).

Previous studies suggest that analysis of spindle whorls can reveal the types of fiber the whorls were used to spin (Clark 1993; Keith 1998). Determining the type of fiber spun with spindle whorls found at a site is important, especially in the Andes, where the two major types of fibers used—cotton and camelid fleece—have distinct ecological and geographic distributions.

Evidence for textile manufacture at Marcaya came indirectly in the form of spindle whorls. A total of forty-five ceramic disks, both complete and fragmented, were recovered in excavations. The ceramic disks were

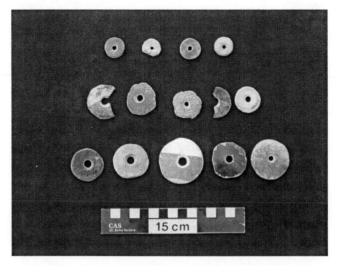

FIGURE 7.1    Sample of spindle whorls found at Marcaya.

classified into one of two categories, depending on the presence of a centrally located hole. Twenty-five disks with holes were designated as spindle whorls (fig. 7.1). No other spinning or weaving implements — or any other direct evidence of textile manufacture, such as textiles or fibers — were found at Marcaya. The distribution of spindle whorls in structures excavated and surface-collected at Marcaya suggest that most, if not all, households spun (see table 5.2). Other evidence for spinning included small fragments of gypsum, which was found in many excavated structures. The gypsum was probably used to coat the hands to facilitate rapid spinning of the spindle.

All but one spindle whorl collected were made from wall sherds of large ceramic vessels. The sherds were first ground down to a roughly circular form and a hole was drilled in the middle from both sides, probably using the chalcedony drills described previously. The only exception to this pattern of production was evidenced in one stone spindle whorl.

While a number of variables can be recorded in the analysis of spindle whorls, according to some studies, whorl diameter and weight are the best indicators of a whorl's function (Clark 1993:397; Keith 1998; Parsons 1972, 1975).[4] Other studies (Winthrop and Winthrop 1975) have shown that the size of the spindle rather than the whorl itself is a good indication of function. Because of lack of preservation, archaeologists rarely recover spindles, but a spindle's size can be approximated by the size of the hole in the spindle whorl. Therefore, whorl diameter, weight, and hole diameter were recorded for all whole and fragmented spindle whorls from Marcaya. The whorl diameter and the hole diameter of incomplete whorls were not difficult to determine, since the whorls were usually broken in half, thereby retaining their original maximum radius. The weight of these whorls was estimated.

While the sample size is small, several patterns are apparent in the data on spindle whorls from Marcaya. When the weight and diameter of the twenty-five spindle whorls are plotted in a scattergram, the resulting diagram of their distribution indicates that there are two groups (fig. 7.2). The larger group consists of bigger and heavier whorls, while the smaller group consists of smaller and lighter whorls.

The flat, disk-shaped spindle whorls manufactured from ceramic sherds at Marcaya are distinct from other known spindle whorls recovered in excavations throughout Nasca. For example, at Pajonal Alto, a small habitation site dating from the Late Nasca period to the Late Intermediate Period, spindle whorls were smaller and formed from clay (Conlee 2000, 2003). While there are several spindle whorls that were recovered in excavations at Cahuachi bearing some resemblance to spindle whorls recovered at Marcaya (see Silverman 1993:fig. 17.2, 17.6), metric attributes are not reported for these artifacts. Thus, the whorls from Marcaya and Pajonal Alto are the only two spindle whorl assemblages reported in detail in Nasca, and comparison between the two may facilitate understanding of how the whorls were used.

The differences in form of the spindle whorl assemblages from Marcaya and Pajonal Alto follow a very general pattern of highland and coastal spindle whorl types. The whorls from Marcaya are similar in shape and size to those documented in the Andean highlands (e.g., see Schreiber 1992:250; Stanish 1997:49), though there is some variability in the manufacturing technique of whorls in the highlands. That is, while some are formed from raw clay, others are constructed from ceramic sherds. This difference is probably attributable to the fact that not all pottery was manufactured in the vicinity. If pottery was produced in the community, handmade spindle whorls could easily be fired along with the pottery. If

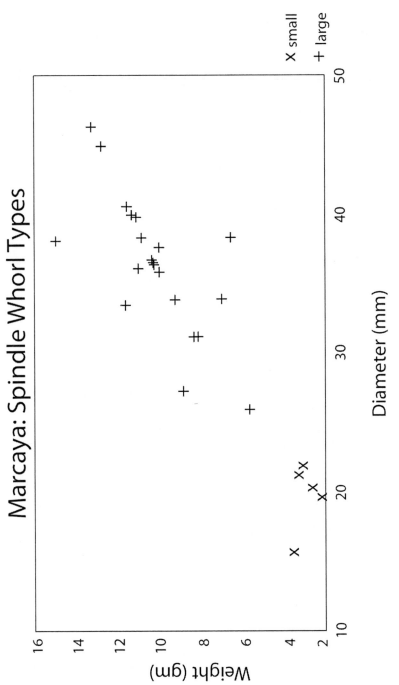

FIGURE 7.2 Scattergram of spindle whorl size from Marcaya.

not, it may have been easier to manufacture spindle whorls from discarded ceramic sherds. The spindle whorls from Pajonal Alto, unlike those at Marcaya, are very similar to whorls documented in archaeological sites from coastal regions in Peru, especially during the later prehistoric period (see Conlee 2000).

Aside from the obvious differences in form, the spindle whorl assemblages from the two sites are remarkably different in the sizes of the spindle whorls (Conlee and Vaughn 1999). The most common explanation for this is that it indicates differences in the types of fiber spun (e.g., Clark 1993; Keith 1998; Parsons 1975). Differences between spindle whorls arise from the spinner's requirements to employ a whorl that (1) controls the speed of a spindle, (2) holds the fiber securely in place, and (3) is the correct weight for the selected fiber. Furthermore, distinct spindle whorls are used in different kinds of spinning and appear to have had long cultural traditions in the Andes (O'Neale 1949).

Drop spinning, used mostly in the highlands to spin camelid fleece, is a method in which both the spindle and the spindle whorl are suspended in air. This method is fast and efficient, and people who employ it can spin while sitting or walking (Gayton 1961). Although efficient, the act of dropping the spindle requires a fairly strong fiber and the method cannot be used to spin more fragile cotton fibers; some suggest that drop spinning is used exclusively for spinning camelid fleece (Franquemont 1986; Goodell 1968; King 1965).

Horizontal spinning, on the other hand, is performed by placing the raw material on the ground, supporting the spindle in either a gourd or ceramic vessel, and drawing out the fiber slowly with the free hand. Horizontal spinning is generally employed on the north coast of Peru, where it is used to spin cotton (Conlee 2000).

At Marcaya, the spindle whorls of the larger-size group are very similar to those used ethnographically in Andean drop spinning. Their form would facilitate drop spinning, and they appear to be too large to spin the more fragile cotton fiber. The only alternative to this hypothesis is to surmise that the larger whorls could have been used to ply cotton. Based on a comparison with the whorls from Pajonal Alto, the smaller spindle whorls may have been small enough to have been used to spin cotton. The majority of the whorls, however, appear to have been of an adequate size and shape to have been used for spinning the fleece of camelids.

TABLE 7.1 Lithic tools at Marcaya and their raw materials. A projectile point and biface were collected on the surface of structures 5 and 8 respectively.

| Tool Type | Material | PG I | PG V | PG X | PG XI | PG XII | Str 17 | Str 20 | Str 40 | Str 5 | Str 8 | Total | % |
|---|---|---|---|---|---|---|---|---|---|---|---|---|---|
| Proj. Point | Obsidian | | 7 | 1 | 2 | 1 | 1 | 1 | 1 | 1 | | 16 | 34.04 |
| Knife | Obsidian | | 1 | | | | | | | | | 1 | 2.13 |
| Knife | Basalt | | | | 2 | | | | | | | 2 | 4.26 |
| Biface | Obsidian | | 4 | | 3 | 1 | | | | | 1 | 9 | 19.15 |
| Biface | R. Chalced. | | | | | 1 | | | | | | 1 | 2.13 |
| Scraper | Obsidian | | 1 | | | | | | | | | 1 | 2.13 |
| Drill | R. Chalced. | | 2 | | 1 | 2 | | | | | | 5 | 10.64 |
| Drill | W. Chalced. | | 1 | | | | | | | | | 1 | 2.13 |
| Util. Flake | Obsidian | 1 | 2 | | 1 | 1 | | | | | | 5 | 10.64 |
| Util. Flake | R. Chalced. | | 2 | | | 1 | | | | | | 3 | 6.38 |
| Util. Flake | W. Chalced. | | | | | 2 | | | | | | 2 | 4.26 |
| Util. Flake | Basalt | | | | 1 | | | | | | | 1 | 2.13 |
| Total | | 1 | 20 | 1 | 10 | 9 | 1 | 1 | 1 | 1 | 1 | 47 | 100 |

## Lithics

Lithic materials recovered in excavations at Marcaya include chipped stone tools, stone debitage, and ground stone. Chipped stone artifacts were found in all excavation contexts at Marcaya, with the highest concentration of debitage and tools found in Structure 11 in Patio Group V (see table 5.2). The lithic assemblage ranged from shatter and flakes, associated with lithic reduction, to blades, retouched flakes, cores, informal tools, small drills, and projectile points. Raw materials included obsidian, andesite, basalt, quartzite, and two types of chalcedony. Formal tools recovered from Marcaya include obsidian projectile points, chalcedony drills, and several basalt knives.

Although it has been suggested that projectile points are rare at Nasca sites (Valdez Cardenas 1994:677), flake tools found at Marcaya include obsidian projectile points, bifacially flaked knives of obsidian and basalt, bifacially flaked tools of obsidian and chalcedony, chalcedony drills, and utilized flakes made of obsidian, chalcedony, and basalt (table 7.1). Virtually all categories of tools and lithics reduction were found in Patio Group V. This fact, and the high quantities of lithic remains in comparison to other patio groups (see table 5.2), suggests that Patio Group V was a locus of lithic production. Most tools in the lithic assemblage were probably reduced by direct percussion flaking and retouched with pressure flaking. Chalcedony drills, however, were probably formed using some sort of crude blade technology, as several blades were found in excavations. Drills most likely were used to bore holes into the centers of spindle whorls manufactured at the site.

Obsidian was utilized primarily for projectile point manufacture (fig. 7.3), though less-formal tools were made from obsidian as well. The full sequence of obsidian reduction is present at Marcaya with cores, primary and secondary waste flakes, and finished tools represented in the assemblage (fig. 7.4). The cores present in the assemblage are small, indicating that the availability of obsidian was probably limited, and that obsidian was reduced efficiently on site. Furthermore, the amount of primary and secondary debitage indicates that exotic obsidian was brought to the community as nodules, rather than as preforms or finished tools, and reduced locally.

Upon initial inspection, there appeared to be three types of obsidian in

FIGURE 7.3  Sample of obsidian projectile points found at Marcaya.

the assemblage based solely on physical characteristics. Type 1 obsidian is black and opaque with reddish magenta spots, Type 2 obsidian is clear with parallel black streaks, and Type 3 is intermediate, exhibiting characteristics of both types 1 and 2. Though some caution was employed against using physical attributes as characteristic of particular obsidian sources in the Andes (Burger and Asaro 1979:301), the working hypothesis was that the different physical types might represent different sources.

While the analysis suggests that obsidian was brought to Marcaya as nodules rather than preforms or formal tools, the two closest known obsidian sources are Quispisisa and Jampatilla. Quispisisa is located in the Department of Ayacucho, ninety-eight kilometers from Marcaya as the condor flies. Prior analysis conducted by Richard Burger and Frank Asaro (1979) demonstrated that this source was used exclusively in the Nasca region. Excavations at Cahuachi (Silverman 1993:285) and La Esmeralda (Isla Cuadrado 1990:75), an Archaic occupation near Cahuachi, revealed small quantities of obsidian artifacts. Both Silverman and Isla Cuadrado assumed that the obsidian from these sites was Quispisisa obsidian. Without the aid of chemical analysis, however, these source identifications remained speculative. Also close to the SNR is the Jampatilla source, located in the Department of Ayacucho, 116 kilometers from the Nasca

a)

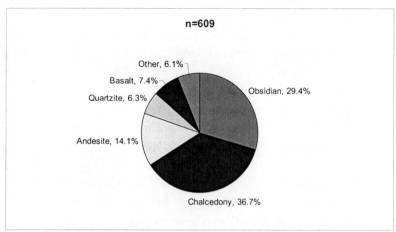

b)

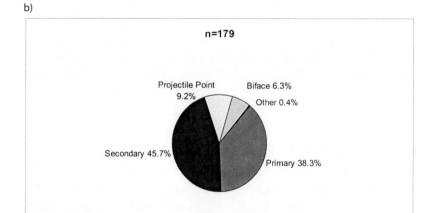

FIGURE 7.4  (a) The lithic assemblage at Marcaya by technological category; and (b) the obsidian assemblage at Marcaya.

region (Burger et al. 1998); however, up to this point, no Jampatilla obsidian has been found in the SNR.

Burger and Asaro's (1979:301) analysis of obsidian from the Quispisisa source revealed a variety of physical characteristics, including different colors—from black to gray to red—and numerous gradients of transparency. A reassessment of the source done by Burger with Michael Glascock of MURR (2000) is consistent with this. Type 1 obsidian from Marcaya bears a strong resemblance to descriptions of Quispisisa obsidian —that is, it is black with red spots. Types 2 and 3 could also be from the Quispisisa source, based on Burger and Asaro's description of the variability of this type of obsidian. Because of the distance between Marcaya and all known obsidian sources, and with Burger and Asaro's caution (1979:282) against sourcing obsidian based on physical attributes alone, an obsidian sample from was subjected to a compositional analysis.

A sample of thirty fragments of obsidian from Marcaya was exported to the United States to undergo INAA at MURR. Specimens were sampled from three different excavated contexts (structures 11, 26 and 29) where obsidian was most frequently found. Glascock supervised the preparation of the obsidian and conducted the statistical analysis. The concentrations of elements in the unknown artifacts were compared to a database of obsidian types in the central Andes. The analysis clearly demonstrates that all thirty fragments of the obsidian sample were from the Quispisisa mine, despite the fact that three visually distinct types were present in the sample (Vaughn and Glascock 2005).

*Ground Stone*

The other major class of lithic artifacts found in excavations at Marcaya was ground stone. Ground stone artifacts were divided into two major categories: subsistence related, and non-subsistence related. Subsistence-related artifacts include large slabs of igneous rock used as a support for grinding food, known locally as *batanes*, and variously sized cobbles (from handheld to thirty-six centimeters in length) that were the companion to these grinding stones. Additionally, pestle fragments and a small mortar round out the subsistence-related ground stone found at Marcaya. Non-subsistence ground stone included several "polishing stones" whose function, while unclear, may have been to polish pottery; a few hammerstones; and a small, modified cobble that could have functioned as a sling stone. The distribution of ground stone artifacts across the site suggests that the preparation of food was an activity that households conducted independently.

## Panpipes

Panpipes (or *antaras*) have been found in numerous contexts in excavations in Nasca. Giuseppi Orefici has found a large cache of hundreds of panpipes at Cahuachi in the Great Temple (Orefici 1993:146). This augments a sample from William Duncan Strong (1957), who found an "unusual amount of broken panpipes" associated with "feasting and sacrificial materials" (1957:31). Similarly, Silverman found more than two hundred fragments of panpipes (1993:241) at Cahuachi in a variety of contexts, including in ceremonial rooms, in fill, and on the surface. In a small excavation at Cahuachi, Lidio Valdez Cardenas (1994:678) found panpipe fragments near an oven that, coupled with the assemblage of artifacts, he considers evidence for feasting activities. Panpipes are also known from other contexts, such as the tomb with six panpipes located in the Copara cemetery in the Trancas Valley (Bolaños 1988:57).

Because they are mostly found in contexts associated with ritual, and because they are portrayed frequently in iconography related to ceremonial activities, panpipes are thought to have played an integral role in Nasca ceremony (Bolaños 1988; Silverman 1993:241). The process by which they were made has been reviewed elsewhere (Bolaños 1988; Dawson 1964; Silverman 1993:241); however, it has yet to be established whether they were manufactured by molds or modeling. César Bolaños (1988:107) argues that panpipes were so precisely made that they were almost certainly produced by a distinct class of specialists.

At Marcaya, fifty-two fragments of panpipes were found in excavations. Because the fragments are fairly small, a minimum number of individuals could not be determined for the assemblage. The panpipes were found in association with other habitation refuse. Their distribution across Marcaya, however, suggests that few households had access to them (table 5.2). This restricted distribution may be evidence for differential access to goods within the community.

Two panpipe fragments found at Marcaya were included in the compositional study described in chapter 6. Both fragments (KJV574 from Patio Group XI and KJV575 from Patio Group XII) were assigned to INAA group 1, the principal polychrome group. This suggests that these panpipes were also produced at the ceremonial center Cahuachi, perhaps by the same specialists.

## Miscellaneous Artifacts

A handful of other artifacts were found in excavations at Marcaya. Several of these were pendants made from a variety of media including ceramic, chalcedony, shell, and polished bone. Other artifacts include a reutilized sherd and a fragment of perforated adobe. No evidence for *Spondylus* or metal artifacts was found in excavations or surface analysis at Marcaya.

A small chalcedony pendant was found in Structure 29. It is broken in two and measures less than two centimeters on a side. A small, incomplete perforation is located near the broken edge, suggesting that the artifact was broken while an attempt was made to perforate it. A broken pendant or bead made of polished bone was recovered in Structure 27. The bead is three centimeters in length and one-half centimeter in width. The surface of the artifact is highly polished and appears to have been burnt prior to polishing, giving it its deep brown color. A pendant made of ceramic was found in excavations in Structure 12. This pendant was made from an Early Nasca (probably Nasca 3) sherd. The sherd's edges were smoothed and a hole was placed in one of its corners. A perforated shell pendant was found in Structure 35. The pendant was made from a fragment of shell with little curvature. Its edges were abraded, and several holes were punctated. A similar pendant was found at Cahuachi (Silverman 1993:fig. 19.2).

## Faunal Analysis

Several analyses provide insight into faunal exploitation in the ancient SNR. The first, by Lidio Valdez Cardenas, focuses on camelids at Cahuachi (Valdez Cardenas 1988). As part of the Proyecto Nasca, directed by Giuseppe Orefici (1993), Valdez Cardenas was able to analyze and quantify the faunal assemblage collected over several years of fieldwork at the site. Based on six thousand bone fragments, the analysis is substantial, and Valdez Cardenas found that the great majority (219 of 245 = 89 percent) of MNI were attributable to camelids. Silverman (1993:304) also briefly addresses the faunal remains at Cahuachi from her excavations. Though quantities of remains are not reported, camelid excrement was found in the excavations. Guinea pigs, in the context of what are interpreted as offerings, were also noted.

Valdez Cardenas suggests that the age ranges of the identified camelids in the analysis demonstrate that the camelids utilized at Cahuachi were domesticated. He argues that they were not kept at Cahuachi, however, as there is an absence of dung and fetuses in excavations (Valdez Cardenas 1988:32), while acknowledging that the remains were recovered from construction fill (see Silverman 1993:221). Silverman (1993:304), in contrast, reports abundant llama dung in her excavations, and she also notes an absence of neonates or immature (juvenile) camelids (ibid.). Since the presence of fetuses would be expected if camelids were raised locally (see Wheeler 1984), Valdez Cardenas suggests that camelids at Cahuachi were probably obtained by trade (Valdez Cardenas 1988:33). Moreover, hunting does not appear to be an exploitation strategy employed for obtaining animals at Cahuachi, as there are few cervids (three elements and one MNI), and lithics (projectile points) appropriate for hunting are not present in Valdez Cardena's analysis.

These conclusions need to be taken with some caution, since it appears that camelids were indeed kept at the site, if Silverman's data are any indication. Silverman does suggest, however, that camelids were probably used in the context of pilgrimages made to Cahuachi. There is also some indication, based on Silverman's excavations, that there may have been hunting activity at Cahuachi, since at least twelve obsidian projectile points were recovered in Silverman's excavations (Silverman 1993:fig. 19.26). Although Silverman does not speculate on the function of these projectile points, an additional obsidian knife found in an excavation (Silverman 1993:fig. 19.25) is thought to be of ceremonial importance. Given the nature of Cahuachi, it is certainly possible that these projectile points were used in ceremonial rather than hunting contexts.

Regardless of the incongruity of the data from Valdez Cardenas's and Silverman's analyses, it appears that domesticated camelids may have formed an integral part of the Nasca subsistence economy (see also Carmichael 1988). They also served as beasts of burden, as depictions on pottery would suggest (Carmichael 1998:fig. 2). The degree to which wild animals formed a part of the subsistence economy is still unknown; however, there are numerous depictions of wild animals in what are interpreted as hunting scenes in Nasca iconography (see Kroeber and Collier: fig. 178 for an example of a guanaco, and fig. 259 for an example of a possible deer or vicuña).

Other animal remains recovered at Cahuachi are undifferentiated rodents (commonly classified with the Spanish term *roedores*, as well as
guinea pigs, or cuy (*Cavia porcellus*). The latter are very rare at Cahuachi (eleven specimens and three MNI), though Valdez Cardenas has
attempted to explain their rarity in archaeological assemblages (Valdez
Cardenas and Valdez 1997). Guinea pigs are present in archaeological
assemblages both as a subsistence good and as animals used in rituals
(Sandweiss and Wing 1997). Silverman's discovery of a cuy offering confirms the importance of guinea pigs in Nasca ritual. Their importance in
the economy of Nasca, however, is unknown, although they were depicted in iconography (Kroeber and Collier 1998:fig. 263). Birds, fish,
and a single specimen from a fox complete the assemblage at Cahuachi.

At the Nasca 5–7 habitation site of Taruga, Katharina Schreiber recovered some faunal remains, including those of an unidentified large
mammal of the *Lama* genus (camelid), an unidentified small mammal, an
unidentified marine mammal, and an unidentified bird. Although cuy
bones were not found, cuy hair and droppings were recovered in excavations. The camelid assemblage included podial fragments, vertebrae, cranial fragments, as well as elements of the articulated skeleton, including
legs. Thus, it appears that whole animals were present at Taruga, not just
choice cuts (Schreiber personal communication).

Excavations at Pajonal Alto demonstrate that camelids were an important part of the economy at that site from the Early Intermediate Period
through the Late Intermediate Period (Conlee 2000:286). Evidence at
Pajonal Alto also suggests that the cuy and unidentified birds were also
important. Overall, however, camelids appear to have been far more important than any other animal in the diet at Pajonal Alto.

Specimens comprising the faunal assemblage at Marcaya were analyzed by structure to evaluate the minimum number of individuals and
species per structure. The majority of fragments were small and unidentifiable; however, it was usually possible to classify them into five general
taxa: adult camelid, juvenile camelid, rodent, viscacha, and bird. Deer
remains were noticeably absent from the faunal assemblage.

All faunal material from Marcaya was first classified into one of the taxa
defined above. The body part (element), element part (feature), and side
of each specimen was subsequently recorded, if possible. If the specimen
was fragmentary, the element part or feature was recorded (for example,

TABLE 7.2 Fauna at Marcaya.

| | | Adult Camelid | Juvenile Camelid | Cavia | Ave | Lagidium | Cervid | Total |
|---|---|---|---|---|---|---|---|---|
| Structure 3 | NISP | 0 | 0 | 1 | 0 | 0 | 0 | 1 |
| | MNI | 0 | 0 | 1 | 0 | 0 | 0 | 1 |
| Structure 11 | NISP | 10 | 2 | 1 | 4 | 0 | 0 | 17 |
| | MNI | 5 | 1 | 1 | 2 | 0 | 0 | 9 |
| Structure 12 | NISP | 1 | 0 | 0 | 0 | 0 | 0 | 1 |
| | MNI | 1 | 0 | 0 | 0 | 0 | 0 | 1 |
| Structure 26 | NISP | 31 | 4 | 0 | 4 | 1 | 0 | 40 |
| | MNI | 14 | 4 | 0 | 2 | 1 | 0 | 21 |
| Structure 27 | NISP | 4 | 0 | 0 | 0 | 0 | 0 | 4 |
| | MNI | 4 | 0 | 0 | 0 | 0 | 0 | 4 |
| Structure 29 | NISP | 1 | 0 | 2 | 0 | 0 | 0 | 3 |
| | MNI | 1 | 0 | 1 | 0 | 0 | 0 | 2 |
| Structure 30 | NISP | 1 | 0 | 0 | 0 | 0 | 0 | 1 |
| | MNI | 1 | 0 | 0 | 0 | 0 | 0 | 1 |
| Structure 36 | NISP | 2 | 0 | 0 | 15 | 0 | 0 | 17 |
| | MNI | 2 | 0 | 0 | 2 | 0 | 0 | 4 |
| | Total NISP | 50 | 6 | 4 | 23 | 1 | 0 | 84 |
| | Total MNI | 28 | 5 | 3 | 6 | 1 | 0 | 43 |

as proximal or distal). Whole elements were labeled as "whole," while indistinguishable elements were labeled "undifferentiated." Body side was recorded, when possible, to evaluate the minimum number of individuals. Obvious axial skeletal elements (vertebrae, for example), were labeled "n/a," while appendicular elements where side could not be determined were labeled with a "?."

The distribution of faunal material was inconsistent across the site, as certain structures (2, 24, 3) had surprisingly few remains (with few or no minimum number of individuals), while other structures (11 and 26) had abundant faunal material, especially of adult camelid (table 7.2). The most abundant identifiable taxon across the site was adult camelid. All specimens were identified as domesticated camelid, though it was unclear whether these were llama (*Lama glama*) or alpaca (*Lama pacos*). The results of the analysis suggest that residents of Marcaya had access to camelids; furthermore, the fact that there were juvenile animals in the sample favors the interpretation that residents of Marcaya herded camelids (see Baied and Wheeler 1985; Shimada and Shimada 1985).

## Shellfish Remains

The role of marine resources in the Nasca economy has been the subject of some inquiry over the last decade (Kennedy and Carmichael 1998; Rodríguez de Sandweiss 1993). In particular, Brenda Kennedy and Patrick Carmichael have been instrumental in demonstrating that marine resources had limited importance in the Nasca diet (1998:40) by employing isotopic analysis on a sample of human remains from Nasca burials. Additionally, María del Carmen Rodríguez de Sandweiss (1993) analyzed the shell remains recovered from excavations at Cahuachi by Silverman (1993). Citing the contexts in which the remains were found, Rodríguez de Sandweiss suggests that some of the shells found in excavations were used in ritual rather than strictly for subsistence purposes (1993:298). This would concur with Silverman's interpretation of Cahuachi in general, as well as with the interpretation of several ritual contexts at the site (e.g., see Silverman 1993:150). The assemblage is fairly substantial, however, and consists of at least seventeen different species of mollusks.

At Taruga, Schreiber (1994, personal communication) recovered the remains of mussels (Mytilidae), sea urchins (Strongylocentrotidae), and small amounts of jewel boxes (Chamidae), soft-shell clams (Myacidae), chitons (Amphineaura), top shells (Trochidae), barnacles (Balanus), and crabs (Canceridae).

Christina Conlee (2000:286) documents an increase and intensification of marine resource use in the Late Intermediate Period with remains found at Pajonal Alto. She also documents an increase in the use of *Choromytilus chorus* during the onset of the Late Intermediate Period. She attributes this increase to the documented larger and more permanent occupation in the littoral zone of the Nasca region (Carmichael 1991).

A small amount of shellfish remains was recovered in excavations at

TABLE 7.3 Shellfish remains at Marcaya.

| Family (Species) | # of Specimens | % |
|---|---|---|
| Mytilidae | | |
| (*Aulacomya ater*) | 322 | 43.87 |
| (*Chorro mytilus*) | 254 | 34.60 |
| (*Perumytilus pupurata*) | 15 | 2.04 |
| (unidentified) | 61 | 8.31 |
| Total Mytilidae | 652 | 88.83 |
| Strongylocentrotidae | 49 | 6.68 |
| Acmaeidae | 1 | 0.14 |
| Cypraeidae | 4 | 0.54 |
| Pectinidae | 5 | 0.68 |
| Melongenidae | 3 | 0.41 |
| Unidentified | 20 | 2.72 |
| Total | 734 | 100.00 |

Marcaya. The distribution of shellfish remains was similar to the terrestrial faunal assemblage, with most households appearing to have access to a small amount of marine resources. Given the relatively small quantity noted above, these resources would have amounted to a small portion of the diet.

All malacological material was first classified into one of six families of mollusks identified in the assemblage: Mytilidae (edible mussel), Strongylocentrotidae (sea urchin), Acmaeidae (limpet), Cypraeidae (cowry), Pectinidae (scallop), and Melongenidae (conch). Because the assemblage consists mostly of small fragments, it was usually impossible to identify specific taxa; however, many specimens from the Mytilidae family were large enough for classification into one of three Mytilidae species: *Aulacomya ater*, *Chorro mytilus*, and *Perumytilus pupurata*. The entire assemblage is summarized in table 7.3. Clearly, the family Mytilidae dominated the assemblage, making up 89 percent. This is consistent with known assemblages in the south coast, in particular Cahuachi, where the percentage of Mytilidae was greater than 60 percent. While *Chorro mytilus* is the most common mussel species in the assemblage at Cahuachi, *Aulacomya ater* is more common at Marcaya.

## Human Remains

The analysis of human burials and their remains inspired initial research in Nasca and continued to be an important component of Nasca studies in later research agendas. Despite the abundance of tombs in the lower valleys of the region, formal tombs were not found in excavations at Marcaya, although human remains were present. This lends support to the argument that burial of the dead was coupled with group-oriented ceremonial activities at Cahuachi and its surrounding region (Schreiber and Lancho Rojas 2003; Silverman 1993:214–217), including other portions of the lower valleys with concentrations of cemeteries and ceremonial architecture (Silverman 1993:216; Schreiber and Lancho Rojas 2003).

Aside from two intrusive burials within Structure 72, human remains were only present in two structures at Marcaya: Structure 11 and Structure 26. The remains found in the latter two structures consisted of four molars and the proximal end of a right tibia. The partial remains of two humans were found on the surface of Structure 72. These remains were found lying near a small, shallow hole in which they apparently had been casually interred. Modern disturbance has revealed the remains. These human remains have been thought to post-date the primary occupation of the site for several reasons. First, they are located on the surface of a structure situated within an arroyo that effectively cuts through loci 1 and 3 of the site. Second, the preservation of the remains is fairly good, especially when compared to that of faunal and other human remains excavated at Marcaya, suggesting that they are more recent.

Based on skull size and bone morphology, the human remains found in Structure 72 were assumed to be from two individuals: an adult and a sub-adult. Specimens were classified according to body part (element), side, and feature. Though some elements were clearly either adult or sub-adult and were classified as such, most remains were so fragmentary that even a general age classification could not be made. These remains were classified as "human." Neither a cemetery nor formal tombs were found in any excavations or surface analysis at Marcaya.

## Summary

Excavations at Marcaya revealed numerous non-pottery artifacts. Excavations demonstrated that households were active in textile production.

Although poor preservation conditions prevented the survival of the textiles themselves, evidence for their manufacture was found indirectly through spindle whorls, used for spinning fibers, as well as gypsum, which was used to facilitate the spinning process. All households at Marcaya were involved in spinning yarn. Functional analysis of the spindle whorls and comparison with another spindle whorl assemblage from the region suggests that almost all the spindle whorls recovered at Marcaya were used to spin camelid fleece.

Additionally, each patio group investigated had evidence for lithic production, although Patio Group V's great quantity of lithics suggested the highest intensity of lithic production. While lithics included a variety of raw materials, nonlocal obsidian made up almost 30 percent of the lithic assemblage. Instrumental neutron activation analysis revealed that the obsidian at Marcaya came from the Quispisisa source located in the Huancavelica highlands ninety-eight kilometers from Marcaya. Formal tools at Marcaya consisted of projectile points, all of which were made of obsidian; some bifacially flaked tools made of obsidian, chalcedony, and basalt; and drills made of chalcedony. Ground stone artifacts were also found in all patio groups, indicating that all households were involved in food processing and preparation. Panpipes found in excavations suggest that some households had access to these rare artifacts. Their distribution across excavated patio groups suggest that their access was restricted to only a few households within the community.

Analysis of faunal material at Marcaya revealed several trends. First, the majority of the assemblage consists of adult camelid remains. Although obsidian projectile points were found at the site, there was very little evidence for hunting found, as the remains were all from domesticated camelids, and no cervid remains were found. The presence of juvenile camelids suggests that camelids were actually reared by residents of Marcaya. Also present in the faunal assemblage, although in much smaller quantities, are the remains of cuy, birds, and one viscacha.

Shellfish remains were also present in excavations. The shellfish assemblage includes a preponderance of Mytelidae, as well as the remains of animals from five other mollusk families. The abundance of specimens from the family Mytelidae is consistent with other shellfish assemblages known in the region. These findings are also consistent with Carmichael and Kennedy's (1998) proposition that marine resources, although present in the Nasca diet, did not compare in importance to agricultural products. Although agricultural products themselves were found infrequently at Marcaya (due to poor preservation), they appear to have played an integral role in the subsistence economy, as indicated by the presence of ground stone tools in all patio groups.

In order to evaluate the Early Nasca village Marcaya, in the following chapter, I will discuss the results of these excavations and analyses. In particular, I will evaluate the kinds of activities present at Marcaya and the significance each has for our understanding of Early Nasca villages.

# 8

# Marcaya, an Early Nasca Village

IN THIS CHAPTER, I summarize the findings described previously and present the Early Nasca village of Marcaya from the perspective outlined in chapters 3 and 4. Specifically, I discuss household identification and organization, status, subsistence and political economies, and ritual activities at Marcaya.

## Archaeological Households

Surface analysis and excavations at Marcaya revealed that patio groups are indeed representative of prehispanic households (fig. 8.1). They are distinct structure clusters, they contain the remains of domestic activities, and they are repeated within the community: all criteria for defining archaeological households. Modern dwellings in the river valley located just downriver from Marcaya are very similar to the prehispanic houses at Marcaya, except for the fact that they were built with river cobbles instead of fieldstone (fig. 8.2).

There are twenty-three identified patio groups at Marcaya, correlating with twenty-three households if each patio group was occupied contemporaneously. There are a number of reasons to believe that patio group occupation was contemporaneous. First, radiocarbon dates from charcoal samples at Marcaya span a relatively short period of time. Although when two standard deviations are taken into consideration, the occupation of the site could encompass several centuries, all three radiocarbon dates overlap within the end of the fourth and the beginning of the fifth centuries AD. Second, the deposit at Marcaya indicates a relatively short occupation. Although some deposits (for example, those in Structure 26) were more than a meter deep, none had sequential occupations with multiple house floors. Furthermore, no stratified middens were found, though this could simply be a preservational factor and is not necessarily the result

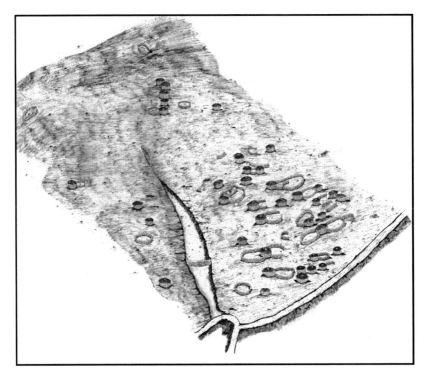

FIGURE 8.1 Hypothetical reconstruction of Marcaya. The modern road has been left in the drawing for perspective. Drawing by Enrique Narciso Bellota.

of a short occupation of the site. Finally, the overwhelming majority of phaseable, fineware ceramics in the vessel assemblage fall into a very short span of the ceramic sequence, Nasca 3 and 4. While there has been some difficulty in dating these phases in absolute terms (see Silverman 1993:38–40), Donald Proulx (1968:100) has suggested that each phase of the Nasca sequence is approximately a century in length.

## Household Organization

Surface analysis and excavations demonstrated the validity of applying the archaeological household concept to Marcaya. Going beyond merely identifying households, what can be securely stated about the organization and composition of households and the overall community? One

FIGURE 8.2 Modern house and patio in the Tierras Blancas valley. Note the similarities between these structures and the ancient structures at Marcaya.

conclusion is that economic activities at Marcaya were organized at the level of the individual household. Archaeological correlates for economic activities are replicated across each patio group, suggesting that each household was economically independent and that households were the primary economic unit at Marcaya. All households contained uniform evidence for food storage and processing, cooking, and consumption. *Collomas*, the only known storage facilities at Marcaya, were found almost without exception within the confines of patios and houses. The location of the collomas suggests that they were primarily used for individual household storage.

*Manejas, chungas, batanes*, and other ground stone artifacts were re-covered within the confines of patio groups, indicating that the processing of subsistence materials was a household activity as well. Additionally, artifacts relating to food preparation and consumption, such as cooking features, cooking vessels, and serving vessels, were found in all patio groups. Other domestic activities, such as lithic production and weaving, took place in households as well, but the intensity of these activities varied from household to household. The one way in which Marcaya households seemed not to be economically self-sufficient was revealed through a lack of evidence for pottery production. Evidence for the community organization of domestic activities is not present at Marcaya. Instead, just as in later periods of prehistory and during the ethnohistoric and historic periods, the household appears to have been the primary economic unit of Nasca society.

## Subsistence Economy

There has been some argument to suggest that the goal in traditional Andean communities was to strive for economic independence among households. This seems to be the case at Marcaya. At this Early Nasca village, each household provided for itself its basic needs (food, shelter, and procurement technologies). Below, I discuss what excavations revealed about the Early Nasca subsistence economy.

### Diet

Settlement survey has demonstrated that Nasca settlements were located on the hillslopes of river valleys, leaving the fertile valley bottoms for cultivation. The combined evidence of past research has indicated that the Nasca diet consisted of a variety of domesticated plants and animals including maize, ají, beans (both common and lima), squash (crookneck and Hubbard), tubers, peanuts, sweet potatoes, and fruit. Additionally, the diet included domesticated and non-domesticated animal products, including adult and juvenile camelids, cuy, birds, and to a lesser extent, marine resources consisting primarily of shellfish. Remains of these foods have been recovered in excavations at Cahuachi, as preservation at the lower valley site is excellent. Marine resources did not appear to make up a large component of the Nasca diet.

*Agriculture.* Unfortunately, excavations at Marcaya neither confirm nor refute statements about the agricultural component of the Nasca diet. Botanical remains did not preserve at Marcaya. The only direct evidence for the consumption of agricultural products consisted of a few charred maize cobs recovered in Patio Group XI. Previous research has shown that maize was probably the most important agricultural component of the Nasca diet. It is the most abundant botanical remain at Cahuachi (Silverman 1993:289), and isotopic evidence demonstrates that maize was indeed an important component of the Nasca diet (Kennedy and Carmichael 1991).

Other agricultural products must have been utilized in the diet at Marcaya as well. The depiction of agricultural products on fineware at Marcaya may indicate that these products were a component of the diet (however, see Carmichael 1994). The most common agricultural product depicted on ceramics is ají. Ají does not preserve well, and given the general conditions of preservation at Marcaya, we would not have expected to find ají remains in excavations. Other agricultural products depicted on the area's pottery include beans, lucuma, and heart-shaped tubers, probably achira, indirectly suggesting that these may have also been components of the diet.

*Camelids.* There is some evidence that large mammals such as deer and wild camelids were hunted during Early Nasca. Iconography on several examples of Nasca ceramics depict scenes of hunting, and it appears that agricultural and herding activities were, at least in part, augmented with some hunting at Cahuachi. While the presence of obsidian projectile points at Marcaya indicates that hunting may have comprised at least a portion of the subsistence activities, surprisingly, no cervid or wild camelid remains were found, suggesting that hunting was an unimportant activity.

Indeed, the faunal assemblage at Marcaya is composed mostly of domesticated adult camelid. Unfortunately, the resolution of the data does not allow for greater specificity, and it is unknown whether these were llamas or alpacas. Overall, however, the assemblage provides evidence that the residents of Marcaya herded camelids and did not rely on hunting wild animals as much as was previously suspected.

Of course, it has been known that domesticated camelids formed a substantial part of the Nasca subsistence economy, but it has not been established whether or not camelids were actually reared in Nasca during the Early Intermediate Period. Using ethnographic, ethnohistoric, archaeological, and physiological data, Izumi and Melody Shimada (1985) argue that llamas were herded on the north coast of Peru extensively by the Middle Horizon and probably before that, beginning in the Early Horizon. Camelids were reared on the north coast by grazing on algarrobo forests and lush side valleys, and north coast peoples utilized camelids for multiple functions — they were the principal source of protein; they were used extensively as pack animals in both vertical and horizontal complementarity strategies; and they were used in ritual sacrifices as well.

Helaine Silverman (1993) states that the abundant faunal remains found at Cahuachi suggest that camelids were used in pilgrimages. Given the amount of camelid dung found at the site, their depiction on Nasca ceramics as pack animals, and their ability to live and even be raised on the coast, I think it is likely that some camelids were herded in the vicinity of Cahuachi. It is likely that camelids were raised at other Early Nasca sites in the region as well, especially in areas located at higher elevations. Were camelids herded by residents of Marcaya?

At Marcaya, the evidence for corrals is weak. The larger isolated structures in Locus 3 of the site were originally considered to be possible corrals; however, limited excavations conducted in those structures did not indicate such activities. The presence of juvenile camelids in the assemblage at Marcaya strongly suggests, however, that residents herded camelids somewhere in the vicinity.

An alternate hypothesis is that residents of Marcaya exchanged for camelid products with pastoralists from the highlands. Ethnographically, it is known that pastoralists often make journeys to lower elevations with llama caravans to participate in highland-coastal exchange (Browman 1974, 1990; Flores Ochoa 1968, 1975, 1985). Coastal products desirable to pastoralists making such a journey include maize, beans, and ají. These could have been exchanged for highland products such as obsidian, camelid meat in the form of charki, camelid fiber, or even the camelids themselves.

It is also documented that camelids were occasionally driven to the coast to feed on agricultural remnants in fields shortly after the harvest (Flores Ochoa 1975:13). In exchange for the opportunity to graze in lower elevations, herders could have traded highland products. Another possibility is that the animals could have been sheared at the lower elevations and their fiber exchanged for grazing rights in the fields of agriculturalists living at lower elevations.

Differential representation of animal body parts in faunal assemblages can reflect patterns of exchange and consumption of Andean camelids (Miller 1979; Miller and Burger 1995). In particular, George Miller has referred to the "charki effect" (Miller 1979) when discussing camelid utilization in the Andes. He demonstrates that where charki was processed, the production and exchange of charki by puna herders has an archaeological correlate characterized by a high representation of podial and cranial elements; in contrast, there is a low representation of these elements in coastal and intermontane valley sites, which received charki from puna dwellers.

Many body parts are present in the camelid assemblage from Marcaya, including podial and cranial fragments as well as portions of the appendicular skeleton, such as femurs, scapulas, etc. If charki was exchanged to Marcaya residents, we would have expected far fewer podial and cranial fragments than were found, since these are generally kept by the charki producers. This indicates that camelid meat was probably not exchanged to Marcaya as charki, and instead that whole camelids were butchered at the site itself, again increasing the likelihood that camelids were herded by the community.

*Marine Resources.* Brenda Kennedy and Patrick Carmichael (1991) argue that marine resources were not an integral part of the Nasca diet. Additionally, through survey of the Ica-Grande littoral, Carmichael (1991) demonstrates that there was never a concerted effort on the part of Nasca society to exploit the coastal zone and its resources. Instead, it appears that most of the Nasca diet focused on a mix of terrestrial resources, both agricultural and faunal. Diet in later centuries, especially during the Late Intermediate Period, shifted to include a high proportion of marine resources (Carmichael 1991; Conlee 2000). The quantity of shellfish remains at Marcaya is not great, but does indicate limited exploitation of the coastal zone.

## Subsistence Economy: Summary

In summary, the subsistence economy at Marcaya is characterized by self-sufficient households that appear to have practiced mixed agro-pastoralism with the occasional exploitation of marine resources. Camelid products were utilized at Marcaya, and most evidence suggests that camelids were herded by Marcaya residents, though it is unclear where camelids were kept. Having documented the Early Nasca subsistence economy, I now turn to the political economy of the village.

## Political Economy

The way power is exercised, manipulated, and resisted can be manifested in a political economy. I have established that there was an emerging political economy in Nasca; however, the way in which this was manifested in a local community remains unclear. I have argued that we can distill emerging political economies into three analytically distinct but interrelated categories: exchange, production, and ideology. Here I focus on evidence for each at Marcaya.

### Exchange

There are few examples of long-distance exchange in the Nasca literature. Exotic animals such as monkeys and parrots are sometimes depicted in the iconography of Nasca ceramics (for example, see Proulx 1983:figs. 25 and 34), and one of the more famous Nasca Lines features an "exotic" animal, the spider monkey (Aveni 1990:9). At Cahuachi, Alfred Kroeber and Donald Collier (1998:fig. 73) recovered the remains of a mummified parrot wrapped in a cloth. The range of this species, identified as *Amazona farinosa* (Kroeber and Collier 1998:259), is limited to the tropical forest of South America and has not been identified on the Peruvian coast. Thus, the parrot is nonlocal and perhaps is evidence of some long-distance exchange. Feathers were recovered at Cahuachi by Silverman (1993:275–276) as well, but species identification were not made, so it is unknown whether the birds were local animals. No evidence for exotic animals was found at Marcaya.

Further evidence of long-distance exchange at Cahuachi is found in the remains of *Spondylus* (Silverman 1993:275). Native to the warm waters of southern Ecuador, *Spondylus* is frequently seen as evidence for long-distance exchange in the central Andes during prehistoric and protohistoric times (Pillsbury 1996). The example at Cahuachi consists of a single piece of worked *Spondylus* found on the surface of the Unit 19 mound (Silverman 1993:275). No evidence for *Spondylus* was found in investigations at Marcaya.

*Obsidian.* The presence of nonlocal obsidian at sites in the region may indicate long-distance exchange in Nasca. At Marcaya in particular, the presence of Quispisisa obsidian may indicate some form of long-distance exchange. The Quispisisa obsidian source is located in the District of Sacsamarca, Province of Huanca Sancos, Department of Ayacucho (Burger and Glascock 2000). This is ninety-eight kilometers as the condor flies from Marcaya, and it is only several days walk from Nasca, up one of the valleys that make up the SNR and across the puna. From Marcaya, one can go directly up the Tierras Blancas Valley until the puna is reached, an estimated two days walk away. From the puna, an additional one to two days is required to reach the obsidian source.

Distances between vertical ecological zones in the Nasca region are actually quite short, and it is not uncommon to hear of people today who make long journeys in one or two days simply to travel to the weekly market in Nasca. For example, near Chuquimaran I spoke with two residents of Uchuytambo (located in the far reaches of the upper Las Trancas Valley), who were traveling to Nasca to sell flowers at the Sunday market. They did not have pack animals, simply carrying their goods in several very large potato sacks. At that point, their journey had already lasted more than ten hours, as they had left at 2 a.m., and they anticipated another ten to twelve hours to get to Nasca (unless they were fortunate enough to catch a bus along the Nasca-Puquio highway).

This example is only given to demonstrate that even today, people travel great distances to exchange goods in the Nasca region. These exchanges would be made that much easier with the use of pack animals. The journey from the puna to Marcaya would have probably taken less than two full days. In exchange for Yunga and Chala products (i.e., maize, ají, etc.), and perhaps even grazing rights, Quispisisa obsidian could have been brought to Marcaya by puna dwellers.

This is the exact scenario envisioned by Richard Burger and Frank Asaro (1979) regarding the distribution of Quispisisa obsidian throughout the central Andes. The authors speculate that puna dwellers, with their camelid herds, traveled to lower elevations during the dry season to trade highland goods for products not available in the puna, such as maize and ají (Burger and Asaro 1979:316). This model, supported by several ethnographic examples (e.g., Custred 1974; Flores Ochoa 1968), suggests that these exchanges were made as reciprocal, household trades. Burger and Asaro postulate other scenarios as well, including one involving an obsidian source that is exploited and distributed via a central agent, thus implying a relatively high level of sociopolitical complexity (Burger and Asaro 1979:317).

While Burger and Asaro's model is derived from Andean ethnography, models of obsidian procurement, exchange, and distribution from other regions of the New World follow a similar dichotomy (though these are not necessarily mutually exclusive) of reciprocal, household exchanges based on kinship ties (either real or fictive) versus redistribution from incipient or established elites. A good example of this is in Jane Peterson et al.'s (1997) article on the acquisition, distribution, and exchange of Hohokam obsidian. They suggest that reciprocal exchange, envisioned within "opportunistic" and "kin-based geographic" models, entails exchanges and/or acquisition of obsidian based on family or kin-based reciprocal ties (Peterson et al. 1997:237–238). A "centralized redistribution model," on the other hand, is far more complex and entails local elites controlling the movement of obsidian (Peterson et al. 1997:237). In the latter model, elites not only used obsidian as a sumptuary good, but also controlled its redistribution.

As a middle-range society with an emerging political economy, we would expect Nasca to have incipient or even established elites who could have controlled the movement of obsidian throughout the Nasca region. However, simpler and more likely explanations for the presence of Quispisisa obsidian in the Nasca region are that it (1) represents small-scale reciprocal exchanges between households — such as those at Marcaya — and puna dwellers, or (2) represents direct exploitation by Nasca residents. Obviously, both of these hypotheses will remain testable until more work is done on obsidian use in the Nasca region, as well as on exploitation of the obsidian source itself.

The full sequence of obsidian reduction was found at Marcaya, suggesting that no matter how obsidian got to Marcaya, it was brought to the site as nodules and not as preforms. While Richard Burger and Michael Glascock (2000) note that the nodules available at Quispisisa are large, with some measuring up to thirty-three centimeters on a side, the nodules brought to Marcaya must have been much smaller than that, since the cores recovered in excavations are quite small.

*Prestige-Goods Exchange.* There seems to have been little in the way of prestige-goods exchange in Early Nasca, especially when compared to later time periods such as the Late Intermediate Period (see Conlee 2003). Cahuachi has little evidence for the presence of nonlocal goods aside from those mentioned previously (Silverman and Proulx 2002:67). Outside of the Nasca heartland, Nasca polychromes were exchanged and used as prestige goods by elites (e.g., Goldstein 2000; Valdez Cardenas 1998); however, within the Nasca heartland, all people had access to polychromes. Because polychromes were not produced at Marcaya, they must have been obtained elsewhere, either through exchange or redistribution. Could access to polychrome pottery in a community that did not produce it provide evidence for an emerging political economy? I explore this possibility below.

## Production

Intensified production is another way in which incipient leaders can build an emerging political economy. With this in mind, I turn to evidence for production at Marcaya.

*Food Production.* No evidence for intensified or communal food production or storage was found in excavations at Marcaya. This suggests that households independently processed food for household members. Subsistence-related features and artifacts were found within the confines of each individual patio group, and there are no loci of community-organized activities related to subsistence production and storage.

*Lithic Production.* All households at Marcaya were involved in some level of lithic production. Each patio group excavated had evidence for lithic production in the form of chipped stone debitage, and less commonly, finished tools themselves. The production of lithics was concentrated mostly on expedient stone tools made of a variety of raw materials, drills made of chalcedony, and obsidian projectile points.

With the exception of the chalcedony drills and a single chalcedony biface, only obsidian was used to produce formal tools. These formal tools included bifaces used as projectile points and knives, as well as unifacially flaked tools that were probably used as scrapers. The efficient reduction of obsidian at Marcaya, and the presence of few cores, suggests that this material was a resource with limited availability and high value.

The most intensive lithic production took place in Structure 11, one of two patios within Patio Group V. Here, a large quantity of lithic material was recovered in excavations. Given the quantity of debitage, I interpret this patio to be a small lithic workshop.

*Textile Production.* Through the recovery and analysis of spindle whorls at Marcaya, it appears that almost the entire community was involved in textile production. Spindle whorls were a ubiquitous artifact in excavations, and the residents of Marcaya appear to have been spinning mostly camelid fiber, possibly augmenting this with a small quantity of cotton.

Much of the camelid fiber spun at Marcaya was surely used for weaving domestic textiles for the community itself. Gayton (1961:277) has demonstrated that the amount of cloth needed for even a small community of twenty families (very close to the estimated size of Marcaya) can be quite substantial. This large amount of cloth would not have been difficult to produce, as the drop spindle technique used for spinning camelid fiber is fast, efficient, and easily performed while "walking about" (Gayton 1961:278).

While it appears that most textiles at Marcaya were made primarily of camelid fiber, this is not the case for a sample of Early Nasca textiles recovered from other excavations throughout the region. The majority of known examples of Nasca textile work come from excavations at Cahuachi, where archaeologists working at the site have recovered a large quantity. Other textiles from the Nasca region exist from collections obtained through excavations of burials from various cemeteries or through looters.

The proportion of textiles made of cotton versus textiles made of camelid fiber has not been quantified from the excavations of Silverman at Cahuachi (1993:273). Elena Phipps (1989:221), however, observes that in Duncan Strong's collection from his 1950s excavations of architectural fill and what Phipps (1989:305) interprets as habitation refuse, almost 90 percent of plain, undecorated textiles at Cahuachi were made of cotton. Birrell's (1961, cited in Silverman 1993:273) original study of this material gives roughly the same proportion of textiles made of cotton versus those made of camelid fiber. Rarely were the two fibers combined in the simple garments presumably worn in everyday life that wound up in the fill excavated by Strong. Whatever the interpretation of the nature of

Cahuachi, the separate analyses of textiles demonstrate that the ordinary textiles (i.e., clothing) used there were made primarily of cotton.

The composition of ordinary clothing is very different from finer textiles recovered from burials of known provenience (many of which are from Cahuachi itself) and from the *huaqueros* who opportunistically loot burials. For example, Lila O'Neale (1937) conducted an analysis of the textiles recovered from burials from the sites of Cahuachi, Majoro, and Cantayo (Cantalloq) and several other Early Nasca sites located in the region. In all, 163 textiles were recorded in the excavations. Of the 163 textiles, 31 percent were made of cotton only, 36 percent were made from camelid fiber only, and 33 percent were composed of a combination of both fibers. Additional examples from the region include two fragments of Nasca 2 ceremonial cloth made entirely from camelid fiber (Rowe 1972:70), as well as a single embroidered fragment of an Early Nasca shirt that was composed entirely of cotton (O'Neale and Whitaker 1947).

Although no textiles were found in excavations, a rough estimate of the proportions of cotton versus camelid fiber textiles can be extrapolated from the spindle whorl data. I estimate that roughly 95 percent of the textiles produced at Marcaya were composed of camelid fiber, while only 5 percent were composed of cotton, based on the sizes of spindle whorls found at Marcaya (table 8.1).

This analysis draws attention to several differences in the composition of textiles from the Early Nasca period. First, while nearly all domestic textiles from Cahuachi were made of cotton, nearly the reverse is true at Marcaya if the spindle whorl data are any indication. Second, known ceremonial cloths from the time period were made of a roughly even proportion of pure wool, pure cotton, and a mixture of the two fibers. In summary, then, the composition of textiles in the region during the early Nasca period appears to vary considerably. Environmental factors (affecting the availability of resources) and the type of textile produced (fine vs. domestic) appear to be influencing the composition of (that is, the type of fiber used for) textiles.

Differences between ceremonial/burial and ordinary cloth have been noted in other culture areas. For example, Ran Boyntner (1998:332) notes that among the coastal Tumilaca/Cabuza and Chiribaya peoples, while cotton was clearly available and used for cloth, camelid fiber was of great

TABLE 8.1 Composition of known textile specimens dating to Early Nasca. The final column is the speculated composition of textiles in use at Marcaya.

| | Cahuachi (Strong Collection) | Cahuachi (Strong Collection) | Cahuachi, Cantalloq, Majoro | ? | Unknown | Marcaya |
|---|---|---|---|---|---|---|
| Phase | Early Nasca | Early Nasca | Early Nasca | Nasca 2 | Early Nasca | Nasca 3-4 |
| Textile | Clothing | Clothing | Ceremonial Cloth | Ceremonial Cloth (n=2) | Shirt (n=1) | Clothing |
| Cotton % | 90 | 84 | 31 | 0 | 100 | 5? |
| Camelid Fiber % | 10 | 16 | 36 | 100 | 0 | 95? |
| Combined % | 0 | 0 | 33 | 0 | 0 | ? |
| Source | Phipps (1989:221) | Birrell (1961, cited in Silverman 1993a:273) | O'Neale (1937) | Rowe (1972) | O'Neale (1947) | |

importance and used in ceremonial cloth for burial contexts. Additionally, both John Murra (1989) and Anne Rowe (1986) have observed that both cotton and camelid fiber yarns were often incorporated together in ceremonial cloth of coastal societies.

It is possible that beyond domestic needs, extra camelid fiber yarn was produced between regular household tasks, and especially between the sowing season and the harvest, when there would have been more time for domestic tasks not associated with agriculture. This is the time of year when it is thought that pottery was produced (see Carmichael 1994:231). Since there is no evidence for pottery production at Marcaya, the production of camelid fiber yarn during the time period between sowing and the harvest would have provided the residents of Marcaya with a valuable commodity to exchange with other communities — and perhaps to use as tribute to the elites at Cahuachi, especially given the great importance imparted on camelid fiber for its use in ceremonial/burial contexts. This, of course, is difficult to verify with the data presented here, but the idea is presented as a testable hypothesis with the hopes that future work may be able to resolve this issue.

*Pottery Production.* One of the more surprising results of the fieldwork conducted at Marcaya is the lack of evidence for pottery production. Although activities associated with pottery production are notoriously difficult to locate in the archaeological record, there are at least two additional lines of evidence beyond the lack of loci for firing pottery at Marcaya that suggest its manufacture did not take place in the community. First, no pottery-making implements or caches of clay or pigments were found in surface analysis or excavations. Second, spindle whorls, which were ubiquitous at the site, were made from broken pieces of pottery. The process of grinding a sherd into a circular form and drilling a hole in the middle so as to create a perforation suitable for a spindle is a fairly labor-intensive process. If the community were firing pottery, it would have been very simple to fire a few whorls modeled by hand along with the pottery.

With no evidence for pottery production, the data resulting from the compositional analysis conducted at MURR have added importance. Some of the possible scenarios regarding pottery production and distribution/exchange were discussed in chapter 6, but given the evidence, it is clear that a large proportion of Nasca fineware (at least the fineware that is present in the assemblage at Marcaya) was actually produced at Cahuachi. The scenarios of pottery production at Cahuachi, and the implications this may have in our understanding of Nasca society, is the subject of some discussion in chapter 9.

### Economy: Conclusions

Norio Yamamoto (1982:40) has suggested that Andean scholars have focused too much attention on distribution (namely reciprocity and redistribution) and not enough on production. As a result, anthropologists discuss complex trade networks when evaluating complementarity at the expense of self-sufficient production systems characteristic of a mixed agropastoral economy. In other words, there is often no need for complex models of interregional exchange in many Andean scenarios. Instead, a model relying on economic self-sufficiency is more than adequate to explain much of the evidence. Certainly, the data at Marcaya indicate that the community was economically self-sufficient and the subsistence base was that of a mixed agropastoral economy. The exception to this self-sufficiency was that the community did not produce pottery.

Marcaya's mixed economy consisted of the exploitation of the various ecological zones, from the Pacific Ocean to the puna, in the vertically compressed topography of the Nasca region. Although residents of Marcaya were not overly concerned with marine resources, the presence of shellfish remains indicate that the Pacific littoral was occasionally exploited. The remainder of the subsistence economy concentrated on the cultivation of domesticated crops — primarily maize, likely augmented with ají, squash, and beans — as well as the herding of camelids. This pattern of mixed subsistence economies coupled with occasional exchanges is one that characterizes many indigenous Andean communities (Alberti and Mayer 1974; Camino 1982; Mayer 2002; Paerregaard 1992; Webster 1971; Yamamoto 1982).

### Ritual Activities

The final avenue towards an emerging political economy for ambitious individuals is through ideologically charged ritual. Given excavations at Marcaya, what can we say about ritual activities?

In evaluating Nasca iconography, Patrick Carmichael (1992:187) has suggested that Nasca researchers have implicitly assumed a sacred vs. secular dichotomy in Nasca art whereby mythical beings represented the sacred realm and agricultural products, while "naturally" depicted human beings represented the mundane and secular realm. Carmichael asserts that this is essentially a Eurocentric view of Nasca iconography, and that no such dichotomy existed in the ancient Andean world. Instead, Nasca iconography should be analyzed contextually, and if a sacred/secular dichotomy is not assumed, the entire body of images can be seen as interrelated visually with no clear division between the sacred and secular realms of life.

Similarly, I submit that excavations demonstrate no clear separation between these two spheres in prehispanic Nasca. Even in two of the most mundane of human acts—eating and drinking—no such division existed between the sacred and the secular. Eating and drinking took place within the household using polychrome pottery, and the process of consumption must have been a ritually charged event.

Having said this, at Marcaya, there is no evidence for *communal* ritual activities in that there are no architectural or special spaces that appear to have been reserved for ritual, feasting, or ceremony. Instead, the built environment was limited to domestic structures. All communal activities involving ceremony appear to have been limited to the ceremonial center Cahuachi, the Nasca Lines, and smaller secondary centers such as Los Molinos in Palpa.

Additionally, it is clear that certain artifacts were used in ritual—especially polychrome pottery and panpipes. These are found in the domestic assemblage at Marcaya, and because they weren't produced there, this must indicate that people had access to activities beyond the village.

## Status at Marcaya

The emergence of inequality is initiated and propelled by individuals or households with varying agendas and strategies to compete for eminence. As discussed previously, this should have a material correlate in the archaeological record. While a continuum of increasing status differences has been identified in Nasca society, most notably in the existence of disparities in burials, up until now, status differences had not been identified at local communities. Excavations at Marcaya revealed that there were status differences at Marcaya. These differences are indicated by differential size of patio groups, differential labor investment as evidenced by the variability in construction quality in structures, and differential access to particular material goods. Two patio groups in particular, X and XII, exhibit signs of status differences.

## Patio Group Size and Architectural Quality

As outlined in chapter 5, several patio groups were designated as belonging to high-status households based on patio group size and architectural quality: patio groups X, XII, and XIV. Of these three, excavations were only undertaken in patio groups X and XII, but these excavations revealed differential access to goods when compared to the low-status patio groups.

## Differential Access to Goods

Although all households had access to most goods found in excavations at Marcaya, including plain and polychrome pottery, ground stone, spindle whorls, lithics, and the remains of domesticated camelids, the degree to which they had access varies considerably from patio group to patio group. Furthermore, the distribution of certain goods — for example, panpipes and particular vessel forms, such as headjars — was restricted to a few select households.

*Polychromes.* Nasca fineware was recovered in virtually every context excavated. All households had access to this particular artifact class. The presence of fineware in all contexts and within all patio groups confirms earlier statements by Carmichael, who suggested that because of their presence on the surfaces of domestic sites and the apparent use-wear on fineware found in burial contexts, the Nasca "ceramic complex" was an "open, shared system to which all members of society had access" (Carmichael 1995:171, 1998a).

Despite the temptation to classify polychrome finewares as such, however, they are not a single undifferentiated class of artifacts. In the past, several vessel shapes have been classified as "prestigious" forms associated with high status: the double-spout bridge and bottle, paired and miniature vessels, cup bowls, and collared jars. Proulx (1968:13) designated the most recognizable form of the Nasca style, the Nasca double-spout and bridge bottle, as Nasca's most prestigious vessel type. Carmichael's (1995:171) analysis revealed only two polychrome vessel shapes reserved for mid- to high-status graves: paired and miniature vessels. He also noted that particular vessel shapes, such as the double-spout and bridge bottle, the cup bowl, and the collared jar (Carmichael 1988:313, 396) were *primarily* associated with mid- to high-status graves, though they were occasionally found in low-status graves as well.

Double-spout and bridge bottles, miniature vessels, and paired vessels were not found at Marcaya. Apparently, none of these were part of the domestic vessel assemblage, and their absence suggests that they may have been reserved for burials. There were, however, notable differences in polychrome pottery consumption among households defined as high and low status (see tables 5.1 and 5.2). While polychrome pottery at Marcaya was consumed in high quantities at all patio groups, a higher quantity was consumed in two high-status households: those of patio groups X and XII. There were also several vessel shapes found solely within these two high-status households. In particular, headjars were found only in excavations here. At least four headjars, and possible fragments of more, were found in Structure 29 (Patio Group XII), while one example was found in Structure 35 (Patio Group X). Of the headjars found at Marcaya, three are complete enough to evaluate the person depicted. All three are "alive" in that their eyes are open, and they do not have spines through their lips (fig. 8.3).

In addition to headjars, other vessel types were restricted to patio groups X and XII. Patio Group XII yielded one of the only examples of a fineware collared jar and two of the three cup bowls found. Furthermore, Patio Group X contained the only example of a very deep-bottomed bowl, and the only modeled effigy vessel in the shape of an unidentified animal. All of these vessel shapes must have been used for serving, with headjars, cup bowls, and collared jars used specifically for drinking (see Silverman and Proulx 2002:132 for discussion of the cup bowl as a ritual drinking vessel), and because of its size, the very deep-bottomed bowl was probably used for serving. Therefore, although their distribution was limited, these high-status vessels served essentially the same function as bowls and vases that were found in all households at Marcaya (fig. 8.4).

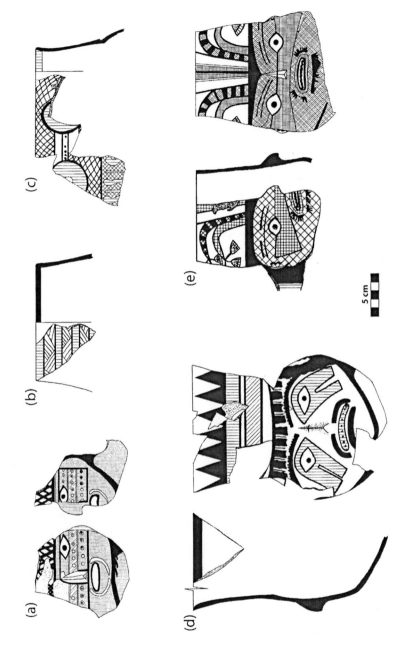

FIGURE 8.3 Headjars that were found in Patio Groups X and XII. (a) Structure 29; (b) Structure 29; (c) Structure 29; (d) Structure 29; (e) Structure 35.

## Low-status vessels

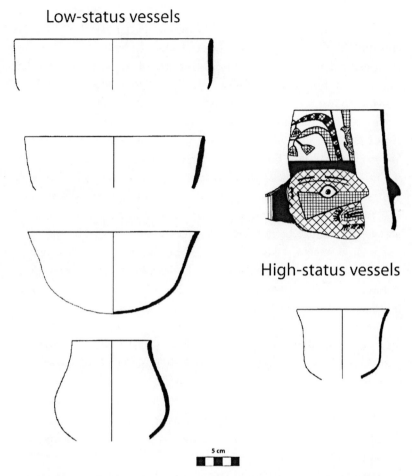

## High-status vessels

5 cm

FIGURE 8.4 While all households at Marcaya had access to Nasca poly-chromes (especially bowls and vases), only high-status households had access to special vessel forms such as headjars and cup bowls shown on the right.

*Headjars.* There are several vessel types at Marcaya that appear to have restricted consumption, which correlates with defined status differences. These vessel types include cup bowls, collared jars, modeled vessels, very deep-bottomed bowls, and headjars. While all were used for drinking and serving, why were these particular shapes highly valued? I believe that evaluating the headjars in particular may provide clues as to the importance of these vessel shapes.

In a treatise on a headless burial found in the Ica Valley, Lisa De-Leonardis argues that the head was the most important symbol of fertility and the "life-force essence" of Nasca (DeLeonardis 2000:381). As the most important symbol, actual heads (such as "trophy" or disembodied heads) or even representations of heads (in iconography or as headjars) provided powerful symbols to those who used them. The correlation of heads to agriculture and symbols of fertility is well known in analyses of Nasca iconography (see Carmichael 1992, 1994; Proulx 1989; Sawyer 1966; Silverman and Proulx 2002), and the correlation is often direct, with the "sprouting head" motif as a clear example (Carmichael 1992). Furthermore, the act of burying caches of trophy heads, as was often done in Nasca (e.g., Browne et al. 1994; Frame 2004), must have been a deliberate act meant to access the life-giving forces of disembodied heads.

While headjars at Marcaya appear to be representations of live individuals, their potency was probably no less than those "disembodied" heads representing dead individuals, especially because the distinction between life and death was blurred in the Andean world (see, for example, Allen 1988:63, as well as Carmichael 1994 for a Nasca example). If headjars were representations of specific individuals (DeLeonardis 2000:381) — and perhaps, given the elaborate headdresses and facial markings, *high-status* individuals — the representation of their heads in ceramic form would have captured the most important element of that persona. It is therefore not surprising to see that their physical representations, expertly manifested in modeled headjars, became the most prestigious vessels at domestic sites.

The use of headjars would have provided a direct link to important individuals. Although we are in no position to determine who these individuals were, we can speculate that they were important ancestors or perhaps important living individuals. Since headjars were vessels from which to drink, I suggest that they provided a very direct link between Nasca religion incorporating fertility concepts, specific important individuals, and the very act of consumption itself.

*Panpipes.* Panpipes were rare and restricted to four patio groups. The highest quantity of these artifacts was found in patio groups X and XII. The frequency of panpipes in patio groups X and XII correlates with the high quantities and diversity of polychromes associated with those patio groups. Because of their use in ceremonial contexts (see Silverman 1993), presumed specialized manufacture (Dawson 1964), and restricted distribution, panpipes also seem to correlate with higher status at Marcaya, with high-status households having access to more of these goods.

*Patio Groups X and XII: High-Status Households.* In summary, the evidence from surface analysis and excavations suggests that the households occupying patio groups X and XII were of higher status than other households at Marcaya. While other patio groups had high-quality architecture, some fineware, and panpipe remains, these two patio groups had all of the criteria used to signify high status at Marcaya. They were two of the larger patio groups, their houses were constructed of worked stone, they had high quantities of fineware, including restricted vessel types such as head-jars, and they had access to a significant quantity of panpipes.

In middle-range societies, status and differentiation are flexible and dynamic. Access to power and building emerging political economies are often resisted by other members of society. I argued previously that there are several ways in which individuals and groups can gain power and build a political economy: through long-distance exchange, craft production, and accessing ideology.

While the religious symbols displayed on polychromes must have appealed to all members of society and created a demand for these crafts, the differential consumption of certain vessel types among households at Marcaya suggests that certain individuals engaged in activities aimed at enhancing their own prestige. This is not surprising, as all people at residential sites engage in power relations (Goldstein 2000:336), with self-interested individuals and groups often attempting to gain control of relatively high-value goods (Blanton 1995; Goldstein 2000; Helms 1993; LeCount 1999; Stein 1998). In fact, the very emergence of inequality is initiated and propelled by individuals (or groups) with disparate agendas and strategies to compete for eminence (see, for example, Blanton et al. 1996; Brumfiel and Fox 1994). The artifactual evidence from Marcaya indicates that the households of patio groups X and XII may have been making such efforts.

A traditional Andean group may illuminate the patterns apparent at Marcaya. In modern Sonqo, *alcaldes* (mayors) serve as the ritual leader of the *ayllu* (Allen 1988:117). The alcalde is responsible for heading communal work parties and initiates dances at important feasts (Allen 1988:117). Catharine Allen indicates that his very presence "validates public functions in which the *Runakuna* (people) act as a collective body and are actualized as an *ayllu*" (Allen 1988:117). The alcalde has no real coercive political power and instead his authority lies in his "capacity to serve as a focus around which the *ayllu* coheres" (Allen 1988:117). Perhaps the high-status households at Marcaya served in similar capacities in Nasca rituals and processions, in which they represented the community as a whole and acted as intermediaries between the community and activities at Cahuachi.

Indeed, any individual or household in Nasca society who appeared to have access to the esoteric and sacred knowledge of group ritual and feasting taking place at Cahuachi would have enhanced their own prominence within their community. Some activities in patio groups X and XII may have taken the form of small-scale ceremony within the patio groups themselves, involving the serving of libations in headjars and panpipe playing. These ceremonies most likely incorporated the same types of ceremonies that took place at Cahuachi, although on a much smaller scale.

## Conclusions

The village of Marcaya was an Early Nasca community dating to the late fourth and early fifth centuries AD. It was composed of about two dozen self-sufficient households that engaged in a variety of domestic activities. These activities included subsistence production and storage, with evidence for a mixed agropastoral economy utilizing resources from the highlands to the coast. Similar to ethnohistoric and ethnographic examples of Andean communities, the residents of the village Marcaya employed this mixed agro-pastoral economy and augmented it with reciprocal exchanges for goods such as obsidian. All households engaged in lithic and textile production as well. Lithic production focused on expedient tools and finished obsidian projectile points. Most textile production focused on wool textiles, and a small surplus of camelid fiber may have provided a valuable commodity for residents of the community.

Additionally, all households at Marcaya used elaborately decorated polychrome pottery produced at the ceremonial center Cahuachi. The consumption of polychromes was widespread, as all households had access to certain vessel shapes, including bowls and vases. Other vessel shapes, however, in particular headjars and cup bowls, were restricted to high-status households. These high-status households are evidence within Marcaya of individuals or groups that were involved in prestige-building activities associated with the ceremonial activities taking place at Cahuachi.

The results of investigations at Marcaya can only be understood in the broader context of Nasca society, the focus of the next chapter. Considering Marcaya in this broader context, I will argue in the following chapter that there is clear evidence for an emerging political economy in Early Nasca centered around group ritual, feasting, and the production of ideologically charged, iconographically rich polychrome pottery.

# Conclusions

POLITICAL ECONOMY AND
POWER IN ANCIENT NASCA

IN CHAPTER 2, I ARGUED that in order to fully understand Nasca as a prehispanic middle-range society, it was necessary to take a village approach that would allow archaeologists to evaluate agency and emerging political economies in a residential village. Analysis of a village has enabled us to gain fresh insight into a prehispanic culture that has been poorly understood even after almost a century of research. In this chapter, I conclude this book by discussing Marcaya in the context of Early Nasca society, as well as more broadly within the context of agency, political economy, and power in middle-range societies. Towards that end, because it is difficult to understand Marcaya in the absence of a wider sociopolitical context, I discuss Cahuachi in light of the findings of this research. By comparing the domestic assemblage from Marcaya with excavations at Cahuachi, I suggest that there is at least indirect evidence for a permanent, elite residence at the ceremonial center. I hypothesize that these elites orchestrated ritual feasts and were involved in the production of polychrome pottery bearing the Nasca religion's major motifs, which focused on agricultural fertility and propagation. This revised view of Cahuachi has profound implications for our understanding of the nature of power and the political economy in Early Nasca. With this new perspective, I return to the Early Nasca village Marcaya and reevaluate agency as seen in this residential community.

## Early Nasca Society

While Marcaya was self-sufficient in terms of its subsistence economy, the Early Nasca village cannot be fully understood without considering its wider cultural context. This context included not only other Early Nasca villages that were part of the settlement system, but also Cahuachi. Early Nasca society appears to have been integrated by activities taking place at the ceremonial center. As such, any discussion of Early Nasca society must take the site into account. How does Cahuachi fit into this context?

## Cahuachi

Interpretations of Cahuachi have undergone several interpretive shifts over the past century. Prior to the 1980s, the site was canonized in the literature as the capital of the Nasca state (e.g., Rowe 1963). Following the fieldwork of Helaine Silverman and Giuseppe Orefici during the 1980s and 1990s, Cahuachi was viewed as an empty ceremonial center. Since that time, this view has been entrenched in the archaeological literature, and ironically, the effort to refute the earlier "capital" model has resulted in an interpretation of Cahuachi that is equally rigid, though a growing number of scholars have questioned this view (Isla Cuadrado and Reindel 2006; Schreiber and Lancho Rojas 2003).

*The Nature of Habitation at Cahuachi.* While Orefici has produced evidence for habitation at Cahuachi, many of Silverman's interpretations can be reevaluated in light of the excavations conducted at Marcaya. For example, Silverman (1993:301) suggested that the "ceramic analysis [at Cahuachi] . . . has shown an outstanding predominance of fineware rather than utilitarian ware, on the order of 70 percent to 30 percent. The proportions would be reversed at a habitation site." This is a reasonable expectation; however, as the vessel assemblage from Marcaya demonstrates, it is not an appropriate expectation for Early Nasca society. The proportion of fineware to utilitarian ware at Marcaya was 56 percent to 44 percent, suggesting that polychrome finewares dominate ceramic assemblages *even at habitations* in Nasca. Therefore, the presence of a large amount of fineware alone does not indicate a lack of habitation at Early Nasca sites.

Silverman recovered an abundance of artifacts that "were of a potentially domestic nature" (1993:301). These included plainware pottery, spindle whorls, plain gourds, plainweave textiles, an abundance of botanical remains, etc. Silverman favors explanations that suggest that artifacts such as these were found in the Cahuachi assemblage as the result of numerous and frequent pilgrimages (1993:300). A good example of this argument is the explanation for the presence of plainweave textiles at Cahuachi. While Elena Phipps (1989), who analyzed William Duncan Strong's collection of textiles from the site, suggested that the abundance of plain textiles and artifacts related to textile production (spindle whorls, yarn, etc.) was indicative of habitation, Silverman imagines pilgrims coming to Cahuachi and exchanging textiles. "I also envision a situation — similar to the one posited for pottery — of fine new textiles being taken into the site and ritually exchanged and taken out again, with worn cloths ending up as refuse" (Silverman 1993:274). While the scenario is compelling, it is a difficult one to test. I believe that the simpler explanation — that the textiles were the result of habitation — is more plausible.

The agglutinated rooms at the base of Unit 2 provide some evidence for centralized storage facilities at Cahuachi (Silverman 1993:302). These, however, did not provide storage for subsistence and other utilitarian goods; instead, they were used for storage of ritual paraphernalia. Thus, there is little evidence for centralized redistribution of subsistence goods at Cahuachi. There is, however, evidence of efforts to store foodstuffs. "Food-storage facilities at Cahuachi appear to be small-scale (consisting of ceramic vessels placed alongside walls or sealed in floors) and dispersed across the site; they are neither large nor formal in any one locus" (Silverman 1993:340). Although these facilities may provide evidence for storage during pilgrimage as Silverman suggests, they could provide evidence for permanent habitation as well.

Finally, Silverman did not recover deep, stratified kitchen middens in excavations, and this is one principal criterion for defining major habitation. "Kitchen midden-type garbage," however, was found in surface survey of the site at Unit QQ1 (Silverman 1993:84). While it is suggested that "this mound should be excavated in the future" (ibid.), ceramics associated with the midden that would date it are not described, nor are further details given. Although quantities of material are not published, the excavations in the open areas (including the test pits), which comprise the majority of Silverman's fieldwork at Cahuachi, revealed artifact assemblages very similar to those that were produced at Marcaya. Based solely on the artifact assemblage and the absence of stratified middens, it might have been concluded that Marcaya was not a permanent habitation either.

In short, given the amount of material that Orefici has recovered in excavations at the site, and taking into account the nature and the quantity of material that Silverman recovered, it is difficult to continue to fully support the model — as it was originally proposed almost two decades ago — of Cahuachi as an empty ceremonial site. In light of continued excavations, and using the assemblages at Marcaya — an unambiguous habitation site — as a comparison, clearly there was a permanent habitation at Cahuachi, even if the population living there was small. The reluctance to accept that there was a small habitation at Cahuachi was an understandable response to the urban-center model that had been proposed for so many years previously. Cahuachi was certainly not a teeming city of thousands upon thousands of people: That much was evident from Silverman's fieldwork. However, it seems fairly evident now that there were permanent residents at the site.

Acknowledging that there was a small, permanent population in residence at Cahuachi does not refute the notion that it was a ceremonial center, however. The presence of temple mounds and other ceremonial constructions, the ritual paraphernalia, the numerous offerings, and the "sacred burial grounds" (Silverman 1993:305), as well as comparisons to other Andean examples of ceremonial centers, suggest that Cahuachi functioned, at least in part, as a place where pilgrims from throughout the south coast congregated. The habitation material recovered from Cahuachi simply demonstrates that it was not an *empty* ceremonial center.

*Elites at Cahuachi.* So, who lived at Cahuachi? Ironically, Silverman has already proposed that there may have been elites living at Cahuachi, though this has not been emphasized in various publications. She compares Cahuachi to Pachacamac (Silverman 1993:311–312), the paramount Andean pilgrimage center first constructed in the Early Intermediate Period and later utilized extensively by the Inca empire (Shimada 1991). Silverman argues that "Cahuachi's *ayllu* temples are the equivalent of Pachacamac's provincial temples" (Silverman 1993:311). While the site of Cahuachi served as a pilgrimage center, Silverman argues that certain buildings may have *also* functioned as elite residences. For example, the "acropolislike grouping (of the unit 2, 1, 9, and 8 mound complex) could have fulfilled some of the 'palace' functions described by Schele and Miller (1986:133–134) for the Lowland Maya: elite residences, the settings for dramatic rituals, administrative hubs, and the places where visiting dignitaries were received, leaders installed, tribute presented, and captives displayed and dispensed" (Silverman 1993:312). While the latter functions of these Maya temples may not be appropriate analogies for activities that took place at Cahuachi, I argue that elite residences and the settings for dramatic rituals were likely functions of the larger "temple mounds" at the ceremonial center.

In light of this analogy and the nature of habitation at Cahuachi, it seems probable that elites were living at the site, perhaps with a small retaining community. The idea that elites lived at Cahuachi fits well into the model of Early Nasca society with a central ceremonial center and autonomous, self-sufficient villages coming together on occasion for the sake of pilgrimage and group-oriented ceremony. It also fits well with John Rowe's (1963) definition of a ceremonial center (see chapter 3).

Who were these elites? Silverman calls the elite of Early Nasca "priests / shamans" and she argues that they retained their status through their access to ritual and esoteric knowledge (Silverman 1993:338). Her view has since been modified and she, along with Donald Proulx (Silverman and Proulx 2002:196), argue that Nasca religion was "shamanistic" and that Nasca did not have "full-time specialists officiating over temples and shrines" as would be the case with priests. They argue this based on the fact that there is "no unambiguous evidence that Nasca's religious officiators were a group of full-time occupation specialists [priests] nor is there direct archaeological evidence to that effect [unlike the Moche situation]" (Silverman and Proulx 2002:197).

I believe that the jury is still out on who exactly these individuals were and what exactly characterized the nature of their power. There are certainly different ways in which this power can be manifested, and just because the Nasca elite did not materialize their power in the same way that the Moche did doesn't mean that they were not full-time officiators of Nasca religion. I only point to differences evoked by Richard Blanton et al. (1996) between the relatively "faceless" rulers of Teotihuacan and the more exclusionary rulers of the Maya. Obviously, more detailed reports of the current excavations undertaken at Cahuachi will be needed before archaeologists are able to make this fine distinction.

*The Nature of Power in Nasca.* While at this juncture we may not be able to reconstruct exactly who the Cahuachi elites were, we can reconstruct some of their activities and the nature of their power in Nasca society. As iconographers have demonstrated (Carmichael 1994; Proulx 2006; Sawyer 1961, 1966), ritual and esoteric knowledge held by the elite of Nasca was intimately related to agricultural fertility, as this is the predominant iconographic theme in pottery. Based on the major themes of Nasca iconography, Silverman (1993:323) hypothesizes that "Nasca religion appears to have sought to control, through ritual, such fundamental fertility factors as the life-giving power of water, the growth potential of seeds, and the productivity of plants."

These important concepts of human and plant fertility were enacted and materialized in large public ceremonies and feasting. Iconographic and archaeological evidence supports the view that these group ceremonies and feasts took place at Cahuachi. Silverman and Proulx suggest that ceremonies and feasts were critical to the sociopolitical elite of Nasca. Indeed, as is expected in middle-range societies where status is negotiated, resisted, and in a constant state of flux, the elite of Nasca must have been constantly attempting to remind participants of their status. "[P]ublic performances at Cahuachi were not just religious acts. They were also political acts clothed in ritual and embodying Nasca ideology. Cahuachi was a locus for status display and negotiation" (Silverman and Proulx 2002:132).

It has been argued that these ceremonies probably centered on rituals that welcomed annual harvests, or perhaps the renewed flooding of the rivers each year, which provided water for fields (Carmichael 1998:224; DeLeonardis 2000). The location of Cahuachi, where the water emerges from the dry lower valley, would have added to the sacred power of the individuals who orchestrated the feasts and ceremonies. Their activities would have directly linked them to water and agricultural fertility: the very essence of life in the dry desert that is Nasca.

Cross-culturally, it is through ritual that emerging elites can simultaneously express social solidarity and social differences, what Pierre Bourdieu referred to as collective misrecognition. Emerging elites can claim that their action benefits everyone by expressing social solidarity through events that appear to integrate society, such as the building of monumental public works (Lucero 2003:524). Lisa LeCount (2003:547) argues that public ritual among the Classic Maya had similar effects in consolidating power among Maya leaders: "Although I agree that public rituals

consolidated community ties via group participation in Classic Maya rituals, I would contend that asymmetrical practices were also important in
the emergence of leaders. While public rituals performed the delicate task
of demonstrating the inclusion of commoners in the civic arena of political
action, they also celebrated elite prerogatives."

I argue that in Nasca, it was this aspect of ritual that was critical in the
transformation of Nasca's social structure. The group rituals organized
and enacted by the sociopolitical elite of Nasca were transformative events
because while all agents were participants, it was ultimately the sponsors
who emerged as leaders and who benefited directly from the events that
transpired at Cahuachi. Those individuals who sponsored feasts and public rituals tied to major agricultural events and cycles, and those who
associated themselves directly with places on the landscape that literally
evoked agricultural fertility, must have been able to gain much status in
the Nasca world.

*Craft Production at Cahuachi.*  The ceremonies and public rituals that took
place at Cahuachi were important sociopolitical arenas for the elites of
Nasca society. As such, their association with an ideology was a critical
component of their ephemeral power. Elites often turn to materializing
this ideology in order to promote it at the expense of others and to make
ideology an important component of their own political strategy. Therefore, the materialization of Nasca ideology would have made it possible
for an elite group sponsoring public feasts and rituals to establish, reinforce, and maintain their power. Materialization takes many forms, such
as monumental buildings and even ceremonial feasts themselves. One
important form that was highly portable and that served to remind people
on a daily basis of elite-serving ideologies was polychrome pottery.

A growing body of evidence suggests that craft production, in particu-
lar ceramic production, was an activity that took place at Cahuachi. To
summarize my research that speaks to this issue, the majority of Early
Nasca polychromes collected from multiple sites in the SNR, including
Marcaya, have a homogeneous paste composition. Along with colleagues,
I have also determined that there were specific, uniform recipes used in
Early Nasca paints. Although the clays in the region are geologically variable, one particular clay, a prehispanic adobe collected near Cahuachi,
matches the composition of the polychrome pottery. Using this evidence,

I argue that Cahuachi was a locus for the production of the majority of Early Nasca polychromes in the SNR.

That Cahuachi is the most likely source of pottery production in the SNR during Early Nasca is not entirely surprising. Silverman originally stated that some pottery was probably produced at the site (Silverman 1993:302), and this has been reiterated by Silverman and Proulx (2002:60). The evidence for pottery manufacture from Silverman's excavations at Cahuachi is not substantial but comes in the form of pigment-stained rocks and what might be paintbrushes (Silverman 1993:302). Unfortunately, data from continued excavations at Cahuachi by Orefici — to evaluate the contexts of pottery production — are lacking, though recent reports demonstrate that production did take place, as artifacts related to the manufacture of ceramics, such as potter's plates, spatulas for wiping ceramics, and paintbrushes have been reported (Carmichael 1998:fig. 3; Orefici 1993:100). More recently, Orefici and Andrea Drusini (2003:144) report evidence for production at Cahuachi consisting of kilns, as well as additional production-related materials such as paintbrushes, caches of pigments, and unfired clay. In addition, although reports of them are not published, many artifacts related to pottery production recovered from recent excavations at Cahuachi are currently displayed at the Antonini Museum in Nasca (personal observation). Finally, the environmental conditions at Cahuachi are certainly amenable to the manufacture of pottery. There is easy access to a permanent source of water in this location of the valley, and the high winds necessary to create temperatures hot enough for firing fineware are prevalent virtually year round.[5]

Thus, there is a growing body of evidence that has traced the source of polychrome production to Cahuachi, the largest, most monumental site in the Nasca region during Early Nasca. We can say this because (1) as of yet, we have no evidence for household production of polychromes at residential sites; (2) polychromes bearing the principal motifs of Nasca ideology are compositionally homogeneous when it comes to pastes and pigments, suggesting a restricted zone of production indicating specialization; (3) we can trace the clays used in the composition of polychromes to a production zone that includes Cahuachi; and (4) now archaeologists are beginning to find actual evidence for production at Cahuachi. All of this has profound implications for understanding Early Nasca society. The production of the most important artifact in materializing ideology has been traced to the very place where the most important public ceremonies and feasts took place in the region. Based on this growing body of evidence, I believe that we can make a strong case that the control of craft production was one of the principal means through which elites in Early Nasca attempted to maintain their power.

We lack the necessary excavation data from Cahuachi to evaluate the exact contexts of pottery production at the site. The very act of manufacturing the sacred pottery, rich with the images of Nasca religion, must have been ritually charged and permeated with special significance. While we cannot say exactly who the makers of the pottery were, it would not be surprising to find evidence for attached specialists in the future. Along with co-author Hector Neff, I originally speculated that the contexts of production may have been what Katherine Spielmann (1998) calls "ritual craft production" (Vaughn and Neff 2000:88), in which artisans who produced ritual objects are the ritual practitioners themselves. Clearly, we need more data from specific excavation contexts at Cahuachi to understand this issue better, but the important point remains: As materialized ideology, polychrome pottery was produced at Cahuachi, the primary seat of Nasca power.

But the importance of polychrome pottery goes beyond its role in materializing the important themes of Nasca religion. Polychromes were actually integral to feasts and ceremonies, as they were the principal vessels in which food and drink were served. This is clear not just from the domestic vessel assemblage at Marcaya, but also from the fact that they are the most common vessels appropriate for serving found at Cahuachi.

Of course, an important component of elite power was how other individuals and groups of Nasca incorporated their materialized ideology into their daily lives. To evaluate the wider social realms of Nasca society, it is important to understand not just in what contexts these polychromes were produced, but also how they were circulated and who consumed them. Silverman (1993) has provided one attempt to model the distribution and exchange of polychromes in Early Nasca society. She suggested that different groups from around the region made polychromes and brought them in pilgrimages to Cahuachi, where they were then ceremonially redistributed and exchanged. Following ceremonies, intact vessels were taken back to residential sites and the vessel assemblages at domestic sites would comprise various styles of Nasca polychromes, including non-local styles (Silverman 1993:302). According to this scenario, we would expect these vessels at a domestic site to be compositionally heterogeneous, since they would have come from throughout the region. While this is compelling, archaeological and compositional data now indicate that this is an unlikely scenario of production and exchange.

Instead, I propose that the most likely scenario of polychrome circulation is one in which, from the source of their production at Cahuachi, polychromes were distributed during feasting ceremonies conducted at the site. This is consistent with ethnographic and archaeological examples of feasting and the manner in which highly valued material goods can be distributed in middle-range societies. Feasts were politically charged events that enabled individuals and groups to enhance their own status, often through the gifting of important material items and the serving of large quantities of food and drink.

In Nasca, a clear link existed between agricultural fertility and polychrome pottery. Ceremonial feasts that involved large amounts of polychrome pottery, and perhaps the distribution of this pottery, would have provided the sponsors of these feasts an opportunity to link themselves directly to agricultural fertility — the most important concern in Nasca ritual life — thus greatly enhancing their status.

The way in which secondary ceremonial centers fit into this reconstruction is unclear at this juncture of research. These secondary centers include Los Molinos in Palpa (Isla and Reindel 2005), as well as several located in Nasca proper (such as Pueblo Viejo and Cantalloq; Isla Cuadrado et al. 1984). While having slightly different styles of adobe used in its construction (Reindel and Isla 2005:62), Los Molinos has many structures that are identical to structures found by Orefici at Cahuachi (Isla and Reindel 2006:395). Exactly how these centers fit into the ceremonial and sociopolitical milieu of the region remains unclear (though Johny Isla Cuadrado and Markus Reindel strongly argue that these secondary centers are actually secondary *political* centers).

With regards to the relationship between Cahuachi and these secondary centers, Schreiber and Lancho (2003:16) speculate that "we cannot know . . . if a single ruling family or chief served the entire region in which

Early Nasca culture is found, or if each valley or group of valleys had their own rulers, who in turn paid homage to a paramount chief at Cahuachi. It is likely, however, that there was some degree of elite power structure in place, and that certain individuals or groups had the power to organize large labor projects: specifically, the building and rebuilding of monumental architecture at Cahuachi and its subsidiaries." With the work reported here, we can add to this that certain individuals or groups appear to have had the power to orchestrate ceramic production as well. Currently, there is no evidence to suggest that these secondary ceremonial centers were involved in ceramic production, and it is also unclear how they fit into the scenario of pilgrimage, feasting, and ceremony. Obviously, more work needs to be done at these secondary centers before we can address these issues fully.

*Power and Political Economy in Nasca*

At the outset of this study, I suggested that a growing concern for anthropological archaeologists was to understand power and agency in middle-range societies. In particular, I argued that one way to focus on the way power is exercised, manipulated, and resisted is by focusing on political economy and how economies in middle-range societies emerge and are manipulated by individuals for their own benefit. Emerging political figures attempt to control political economies by focusing on any combination of exchange, production, and the manipulation of ideology through ritual feasting or through materialization.

Status in middle-range societies is characterized by transient, cyclical "offices" usually held by virtue of an emerging elite's ability to attract followers based on their personal prominence and their access to esoteric knowledge. I have argued thus far that the status of the Nasca elite was based on their ability to materialize their ideology through the production of polychrome pottery, to orchestrate feasts, and to conduct ceremonies for the wider Nasca populous. Indeed, those who had access to the supernatural world and who appeared to have the ability to control such vital resources as water and agricultural fertility could have attracted a following in this dry desert landscape.

While the production of polychrome pottery bearing the principal motifs of Nasca ideology was critical to power building in Early Intermediate Period Nasca, long-distance exchange appears to have been less important. Exchange for goods from outside the region was limited to obsidian and, far less frequently, *Spondylus*. Llama caravans may have brought Quispisisa obsidian to Nasca, where it has been found at small residential villages such as Marcaya. Obsidian has been recovered widely in the region through excavation and survey (Silverman, 2002). *Spondylus* is found much more rarely in the region. None was found in excavations at Marcaya, while survey revealed fragments in the Ingenio Valley (Silverman, 2002). Long-distance exchange, then, appears to have been less of a concern in Early Intermediate Period Nasca than the production of material symbols of power.

Outside the region, however, it was exchange and imitation of these very material symbols of power that was important for emerging elites in far-reaching regions. Far to the south in Moquegua, local elites attempted to associate themselves with the distant powers of Nasca (and in particular, I would argue the Cahuachi elite) by having access to small quantities of Nasca ceramics (Goldstein 2000). Closer to the Nasca heartland, in Acarí and in Pisco, local elites were engaged in similar activities.

The ceremonies that took place at Cahuachi were probably only one of several different kinds of public rituals that were important in associating specific people with the major concepts of Nasca religion. The vast "monuments" of the Nasca Lines to the north of Cahuachi were important parts of Nasca religion as well. These regional features evoked agricultural fertility and were probably associated with rituals related to rain and propagation. It is no accident that many of the geoglyphs recorded throughout the region are constructed in flat areas of Nasca and Palpa that were completely inadequate for agriculture. Reindel and Isla Cuadrado (2006:172) suggest that this placement of geoglyphs on locations that were too arid for agriculture must have been a deliberate attempt to incorporate these economically unviable areas into the social and ritual landscape of Nasca, yet again directly associating Nasca elites with agricultural potential and success.

Isla Cuadrado and Reindel (2005:66) also suggest that the vast array of Nasca Lines located in Nasca and Palpa were constructed through some form of occupational specialization. Perhaps the construction of these regional monuments was also part of the efforts of Early Nasca elites to orchestrate endeavors that would have materialized ideology.

## Marcaya and Cahuachi

Of course, Early Nasca elites were not the only members of society to exercise agency. Their efforts were only possible within a given socio-political and environmental context. Indeed, an agency approach will recognize that the efforts of elites are not the only relevant behaviors that archaeologists can evaluate (see Pauketat 2000:84). The question, then, is: How were the events that transpired at Cahuachi affected by what transpired in the local village?

In the Nasca scenario, if polychrome pottery was a vehicle for ideology, and if materialization extends ideology "to communicate the power of a central authority to a broader population" (DeMarrais et al. 1996:16), then the variability of polychrome consumption at residential sites should provide an indication of whether people not directly responsible for this ideology accepted it and incorporated it into their daily lives. Additionally, from an agency approach, we would expect all individuals to engage in power relations, and so we might look for different ways in which these symbols were incorporated into daily lives.

Published data for the consumption of polychrome pottery outside of Cahuachi include those from the smaller ceremonial centers of Los Molinos and Pueblo Viejo, and now from the unambiguous residential site Marcaya. The excavations reported here demonstrate a vessel assemblage composed of 56 percent polychromes versus 44 percent plain pottery. Most polychrome vessel shapes, especially bowls and vases, were employed as the most common serving vessels at Marcaya. All households had access to these vessels, and they were the only vessels in the recovered assemblage that were appropriate for eating and drinking.

In an earlier attempt to understand the apparent distribution of polychromes throughout the Nasca region, Silverman and Proulx suggest that Nasca "pottery was widely circulated . . . for the purpose of widespread participation in Nasca ritual" (Silverman and Proulx 2002:246). Furthermore, fine pottery "in Nasca domestic contexts could have acted . . . to maintain the relationship between distant ritual and supracommunal sacred settings and the dynamic, localized social order" (Silverman and

Proulx 2002:264). Finally, they propose that panpipes at habitations found on survey suggest "home rituals and portage to other ritual sites" (Silverman and Proulx 2002:201).

The data from Marcaya are consistent with and confirm these propositions by Silverman and Proulx. I suggest that polychromes may have been used in Nasca villages in small-scale rituals, perhaps to continue to ensure agricultural success, which must have been a constant concern in this dry desert landscape. As communal feasting areas and spaces were not present at Marcaya, rituals must have been limited to the household rather than including the community as a whole.

This implies that public rituals in Nasca were limited to Cahuachi, while smaller, household rituals were limited to local villages. As I described previously, the contemporary highland community of Sonqo makes distinctions between *ayllu* public rituals in communal festivals taking the form of processions and pilgrimages led by community leaders, and those small-scale rituals such as the *despacho*, where heads of households made libations within the house. We can surmise that similar distinctions were made in prehispanic Nasca, where large processions and pilgrimages to Cahuachi were followed by public feasts and communal celebrations, while smaller rituals were conducted within the household.

Using the Sonqo as an example, I also described "power objects" called *enqa* and *istrilla* used on special ceremonial occasions from their holding places (Allen 1988:201). As *kawsaqkuna* ("living ones"), they were the source of health and fertility for the household, as well as for crops and livestock. As the source of health and fertility, they were very important objects that "store[d] vitality and well-being by forging a connection between the household and the Sacred Places" in Sonqo (Allen 1988:201). We can speculate that polychromes were power objects in the same sense that the residents of Sonqo saw *enqa* and *istrilla*, since they provided a connection between the activities taking place at sacred places such as Cahuachi directly with households in Nasca. Perhaps their use in the village served as a constant reminder of the ideology that was directly associated with the Nasca elites, and their frequent consumption in the village suggests that people away from the centers of power were incorporating these symbols of Nasca religion into their daily lives.

While the symbols displayed on polychromes appear to have appealed to all members of society, as all households at Marcaya consumed polychromes, the differential consumption of some vessel types among households at Marcaya suggests that certain individuals or groups, in particular the households in patio groups X and XII, engaged in activities aimed at enhancing their own prestige.

In the context of discussing the Terminal Classic Lowland Maya sites, Lisa LeCount (1999) suggests that specific individuals of elevated status who may have had greater access to elite ideologies could have used artifacts that materialized this ideology as political currency to further group and individual political ambitions. The artifacts used by these local elites included polychrome pottery. Similarly, I submit that status differences at Marcaya were a result of the affiliations that high-status households had with the activities transpiring at Cahuachi. In the Nasca scenario, serving as intermediaries between local communities and the ceremonial center provided an avenue towards prestige-building at the local village for those who wished to enhance their own status. As intermediaries, I suggest that these individuals may have had direct access to the ceremonial and feasting activities at Cahuachi, and they perhaps even had access to the esoteric knowledge retained by the elites of Early Nasca at Cahuachi.

Again, we are in no position to reconstruct the nature of this access to activities at Cahuachi, but the increased access to certain vessel shapes, especially headjars and cup bowls, as well as panpipes, suggests that this access was ritual in nature. Again, I point to the intermediary elites of Sonqo, the *alcaldes*, who served as ritual leaders of the ayllu and who were responsible for leading work parties and initiating dances at public feasts.

## Early Nasca Villages

My proposed scenario of the relationship between Marcaya and Cahuachi has important implications for how the region as a whole is understood. With this in mind, how should we understand other Early Nasca villages? What can be stated about these habitations in the context of Cahuachi as a ceremonial center?

*Village Self-Sufficiency.* The Marcaya data indicate that communities in Early Nasca society were economically self-sufficient with the exception of pottery production. There are numerous Early Nasca habitation sites in the SNR, but the ways in which they interacted and were integrated is still unclear. In any case, the settlement pattern during the time period is suggestive of economic self-sufficiency.

Cahuachi's role as a ceremonial center does not appear to have been accompanied by a central economic role. That is, Cahuachi did not serve as a redistributive center for subsistence goods. Since a redistributive economy is not common in middle-range societies (Feinman and Neitzel 1984; see chapter 3), this is not surprising. Furthermore, there are no habitations that would have served as secondary centers in the settlement pattern of Early Nasca in the SNR, while it is possible that Los Molinos may have served as a secondary center in Palpa. Instead, Early Nasca habitations were fairly small and were composed of patio groups similar to those described at Marcaya. At least superficially, based on these initial surface resemblances, we would expect an economic organization characterized by self-sufficiency.[6]

On the other hand, Cahuachi may have served as a redistributive center for polychrome pottery. The scenario that Silverman (1993:302) proposes for the ritual exchange of pottery at Cahuachi may have in fact taken place there. Instead of pottery being manufactured from different areas of the south coast, however, the bulk of polychromes at Marcaya appear to have been manufactured in one location — Cahuachi.

There is evidence for variability in the production of plainware pottery in the SNR, however. Thus, we would expect to find evidence for the production of plainware pottery at Early Nasca habitations. The few polishing stones recovered in excavations at Marcaya may provide us with indirect evidence for the production of some pottery at Marcaya. Given the compositional evidence, though, I suggest that these polishing stones may have been used in the production of plainwares rather than polychromes. Indeed, the compositional work that I have done with colleagues suggests that one plainware group (INAA Group 2) is limited to the upper Tierras Blancas Valley, where Marcaya is located (Vaughn et al. 2006:685). I expect that additional plainware groups will be found with further compositional work in the future.

*Mixed Economy.* The self-sufficient village economies of Early Nasca habitations relied on mixed agropastoralism involving cultivated crops and the herding of Andean camelids. Other habitations are located in the upper valleys of the southern Nasca region, where a similar subsistence pattern could have been pursued. Products such as marine resources and obsidian, which were surely utilized at other habitations, may have been obtained through small-scale reciprocal exchanges with puna dwellers, and perhaps through infrequent exploitation of the littoral. In the context of pilgrimage, some economic products could have been exchanged as well, as Andean pilgrimages are known to have created opportunities for exchange (Rostworowski 1999).

*Status.* While there are status differences at Marcaya, the degree of status differentiation at other Early Nasca habitations is unknown. Although none of the Early Nasca habitations located in the upper valleys have monumental constructions or other overt signs of status, a careful analysis of architectural construction techniques and excavations within differentiated patio groups will determine the degree of differences between them.

I suggest here that localized status differences between households at communities such as Marcaya were due to the affiliation those households had with the activities taking place at Cahuachi. Having access to the ceremonial activities at Cahuachi, and perhaps even the esoteric knowledge retained by the elites of Early Nasca society, would have been of great value to individuals and/or households who sought to build their own prestige. It appears that at least two households at Marcaya attempted to enhance their prestige by appealing to their access to the ceremonial activities taking place at Cahuachi. They may have been able to replicate some of these ceremonial activities, albeit at a smaller, local scale, with the use of such ritual goods as headjars and panpipes. We would expect similar patterns at other Early Nasca habitations.

## Early Nasca Society and Beyond

One of the primary concerns of archaeology is to reconstruct the past. In order to do this, we must look not just at tombs and temples, but also at residences where the majority of people lived in complex societies. Accordingly, does the village approach described here place us closer to this goal with respect to Early Nasca society? Although many questions remain unanswered and many propositions require testing, the Marcaya data furnish the first glimpse into Early Nasca domestic life. Furthermore, the data provide an opportunity to reevaluate not only Cahuachi as a ceremonial center, but also how we understand Early Nasca as a middle-range society. Given the conclusions discussed above, what can be stated about the organization of Early Nasca society?

I have argued that Nasca was a middle-range society composed of relatively self-sufficient villages integrated regionally into a wider social realm centered on group ritual and feasting at Cahuachi, which was orchestrated by elites who controlled the production of polychrome pottery. The act of prestige-building in Early Nasca society was centered around an aspiring elite's ability to secure support based on its access to esoteric knowledge and the ways in which other members of society incorporated the materialized symbols of this esoteric knowledge into their daily lives.

In the Nasca scenario, it was probably the priest/shaman, who may have been intimately involved in pottery production, who had this esoteric/ceremonial knowledge. In the exceptionally dry landscape of the south coast, aspiring political leaders who co-opted and manipulated symbols of agricultural fertility and renewal in iconography would have been in a commanding position to enhance their own political status. Additionally, evaluating Marcaya using the village approach demonstrates that other members of society were actively engaged in the activities taking place at Cahuachi and that they were actively incorporating the materialized symbols of ideology into their daily lives.

Why, then, did this trend fail to persist past Early Nasca times? Cahuachi suffered what has been called a "collapse" at the end of Early Nasca, as construction at the site ceased at that time. The site continued to be used following the Early Nasca time period, however, though the hyper-ceremonialism that characterized the center during Early Nasca apparently became much less frequent. As I discussed previously, there were profound changes throughout the southern Nasca region during the Nasca 5 phase subsequent to Cahuachi's "collapse": *puquios* were constructed, there were so-called "bizarre" innovations in ceramic iconography, and settlement in the SNR shifted dramatically. Additionally, the locus of power appears to have shifted to the north in Palpa at the site of La Muña, where archaeological evidence indicates massive tomb construction with all the trappings of power.

Ice core data from Quelccaya (Shimada, et al. 1991; Thompson, et al. 1985) demonstrate that there were several droughts during the sixth century AD, the century that corresponds to Nasca 5, and several authors have already suggested that significant changes in Nasca prehistory during Nasca 5 may have been due to deteriorating environmental conditions (Carmichael 1998; Schreiber 1998:263).

A severe drought, especially during a time of protracted desiccation — as Bernhard Eitel et al. (2006) have demonstrated — would have had an enormous impact on the tenuous control that aspiring Nasca leaders retained, especially if their power was not coercive but instead was derived from access to supernatural knowledge associated with agricultural fertility. If a drought caused agricultural productivity to fail, elites who served as intermediaries to the supernatural world would have lost much of their authoritative role.

Patrick Carmichael (1998:225, fig. 14) has proposed a model of Nasca 5 ceramic production in light of this possible drought and subsequent societal changes. In his model, Carmichael suggests that the environmental stress caused by a severe drought would have caused accelerated ceramic production as those who manipulated Nasca ideology were forced to reinvent icons. The increased competition in ceramic production would have resulted in experimentation and new innovations. Examples of these new innovations include the "Bizarre sub-style" (Roark 1965) and the color blue being used for the first time in Nasca iconography (Carmichael 1998:225).

Katharina Schreiber (1998:263; Schreiber and Lancho Rojas 2003:fig. 14) has demonstrated that settlement in the region was characterized by greater aggregation into larger habitation sites by Nasca 5. The largest of the settlements are referred to as "small towns" in Schreiber's scheme, and form the highest of a three-tiered settlement hierarchy. Carmichael (1998a:225) suggests that perhaps it was in these larger communities that potters "would have been in a position to interact more frequently, fostering exchange of ideas and experimentation."

The scenario proposed by Carmichael fits well into the hypothetical model that I outline for Early Nasca society. In my model, the hyperceremonialism at Cahuachi peaked in Early Nasca during a time period at which the entire region was suffering from desiccation (table 3.1). This must have made Early Nasca elite power that much more tenuous. The prestige associated with elites living at Cahuachi collapsed with environmental degradation and resource depletion in Nasca 5. This forced a realignment of the existing system, and the cyclical, transient "office" that was held by Nasca elites became vulnerable to competitive rivalry, perhaps resulting in a power shift to the north.

## Conclusions

In this book, I have attempted to investigate the importance of villages in the development of early Andean complex societies. I have demonstrated that a village approach focusing on archaeological households has illuminated our understanding of power and inequality, political and subsistence economies, and ideology as seen through ritual in ancient Nasca.

I believe that this method has broader applications in other archaeological examples of middle-range societies. Emphasis on larger, more spectacular centers comes at the expense of understanding smaller, more modest settlements that are not only responsible for the majority of a society's population, but are also where daily life is practiced. Again, if archaeologists are concerned with agency, we cannot ignore villages.

Employing this methodological approach results in a unique perspective on Nasca society. Excavations have demonstrated that Marcaya was a community dating to the late fourth and early fifth centuries AD, composed of several dozen economically self-sufficient households that were engaged in a variety of domestic activities, including subsistence production and storage, lithic production, textile production, and small-scale ritual activities involving finely painted polychrome pottery and, for some, panpipes. Similar to the ethnohistoric and ethnographic examples of other Andean communities, the village of Marcaya employed a mixed agropastoral subsistence economy with the use of camelids for meat and wool augmented with Andean domesticated staples. This basic subsistence economy was augmented with goods such as obsidian obtained from the highlands. With the exception of polychrome pottery production, households were economically self-sufficient with no evidence for communal organization of storage, production, or consumption.

Polychrome pottery, especially bowls and vases, which enjoyed unrestricted access, made up more than half of the vessels that were used at Marcaya and comprised the vast majority of vessels that were used for serving food and drink. The remaining vessels were utilitarian cooking and storage wares. This is a high frequency of polychrome pottery compared to that found in other agrarian societies, especially considering that the majority of the polychrome pottery was produced at Cahuachi. Using this evidence, I argue that residents of Marcaya, no matter what their status, were participating in Nasca ritual, probably first carried out at the ceremonial center Cahuachi. With evidence of production of polychrome pottery at the ceremonial center, and now evidence that the polychromes were then distributed to Nasca commoners, I suggest that this provides convincing evidence that both activities served to reinforce elite power, reminding commoners of elite access to the supernatural world. In fact, this reinforcement didn't just occur at the ceremonial center, but transpired on a daily basis, since the pottery was being used for basic consumption in villages.

Evidence for an emerging political economy is seen by status differences at the site in the form of larger households, higher labor investment in domestic dwellings, special architectural features, and restricted access to certain artifact classes—particularly, polychrome vessel types such as headjars and cup bowls. Based on ethnographic comparisons of modern indigenous Andean groups where *ayllu* (community) leaders serve as ritual leaders and represent villages at important feasts and communal ceremonies, I suggest that these individuals at Marcaya were lineage heads who represented the wider community at the ceremonial feasts that took place at Cahuachi.

Ultimately, however, archaeologists are still limited in our reconstructions by our data. More projects that take the village approach in an effort to reconstruct Nasca society, as well as the changes that occurred over time, are necessary before we can fully understand the prehistory of the region. I propose that the scenario I reconstruct here is a testable hypothesis, ultimately modifiable as new research is conducted.

It has been nearly a full century since archaeological exploration was first initiated on the south coast of Peru. Since those initial forays into the region, archaeological research has developed from the "tombs and temples" approach that characterized much of the twentieth century to regional approaches with broader research perspectives in the last few decades. The research presented in this book continues this trend, further enhancing an ever-broadening view of Nasca society by introducing the village approach, which focuses on individual agency from the perspective of small, rural villages.

As early as the 1950s, the Nasca region was described as "one of the most famous, and at the same time, one of the least known cultural provinces in Peru" (Strong 1957:1). Decades of scientific research, particularly that using the regional approaches of the last twenty years, have shed considerable light on Early Nasca society, and my research has been an extension of those regional approaches. While we have gained a more complete picture of Early Nasca society, questions remain — stimulating the need for continued research before we can fully comprehend the lasting legacy of Nasca prehistory.

# Notes

1. The Taruga Valley in the Nasca region becomes the Chuquimaran Valley as one moves up in elevation.

2. Structures 35 and 51 have associated collomas just outside the confines of the structures themselves.

3. Feature numbers were assigned consecutively in the order they were found in the field. Because excavations were undertaken simultaneously in multiple patio groups, the sequence of feature numbers within patio groups was often nonconsecutive.

4. The analysis of spindle whorls at Marcaya is based on a comparison with the assemblage of spinning equipment at the Late Intermediate Period site Pajonal Alto, excavated by Christina Conlee. At this site, nearly all spindle whorls appear to have been used for spinning cotton (Conlee and Vaughn 1999).

5. The evidence for pottery production is accompanied by artifacts related to textile production as well (Orefici 1993; Phipps 1989; Silverman 1993:274; Strong 1957:28), although the nature of textile production at Cahuachi remains unclear.

6. To address some of these questions, in recent years I have been working at some of these habitations that have Early Nasca components (e.g., Vaughn 2005; Vaughn and Linares 2006).

# References Cited

Abrams, E. M. 1989. Architecture and Energy: An Evolutionary Perspective. In *Archaeological Method and Theory*, vol. 1, edited by M. B. Schiffer, 47–88. University of Arizona Press, Tucson.

Alberti, G., and E. Mayer. 1974. Reciprocidad andina: ayer y hoy. In *Reciprocidad e intercambio en los Andes peruanos*, edited by G. Alberti and E. Mayer, 13–36. Instituto de Estudios Peruanos, Lima.

Aldenderfer, M. S. 1993. Ritual, Hierarchy, and Change in Foraging Societies. *Journal of Anthropological Archaeology* 12: 1–40.

———. 2005. Preludes to Power in the Highland Late Preceramic Period. In *The Foundations of Power in the Prehispanic Andes*, edited by K. J. Vaughn, D. E. Ogburn, and C. A. Conlee, 13–35. Archeological Papers of the American Anthropological Association, vol. 14. Washington, D.C.

Aldenderfer, M. S., and C. Stanish. 1993. Domestic Architecture, Household Archaeology, and the Past in the South Central Andes. In *Domestic Architecture, Ethnicity, and Complementarity in the South-Central Andes*, edited by M. Aldenderfer, 1–12. University of Iowa Press, Iowa City.

Allen, C. J. 1988. *The Hold Life Has: Coca and Cultural Identity in an Andean Community*. Smithsonian Institution Press, Washington, D.C.

Arnold, B. 1999. "Drinking the Feast": Alcohol and the Legitimation of Power in Celtic Europe. *Cambridge Archaeological Journal* 9(1): 71–93.

Arnold, D. E. 1985. *Ceramic Theory and Cultural Process*. Cambridge University Press, Cambridge.

Arnold, D. E., H. Neff, and R. L. Bishop. 1991. Compositional Analysis and "Sources" of Pottery: An Ethnoarchaeological Approach. *American Anthropologist* 93: 70–90.

Aveni, A. F. 1990. Order in the Nazca Lines? In *The Nazca Lines*, edited by A. F. Aveni, 43–113. American Philosophical Society, Philadelphia.

———. 2000 *Between the Lines: The Mystery of the Giant Ground Drawings of Ancient Nazca, Peru*. University of Texas Press, Austin.

Baied, C. A., and J. C. Wheeler. 1993. Evolution of High Andean Puna Ecosystems — Environment, Climate, and Culture Change over the Last 12,000 Years in the Central Andes. *Mountain Research and Development* 13(2): 145–156.

Bandy, M. S. 2005a. Trade and Social Power in the Southern Titicaca Basin Formative. In *The Foundations of Power in the Prehispanic Andes*, edited by K. J. Vaughn, D. E. Ogburn, and C. A. Conlee, 91–111. Archeological Papers of the American Anthropological Association, vol. 14. Washington, D.C.

———. 2005b. Energetic Efficiency and Political Expediency in Titicaca Basin Raised Field Agriculture. *Journal of Anthropological Archaeology* 24: 271–296.

Bawden, G. 1982. Community Organization Reflected by the Household: A Study of Pre-Columbian Social Dynamics. *Journal of Field Archaeology* 9(2): 165–181.

———. 2001. The Symbols of Late Moche Social Transformation. In *Moche Art and Archaeology in Ancient Peru*, edited by J. Pillsbury, 285–305. Studies in the History of Art, vol. 63. National Gallery of Art, Washington D.C.

Bayman, J. M. 1999. Craft Economies in the North American Southwest. *Journal of Archaeological Research* 7(3): 249–299.

Bender, B. 1989. The Roots of Inequality. In *Domination and Resistance*, edited by D. Miller, M. Rowlands, and C. Tilley, 83–92. Unwin Hyman, London.

Bermann, M. 1994. *Lukurmata: Household Archaeology in Prehispanic Bolivia*. Princeton University Press, Princeton.

———. 1997. Domestic Life and Vertical Integration in the Tiwanaku Heartland. *Latin American Antiquity* 8(2): 93–134.

Billman, B. R. 1999. Reconstructing Prehistoric Political Economies and Cycles of Political Power in the Moche Valley, Peru. In *Settlement Pattern Studies in the Americas: Fifty Years Since Virú*, edited by B. R. Billman and G. M. Feinman, 131–159. Smithsonian Institution Press, Washington, D.C.

Blanton, R. 1995. The Cultural Foundations of Inequality in Households. In *Foundations of Social Inequality*, edited by T. D. Price and G. M. Feinman, 105–128. Plenum Press, New York.

Blanton, R., G. Feinman, S. Kowalewski, and P. Peregrine. 1996. A Dual-Processual Theory for the Evolution of Mesoamerican Civilization. *Current Anthropology* 37(1): 1–14.

Blasco Bosqued, C., and L. J. Ramos Gómez. 1980. *Cerámica Nazca*. Seminario Americanista de la Universidad de Valladolid, Valladolid.

Blitz, J. 1993. Big Pots for Big Shots: Feasting and Storage in a Mississippian Community. *American Antiquity* 58(1): 80–95.

Bohannan, P. 1963. *Social Anthropology*. Holt, Rinehart, and Winston, New York.

Bolaños, C. 1988. *Las Antaras Nasca*. Programa de Arqueomusicología del Instituto Andino de Estudios Arqueológicos, Lima.

Bourdieu, P. 1977. *Outline of a Theory of Practice*. Cambridge University Press, Cambridge.

———. 1990. *The Logic of Practice*. Polity Press, Cambridge.

Boyntner, R. 1998. Textiles from the Lower Osmore Valley, Southern Peru: A Cultural Interpretation. *Andean Past* 5: 325–356.

Browman, D. L. 1974. Pastoral Nomadism in the Andes. *Current Anthropology* 15(2): 188–196.

———. 1990 Camelid Pastoralism in the Andes: Llama Caravan Fleteros, and Their Importance in Production and Distribution. In *Nomads in a Changing World*, edited by C. Salzman and J. G. Galaty. Instituto Universitario Orientale, Dipartimento di Studi Asiatici, Naples.

Browne, D. M. 1992. Further Archaeological Reconnaissance in the Province of Palpa, Department of Ica, Peru. In *Ancient America: Contributions to New World Archaeology*, edited by N. J. Saunders, 77–116. Oxbow Monograph 24. Oxbow Books, Oxford.

Browne, D., H. Silverman, and R. García. 1993. A Cache of 48 Nasca Trophy Heads from Cerro Larapo, Peru. *Latin American Antiquity* 4(3): 274–294.

Brumfiel, E. M. 1992. Distinguished Lecture in Archaeology: Breaking and Entering the Ecosystem: Gender, Class, and Faction Steal the Show. *American Anthropologist* 94: 551–567.

———. 1996 The Quality of Tribute Cloth: The Place of Evidence in Archaeological Argument. *American Antiquity* 61(3): 453–462.

Brumfiel, E. M., and T. Earle. 1987. Introduction. In *Specialization, Exchange, and Complex Societies*, edited by E. Brumfiel and T. Earle, 1–9. Cambridge University Press, Cambridge.

Brumfiel, E. M., and J. Fox, eds. 1994. *Factional Competition and Political Development in the New World*. Cambridge University Press, Cambridge.

Burger, R. L. and F. Asaro. 1979. Análisis de los rasgos significativos en la obsidian de los Andes Centrales. *Revista del Museo Nacional* 43: 281–326.

Burger, R. L., and M. D. Glascock. 2000. Locating the Quispisisa Obsidian Source in the Department of Ayacucho, Peru. *Latin American Antiquity* 11(3): 258–268.

Burger, R. L., K. J. Schreiber, M. Glascock, and J. Cencho. 1998. The Jampatilla Obsidian Source: Identifying the Geological Source of Pampas Type Obsidian Artifacts from southern Peru. *Andean Past* 5: 225–239.

Camino, A. 1982. Tiempo y espacio en la estrategia de subsistencia Andina: Un caso en las vertientes orientales sud-Peruanas. In *El hombre y su ambiente en los Andes centrales*, edited by L. Millones and H. Tomoeda, 11–38. Senri Ethnological Studies, vol. 10. National Museum of Ethnology, Osaka.

Canuto, M. A. and J. Yaeger. 2000. *The Archaeology of Communities: A New World Perspective*. Routledge, New York.

Carmichael, P. H. 1988. *Nasca Mortuary Customs: Death and Ancient Society on the South Coast of Peru*. Ph.D. dissertation, University of Calgary, Calgary.

———. 1991 *Prehistoric Settlement of the Ica-Grande Littoral, Southern Peru*. Social Sciences and Humanities Research Council of Canada, Ottawa.

———. 1992. Interpreting Nasca Iconography. In *Ancient Images, Ancient Thought: The Archaeology of Ideology. Proceedings of the 23rd Annual Chacmool Conference*, edited by A. S. Goldsmith, S. Garvie, D. Selin, and J. Smit, 187–197. Department of Archaeology, University of Calgary, Calgary.

———. 1994. The Life from Death Continuum in Nasca Imagery. *Andean Past* 4: 81–89.

———. 1995. Nasca Burial Patterns: Social Structure and Mortuary Ideology. In *Tombs for the Living: Andean Mortuary Practices*, edited by T. Dillehay, 161–189. Dumbarton Oaks, Washington, D.C.

———. 1998. Nasca Ceramics: Production and Social Context. In *Andean Ceramics:*

*Technology, Organization, and Approaches*, edited by I. Shimada, 213–231. University of Pennsylvania Museum of Archaeology and Anthropology, Philadelphia.

Cashdan, E. 1980. Egalitarianism Among Hunters and Gatherers. *American Anthropologist* 82: 116–120.

Clark, N. 1993. *The Estuquina Textile Tradition: Cultural Patterning in Late Prehistoric Fabrics, Moquegua, Far Southern Peru*. University Microfilms, Ann Arbor.

Clarkson, P. 1990. The Archaeology of the Nazca Pampa: Environmental and Cultural Parameters. In *The Lines of Nazca*, edited by A. Aveni, 117–172. The American Philosophical Society, Philadelphia.

Cobb, C. R. 1993. Archaeological Approaches to the Political Economy of Nonstratified Societies. *Archaeological Method and Theory* 5: 43–99.

——. 1996. Specialization, Exchange, and Power in Small-Scale Societies and Chiefdoms. *Research in Economic Anthropology* 17: 251–294.

Conlee, C. A. 2000. *Late Prehispanic Occupation of Pajonal Alto, Nasca, Peru: Implications for Imperial Collapse and Societal Reformation*. University Microfilms, Ann Arbor.

——. 2003. Local Elites and the Reformation of Late Intermediate Period Sociopolitical and Economic Organization in Nasca, Peru. *Latin American Antiquity* 14(1): 47–65.

——. 2005. The Expansion, Diversification, and Segmentation of Power in Late Prehispanic Nasca. In *The Foundations of Power in the Prehispanic Andes*, vol. 14, edited by K. J. Vaughn, D. E. Ogburn, and C. A. Conlee, 211–223. Archeological Papers of the American Anthropological Association, Washington, D.C.

——. 2007. Decapitation and Rebirth: A Headless Burial from Nasca, Peru. *Current Anthropology* 48(3): 438–445.

Conlee, C. A., and K. Schreiber. 2006. The Role of Intermediate Elites in the Balkanization and Reformation of Post-Wari Society in Nasca, Peru. In *Between King and Commoner: Intermediate Elites in Pre-Columbian States and Empires*, edited by C. Elson and R. A. Covey. University of Arizona Press, Tucson.

Conlee, C., and K. Vaughn. 1999. The Development of Spinning Technology and Implements in the Nasca Region. Paper presented at the Institute of Andean Studies 39th annual meeting, Berkeley, California.

Coupland, G. and E. B. Banning, eds. 1996. *People who Lived in Big Houses: Archaeological Perspectives on Large Domestic Structures*. Prehistory Press, Madison.

Costin, C. L. 1993. Textiles, Women and Political Economy in Late Prehispanic Peru. *Research in Economic Anthropology* 14: 3–28.

——. 1996. Craft Production and Mobilization Strategies in the Inka Empire. In *Craft Specialization and Social Evolution: In Memory of V. Gordon Childe*, edited by B. Wailes, 211–225. University Museum Symposium Series, vol. 6. University of Pennsylvania Museum of Archaeology and Anthropology, Philadelphia.

Cross, J. R. 1993. Craft Specialization in Nonstratified Societies. *Research in Economic Anthropology* 14: 61–84.

Custred, G. 1974. Llameros y comercio interregional. In *Reciprocidad e intercambio en los Andes peruanos*. Peru problema, vol. 12. Instituto de Estudios Peruanos, Lima.

Dawson, L. E. 1964. Slip Casting: A Ceramic Technique Invented in Ancient Peru. *Ñawpa Pacha* 2: 107–112.

DeLeonardis, L. 1997. *Paracas Settlement in Callango, Lower Ica Valley, First Millennium B.C., Peru.* Ph.D. dissertation, The Catholic University of America, Washington, D.C.

——. 2000. The Body Context: Interpreting Early Nasca Decapitated Burials. *Latin American Antiquity* 11(4): 363–386.

DeMarrais, E., L. J. Castillo, and T. Earle. 1996. Ideology, Materialization, and Power Strategies. *Current Anthropology* 37(1): 15–31.

Dietler, M. 2001. Theorizing the Feast: Rituals of Consumption, Commensal Politics, and Power in African Contexts. In *Feasts: Archaeological and Ethnographic Perspectives on Food, Politics, and Power*, edited by M. Dietler and B. Hayden, 65–114. Smithsonian Institution Press, Washington, D.C.

Dietler, M., and B. Hayden. 2001. Digesting the Feast: Good to Eat, Good to Drink, Good to Think. In *Feasts: Archaeological and Ethnographic Perspectives on Food, Politics, and Power*, edited by M. Dietler and B. Hayden, 1–20. Smithsonian Institution Press, Washington, D.C.

Dietler, M., and I. Herbich. 2001. Feasts and Labor Mobilization: Dissecting a Fundamental Economic Practice. In *Feasts: Archaeological and Ethnographic Perspectives on Food, Politics, and Power*, edited by M. Dietler and B. Hayden, 240–264. Smithsonian Institution Press, Washington, D.C.

Dobres, M. A., and J. E. Robb. 2000. Agency in Archaeology: Paradigm or Platitude? In *Agency in Archaeology*, edited by M. A. Dobres and J. Robb, 3–17. Routledge, New York.

Dobres, M. A., and J. E. Robb, eds. 2000. *Agency in Archaeology*. Routledge, New York.

Earle, T. 1991. The Evolution of Chiefdoms. In *Chiefdoms: Power, Economy, and Ideology*, edited by T. Earle, 1–15. Cambridge University Press, Cambridge.

——. 1997. *How Chiefs Come to Power: The Political Economy in Prehistory*. Stanford University Press, Palo Alto.

Eitel, B., S. Hecht, B. Mächtle, G. Schukraft, A. Kadereit, G. A. Wagner, B. Kromer, I. Unkel, and M. Reindel. 2005. Geoarchaeological Evidence from Desert Loess in the Nazca-Palpa Region, Southern Peru: Paleoenvironmental Changes and Their Impact on Pre-Columbian Cultures. *Archaeometry* 47(1): 137–158.

Feinman, G. M., and J. Neitzel. 1984. Too Many Types: An Overview of Sedentary Prestate Societies in the Americas. In *Advances in Archaeological Method and Theory*, edited by M. B. Schiffer, 39–85. Advances in Archaeological Method and Theory, vol. 7. Academic Press, New York.

Feinman, G. M., and L. M. Nicholas, eds. 2004. *Archaeological Perspectives on Political Economies*. University of Utah Press, Salt Lake City.

Flannery, K. V., and M. C. Winter. 1976. Analyzing Household Activities. In *The Early Mesoamerican Village*, edited by K. V. Flannery, 34–44. Academic Press, New York.

Flores Ochoa, J. 1968. Los pastores de Paratia: Una introduccion a su estudio. *Instituto Indigenista Interamericano, Serie: Antropología Social* 10.

——. 1975. Pastores de alpacas. *Allpanchis: Revista del Instituto de Pastoral Andina* 8: 5–23.

——. 1985. Interaction and Complementarity in Three Zones of Cuzco. In *Andean Ecology and Civilization: An Interdisciplinary Perspective on Andean Ecological Complementarity: Papers from Wenner-Gren Foundation for Anthropological Research Symposium no. 91*, edited by Y. Masuda, I. Shimada, and C. Morris, 550. University of Tokyo Press, Tokyo.

Forgey, K. 2006. *Investigating the Origins and Function of Nasca Trophy Heads Using Osteological and Ancient DNA Analyses*. University Microfilms, Ann Arbor.

Frame, M. 2003–2004. What the Women Were Wearing: A Deposit of Early Nasca Dresses and Shawls from Cahuachi, Peru. *Textile Museum Journal* 42–43: 13–53.

Franquemont, E. M. 1986. Cloth Production Rates in Chinchero, Peru. In *The Junius B. Bird Conference on Andean Textiles*, edited by A. Rowe, 309–329. The Textile Museum, Washington, D.C.

Gayton, A. 1961. The Cultural Significance of Peruvian Textiles: Production, Function, Aesthetics. *Kroeber Anthropological Society Papers* 25: 111–128.

Giddens, A. 1984. *The Constitution of Society: Outline of a Theory of Structuration*. University of California Press, Berkeley.

Gillespie, S. D. 2001. Personhood, Agency, and Mortuary Ritual: A Case Study from the Ancient Maya. *Journal of Anthropological Archaeology* 202(1): 73–112.

Glascock, M. 1992. Characterization of Archaeological Ceramics at MURR by Neutron Activation Analysis and Multivariate Statistics. In *Chemical Characterization of Ceramic Pastes in Archaeology*, edited by H. Neff, 11–26. Monographs in World Archaeology, vol. 7. Prehistory Press, Madison.

Goldstein, P. S. 2000. Exotic Goods and Everyday Chiefs: Long-Distance Exchange and Indigenous Sociopolitical Development in the South-Central Andes. *Latin American Antiquity* 11(4): 335–361.

——. 2005. *Andean Diaspora: The Tiwanaku Colonies and the Origins of South American Empire*. University Press of Florida, Gainesville.

Goodell, G. 1968. A Study of Andean Spinning in the Cuzco Region. *Textile Museum Journal* 2(3): 2–8.

Goody, J. 1972. The Evolution of the Family. In *Household and Family in Past Time*, edited by P. Laslett and R. Wall, 103–124. Cambridge University Press, Cambridge.

Hayden, B. 2001. Richman, Poorman, Beggarman, Chief: The Dynamics of Social Inequality. In *Archaeology at the Millennium: A Sourcebook*, edited by G. M. Feinman and T. D. Price, 231–272. Kluwer Academic, New York.

Helms, M. W. 1993. *Craft and the Kingly Ideal: Art, Trade, and Power*. University of Texas Press, Austin.

——. 1999 Political Ideology in Complex Societies. In *Complex Polities in the Ancient Tropical World*, edited by E. A. Bacus and L. J. Lucero, 195–200. Archaeological Papers of the American Anthropological Association, vol. 9. American Anthropological Association, Arlington.

Hirth, K. 1993. Identifying Rank and Socioeconomic Status in Domestic Contexts: An

Example from Central Mexico. In *Prehispanic Domestic Units in Western Mesoamerica*, edited by R. Santley and K. Hirth, 121–146. CRC Press, Boca Raton.

Iannone, G., and S. V. Connell. 2003. Perspectives on Ancient Maya Rural Complexity: An Introduction. In *Perspectives on Ancient Maya Rural Complexity*, edited by G. Iannone and S. V. Connell, 1–6. The Cotsen Institute of Archaeology, Monograph 49, University of California, Los Angeles.

Inomata, T. 2001. The Power and Ideology of Artistic Creation. *Current Anthropology* 42(3): 321–350.

Isbell, B. J. 1977. Those Who Love Me. In *Andean Kinship and Marriage*, edited by R. Bolton and E. Mayer, 81–105. American Anthropological Association, Washington, D.C.

Isla Cuadrado, J. 1990. La Esmeralda: Una ocupación del período arcáico en Cahuachi, Nasca. *Gaceta arqueológica andina* 20: 67–80.

———. 1992. La ocupación Nasca en Usaca. *Gaceta arqueológica andina* 22: 119–151.

———. 2001. Wari en Palpa y Nasca: Perspectivas desde el Punto de Vista Funerario. *Boletín de arqueología PUCP* 5: 555–584.

Isla Cuadrado, J., M. Ruales, and A. Mendiola. 1984. Excavaciones en Nasca: Pueblo Viejo, Sector X3. *Gaceta arqueológica andina* 12: 8–11.

Isla Cuadrado, J., and M. Reindel. 2005. New Studies on the Settlements and Geoglyphs in Palpa, Peru. *Andean Past* 7: 57–92.

———. 2006. Burial Patterns and Sociopolitical Organization in Nasca 5 Society. In *Andean Archaeology III: North and South*, edited by W. H. Isbell and H. Silverman, 374–400. Kluwer, New York.

Janusek, J. W. 1999. Craft and Local Power: Embedded Specialization in Tiwanaku Cities. *Latin American Antiquity* 10(2): 107–131.

———. 2002. Out of Many, One: Style and Social Boundaries in Tiwanaku. *Latin American Antiquity* 13(1): 35–62.

Jennings, J. 2005. La Chichera y el Patrón: Chicha and the Energetics of Feasting in the Prehistoric Andes. In *The Foundations of Power in the Prehispanic Andes*, edited by K. J. Vaughn, D. E. Ogburn, and C. A. Conlee, 241–260. Archeological Papers of the American Anthropological Association, vol. 14. Washington, D.C.

Jennings, J., K. Antrobus, L., S. J. Atencio, E. Glavich, R. Johnson, G. Loffer, and C. Luu. 2005. "Drinking Beer in a Blissful Mood": Alcohol Production, Operational Chains, and Feasting in the Ancient World. *Current Anthropology* 46(2): 275–303.

Johnson, A., and T. Earle. 2000. *The Evolution of Human Societies: From Foraging Group to Agrarian State*, second ed. Stanford University Press, Stanford.

Johnson, D. W., D. A. Proulx, and S. B. Mabee. 2002. The Correlation Between Geoglyphs and Subterranean Water Resources in the Río Grande de Nazca Drainage. In *Andean Archaeology II: Art, Landscape, and Society*, edited by H. Silverman and W. H. Isbell, 307–332. Kluwer, New York.

Junker, L. L. 2001. The Evolution of Ritual Feasting Systems in Prehispanic Philippine Chiefdoms. In *Feasts: Archaeological and Ethnographic Perspectives on Food, Politics, and Power*, edited by M. Dietler and B. Hayden, 267–310. Smithsonian Institution Press, Washington, D.C.

Kantner, J. 1996. Political Competition Among the Chaco Anasazi of the American Southwest. *Journal of Anthropological Archaeology* 15(1): 41–105.

Kantner, J., and N. M. Mahoney, eds. 2000 *Great House Communities Across the Chacoan Landscape*. University of Arizona Press, Tucson.

Kellner, C. A. 2002. *Coping with Environmental and Social Challenges in Prehistoric Peru: Bioarchaeological Analyses of Nasca Populations*. University Microfilms, Ann Arbor.

Kellner, C. M., and M. J. Schoeninger. n.d. Stable Isotope Analyses of Nasca Diet During Wari Imperial Influence. Manuscript on file at the University of California, San Diego.

Keith, K. 1998. Spindle Whorls, Gender, and Ethnicity at Late Chalcolithic Hacinebi Tepe. *Journal of Field Archaeology* 25(4?): 497–515.

Kennedy, B. V., and P. Carmichael. 1991. The Role of Marine Resources in the Nasca Economy. Paper presented at the 31st annual meeting of the Institute of Andean Studies, Berkeley.

King, M. E. 1965. *Textiles and Basketry of the Paracas Period, Ica Valley, Peru*. University Microfilms, Ann Arbor.

Kolata, A., ed. 1994. *Tiwanaku and its Hinterland: Archaeology and Paleoecology of an Andean Civilization*. Smithsonian Institution Press, Washington, D.C.

Kolb, M. J., and J. E. Snead. 1997. It's a Small World After All: Comparative Analyses of Community Organization in Archaeology. *American Antiquity* 62(4): 609–628.

Kosok, P. 1965. *Life, Land and Water in Ancient Peru*. Long Island University Press, Brooklyn.

Kroeber, A. L. 1944. *Peruvian Archeology in 1942*. Viking Fund Publication in Anthropology 4. Viking Fund, New York.

Kroeber, A. L. 1956. Toward Definition of the Nazca Style. *University of California Publications in American Archaeology and Ethnology* 43(3): 327–432.

Kroeber, A. L. and D. Collier. 1998. *The Archaeology and Pottery of Nazca, Peru: Alfred L. Kroeber's 1926 Expedition*, edited by P. Carmichael. Altamira Press, Walnut Creek, CA.

Kroeber, A. L., and W. D. Strong. 192.4 The Uhle Collections from Chincha. *University of California Publications in American Archaeology and Ethnology* 21(2): 1–54.

Lambers, K. 2006. *The Geoglyphs of Palpa, Peru: Documentation, Analysis, and Interpretation*. Forschungen zur Archäologie AuBereuropáischer Kulturen, Bonn.

LeCount, L. J. 1999. Polychrome Pottery and Political Strategies in Late and Terminal Classic lowland Maya Society. *Latin American Antiquity* 10(3): 239–258.

———. 2001 Like Water for Chocolate: Feasting and Political Ritual among the Late Classic Maya at Xunantunich, Belize. *American Anthropologist* 103(4): 935–953.

Lucero, L. 2003. The Politics of Ritual: The Emergence of Classic Maya Rulers. *Current Anthropology* 44(4): 523–558.

Mann, M. 1986. *The Sources of Social Power: Volume 1, A History of Power from the Beginning to A.D. 1760*. Cambridge University Press, Cambridge.

Marcus, J. 1987. *Late Intermediate Period Occupation at Cerro Azul, Peru: A Preliminary Report*. University of Michigan Museum of Anthropology Technical Report, no. 20. University of Michigan Museum of Anthropology, Ann Arbor.

Maschner, H. D. G. and J. Q. Patton. 1996. Kin Selection and the Origins of Hereditary Social Inequality: A Case Study from the Northern Northwest Coast. In *Darwinian Archaeologies*, edited by H.D.G. Maschner, 89–107. Plenum, New York.

Massey, S. A. 1983. Antiguo centro Paracas: Animas altas. In *Culturas precolombinas: Paracas*, edited by J. A. De Lavalle and W. Lang, 134–160. Banco de Crédito, Lima.

———. 1986 *Sociopolitical Change in the Upper Ica Valley, 400 BC to AD 400: Regional States on the South Coast of Peru*. University Microfilms, Ann Arbor.

Mayer, E. 2002. *The Articulated Peasant: Household Economies in the Andes*. Westview Press, Boulder.

Menzel, D. 1959. The Inca Occupation of the South Coast of Peru. *Southwestern Journal of Anthropology* 15(2): 125–142.

Miller, G. R. 1979. *An Introduction to the Ethnoarchaeology of the Andean Camelids*. University of California, Berkeley.

Miller, G. R., and R. L. Burger. 1995. Our Father the Cayman, Our Dinner the Llama: Animal Utilization at Chavín de Huantar, Peru. *American Antiquity* 60(3): 421–458.

Miller, D., and C. Tilley. 1984. Ideology, Power and Prehistory: An Introduction. In *Ideology, Power and Prehistory*, edited by D. Miller and C. Tilley, 1–15. Cambridge University Press, Cambridge.

Mills, B. J. 2000. Gender, Craft Production, and Inequality. In *Women and Men in the Prehispanic Southwest: Labor, Power and Prestige*, edited by P. L. Crown, 301–343. School of American Research Press, Santa Fe.

Moore, J. 1985. *Household Economics and Political Integration: The Lower Class of the Chimu Empire*. Ph.D. dissertation, University of California.

———. 2005. Power and Practice in the Prehispanic Andes: Final Comments. In *The Foundations of Power in the Prehispanic Andes*, edited by K. J. Vaughn, D. E. Ogburn, and C. A. Conlee, 261–274. Archeological Papers of the American Anthropological Association, vol. 14. Washington, D.C.

Moseley, M. E. 2001. *The Incas and Their Ancestors: The Archaeology of Peru*. Revised ed. Thames and Hudson, New York.

Murra, J. 1989. Cloth's Function in the Inka State. In *Cloth and Human Experience*, edited by A. Forsyth, 275–291. Smithsonian Institution Press, Washington, D.C.

Neff, H., M. Glascock, R. Bishop, and M. J. Blackman. 1996. An Assessment of the Acid-Extraction Approach to Compositional Characterization of Archaeological Ceramics. *American Antiquity* 61(2): 389–404.

O'Donovan, M., ed. 2002. *The Dynamics of Power*. Occasional Paper No. 30. Center for Archaeological Investigations, Southern Illinois University, Carbondale.

Oficina Nacional de Evaluación de Recursos Naturales (ONERN). 1971. *Inventario, evaluación, y uso racional de los recursos naturales de la costa: Cuenca del Río Grande (Nazca)*. Oficina Nacional de Evaluación de Recursos Naturales, Lima.

Ogburn, D. E. 1993. *The Cemeteries of Nasca.* M.A. paper, University of California at Santa Barbara, Santa Barbara.

O'Neale, L. M. 1949. Weaving. In *Handbook of South American Indians,* vol. 5, edited by J. Steward, 97–138. Smithsonian Institution Bureau of American Ethnology, Washington, D.C.

O'Neale, L. M., and T. Whitaker. 1947. Embroideries of the Early Nazca Period and the Crop Plants Depicted on Them. *Southwestern Journal of Anthropology* 3(4): 294–321.

Orefici, G. 1992. *Nasca: Archeologia per una ricostruzione storica.* Jaca Books, Milan.

Orefici, G., and A. Drusini. 2003. *Nasca: Hipótesis y evidencias de su desarrollo cultural.* Centro Italiano Studi E Ricerche Archeologiche Precolombiane, Brescia, Italy.

Ortner, S. B. 1984. Theory in Anthropology Since the Sixties. *Comparative Studies in Society and History* 26(1): 126–166.

Orton, C., P. Tyers, and A. Vince. 1993. *Pottery in Archaeology.* Cambridge University Press, Cambridge.

Pacheco Torres, V. R., A. J. Altamirano Enciso, and E. S. Guerra Porras. 1986. *The Osteology of South American Camelids.* Archaeological Research Tools, vol. 3. University of California, Los Angeles Institute of Archaeology.

Paerregaard, K. 1992. Complementarity and Duality: Oppositions Between Agriculturists and Herders in an Andean Village. *Ethnology* 31(1): 15–26.

Parsons, M. H. 1972. Spindle Whorls from the Teotihuacan Valley, Mexico. *Museum of Anthropology Anthropological Papers* 45: 619–639.

———. 1975. The Distribution of Late Postclassic Spindle Whorls in the Valley of Mexico. *American Antiquity* 40: 208–215.

Paul, A., ed. 1991. *Paracas Art and Architecture: Object and Context in South Coastal Peru.* University of Iowa Press, Iowa City.

Perlman, I., and F. Asaro. 1971. Pottery Analysis by Neutron Activation. In *Science and Archaeology,* edited by R. H. Brill, 182–195. MIT Press, Cambridge.

Perodie, J. R. 2001. Feasting for Prosperity: A Study of Southern Northwest Coast Feasting. In *Feasts: Archaeological and Ethnographic Perspectives on Food, Politics, and Power,* edited by M. Dietler and B. Hayden, 185–214. Smithsonian Institution Press, Washington, D.C.

Peterson, J., D. Mitchell, and M. S. Shackley. 1997. The Social and Economic Context of Lithic Procurement: Obsidian from Classic-Period Hohokam Sites. *American Antiquity* 62(2): 231–259.

Phipps, E. 1997. The Great Cloth Burial at Cahuachi, Nasca Valley, Peru. In *Proceedings of the Fifth Biennial Symposium of the Textile Society of America, 1996, Chicago, Illinois,* 111–120. Textile Society of America, Middletown, Del.

Pillsbury, J. 1996. The Thorny Oyster and the Origins of Empire: Implications of Recently Uncovered Spondylus Imagery from Chan Chan, Peru. *Latin American Antiquity* 7(4): 313–340.

Potter, J. M. 2000. Pots, Parties and Politics: Communal Feasting in the American Southwest. *American Antiquity* 65:471–492.

Price, T. D., and G. Feinman. 1995. Foundations of Prehistoric Social Inequality.

In *Foundations of Social Inequality*, edited by T. D. Price and G. Feinman, 3–11. Plenum, New York.

Proulx, D. A. 1968. *Local Differences and Time Differences in Nasca Pottery*. University of California Publications in Anthropology 5. University of California Press, Berkeley.

——. 1971. Headhunting in Ancient Peru. *Archaeology* 24(1): 16–21.

——. 1989. A Thematic Approach to Nasca Mythical Iconography. *Bollettino del Museo Internazionale delle Ceramiche in Faenze* 75(4–5): 141–158.

——. 2001. Ritual Uses of Trophy Heads in Ancient Nasca Society. In *Ritual Human Sacrifice in Ancient Peru*, edited by E. Benson and A. Cook, 119–136. University of Texas Press, Austin.

——. 2006. *A Sourcebook of Nasca Ceramic Iconography*. Iowa University Press, Iowa City.

Reiche, M. 1968. *Mystery on the Desert*. Eigenverlag, Stuttgart.

Reindel, M., and J. Isla Cuadrado. 2001. Los molinos y la muña: Dos centros administrativos de la cultura Nasca en Palpa, costa sur del Perú. *Sonderdruck aus Beiträge zur Allgemeinen und Vergleichenden Archäeologie* 21: 289–319.

——. 2006. Reconstructing Nasca Social and Political Structures: A View from Los Molinos and La Muña. In *Nasca, Wonder of the World: Messages Etched on the Desert Floor*, edited by I. Shimada, H. Baba, K. Shinoda, and O. Masahiro, 165–173. TBS, Tokyo.

Reinhard, J. 1988. The Nazca Lines, Water and Mountains: An Ethnoarchaeological Study. In *Recent Studies in Pre-Columbian Archaeology*, edited by N. J. Saunders and O. de Montmollin, 363–502. BAR International Series, vol. 421. BAR, Oxford.

Renfrew, C. 1974. Beyond a Subsistence Economy: The Evolution of Social Organisation in Prehistoric Europe. In *Reconstructing Complex Societies: An Archaeological Colloquium*, vol. 20 (supplement), edited by C. B. Moore, 69–95. American Schools of Oriental Research, Ann Arbor.

Reycraft, R. M., ed. 2005. *Us and Them: The Assignation of Ethnicity in the Andean Region, Methodological Approaches*. Cotsen Institute of Archaeology, Los Angeles.

Rice, P. M. 1987. *Pottery Analysis: A Sourcebook*. University of Chicago Press, Chicago.

Rick, J. W. 2005. The Evolution of Authority at Chavín de Huantar. In *The Foundations of Power in the Prehispanic Andes*, edited by K. J. Vaughn, D. E. Ogburn, and C. A. Conlee, 71–89. Archeological Papers of the American Anthropological Association, vol. 14. Washington, D.C.

Riddell, F. A., and L. M. Valdez. 1987–88. Hacha y la ocupación temprana del Valle de Acarí. *Gaceta Arqueológica Andina* 16: 6–10.

Roark, R. P. 1965. From Monumental to Proliferous in Nasca Pottery. *Ñawpa Pacha* 3: 1–92.

Robin, C. 2003. New Directions in Classic Maya Household Archaeology. *Journal of Archaeological Research* 11(4): 307–356.

Rodríguez de Sandwiss, M. 1993. Malacological Analysis. In *Cahuachi in the Ancient Nasca World*, edited by H. Silverman, 294–299. University of Iowa Press, Iowa City.

Roseberry, W. 1989. *Anthropologies and Histories: Essays in Culture, History, and Political Economy*. Rutgers University Press, New Brunswick.

Rowe, A. P. 1986. Textiles from the Nasca Valley at the Time of the Fall of the Huari Empire. In *The Junius Bird Conference on Andean Textiles*, edited by A. P. Rowe, 151–182. The Textile Museum, Washington D.C.

Rowe, J. H. 1960. Nuevos datos relativos a la cronología del estilo Nasca. In *Antiguo Perú, espacio y tiempo: Trabajos presentados a la semana de arqueología peruana, 1959*, 29–45. Librería-Editorial Juan Mejía Baca, Lima.

———. 1963. Urban Settlements in Ancient Peru. *Ñawpa Pacha* 1: 1–27.

Sahlins, M. 1972. *Stone Age Economics*. Aldine de Gruyter, Chicago.

Sandweiss, D. H., and E. Wing. 1997. Ritual Rodents: The Guinea Pigs of Chincha, Peru. *Journal of Field Archaeology* 24(1): 47–58.

Sassaman, K. E. 1998. Crafting Cultural Identity in Hunter-Gatherer Economies. In *Craft and Social Identity*, edited by C. Costin and R. Wright, 93–108. American Anthropological Association, Washington, D.C.

———. 2000. Agents of Change in Hunter-Gatherer Technology. In *Agency in Archaeology*, edited by M. A. Dobres and J. Robb, 148–168. Routledge, London.

Sawyer, A. R. 1961. Paracas and Nazca Iconography. In *Essays in Pre-Columbian Art and Archaeology*, edited by S. K. Lothrop, 269–298. Harvard University Press, Cambridge.

———. 1966. *Ancient Peruvian Ceramics: The Nathan Cummings Collection*. Metropolitan Museum of Art, New York.

Schachner, G. 2001. Ritual Control and Transformation in Middle-Range Societies: An Example from the American Southwest. *Journal of Anthropological Archaeology* 20(2): 168–194.

Schele, L., and M. A. Miller. 1986. *The Blood of Kings: Dynasty and Ritual in Maya Art*. Kimball Art Museum, Fort Worth.

Schortman, E. M., and P. A. Urban. 2004. Modeling the Roles of Craft Production in Ancient Political Economies. *Journal of Archaeological Research* 12(2): 185–226.

Schreiber, K. J. 1988. On Revisiting Huaca del Loro: A Cautionary Note. *Andean Past* 2:69–79.

———. 1989. *Proyecto Nasca Sur 1989: Informe final*. Instituto Nacional de Cultura de Peru, Lima.

———. 1992. *Wari Imperialism in Middle Horizon Peru*. University of Michigan, Ann Arbor.

———. 1994. *Proyecto Nasca Sur 1994: Informe final*. Instituto Nacional de Cultura de Peru, Lima.

———. 1998. Afterword. In *The Archaeology and Pottery of Nazca, Peru: Alfred L. Kroeber's 1926 Expedition*, edited by P. H. Carmichael, 261–270. Alta Mira Press, Walnut Creek.

———. 1999. Regional Approaches to the Study of Prehistoric Empires: Examples from Ayacucho and Nasca, Peru. In *Settlement Pattern Studies in the Americas: Fifty Years Since Virú*, edited by B. R. Billman and G. M. Feinman, 160–171. Smithsonian Institution Press, Washington D.C.

------. 2005. Imperial Agendas and Local Agency: Wari Colonial Strategies. In *The Archaeology of Colonial Encounters: Comparative Perspectives*, edited by G. J. Stein, 237–262. School of American Research Press, Santa Fe.

Schreiber, K. J., and J. Isla Cuadrado. 1996. *Proyecto Nasca Sur 1996: Informe Final*. Instituto Nacional de Cultura de Peru, Lima.

Schreiber, K. J., and J. Lancho Rojas. 2003. *Irrigation and Society in the Peruvian Desert: The Puquios of Nasca*. Lexington Books, Lanham, Md.

------. 2006. *Aguas en el desierto: Los puquios de Nasca*. Fondo Editorial PUCP, Lima.

Schwartz, G. M., and S. E. Falconer, eds. 1994. *Archaeological Views from the Countryside: Village Communities in Early Complex Societies*. Smithsonian Institution Press, Washington, D.C.

Service, E. R. 1962. *Primitive Social Organization: An Evolutionary Perspective*. Random House, New York.

Shady Solis, R., J. Haas, and W. Creamer. 2001. Dating Caral, a Preceramic Site in the Supe valley on the Central Coast of Peru. *Science* 292: 723–726.

Shimada, M., and I. Shimada. 1985. Prehistoric Llama Breeding and Herding on the North Coast of Peru. *American Antiquity* 50: 3–26.

Silverman, H. 1993. *Cahuachi in the Ancient Nasca World*. University of Iowa Press, Iowa City.

------. 1996. The Formative Period on the South Coast of Peru: A Critical Review. *Journal of World Prehistory* 10(2): 95–147.

------. 1997. The First Field Season of Excavations at the Alto del Molino Site, Pisco Valley, Peru. *Journal of Field Archaeology* 24(4): 441–458.

------. 2002 *Ancient Nasca Settlement and Society*. University of Iowa Press, Iowa City.

Silverman, H., and D. A. Proulx. 2002. *The Nasca*. Blackwell Publishers, Malden.

Sinopoli, C. M. 1991. *Approaches to Archaeological Ceramics*. Plenum, New York.

Spalding, K. 1984. *Huarochirí: An Andean Society Under Inca and Spanish Rule*. Stanford University Press, Stanford.

Spielmann, K. 2002. Feasting, Craft Specialization, and the Ritual Mode of Production in Small-Scale Societies. *American Anthropologist* 104(1): 195–207.

Stanish, C. 1989. Household Archaeology: Testing Models of Zonal Complementarity in the South Central Andes. *American Anthropologist* 91: 7–24.

------. 1992. *Ancient Andean Political Economy*. University of Texas Press, Austin.

------. 1997. Archaeological Survey in the Juli-Desaguadero Region of the Lake Titicaca Basin, Southern Peru. *Fieldiana* 29: 1–170.

------. 2003. *Ancient Titicaca: The Evolution of Complex Society in Southern Peru and Northern Bolivia*. University of California Press, Berkeley.

------. 2004. The Evolution of Chiefdoms: An Economic Anthropological Model. In *Archaeological Perspectives of Political Economies*, edited by G. M. Feinman, 7–24. University of Utah Press, Salt Lake City.

Stein, G. J. 1998. Heterogeneity, Power, and Political Economy: Some Current Research Issues in the Archaeology of Old World Complex Societies. *Journal of Archaeological Research* 6(1): 1–44.

Strong, W. D. 1957. *Paracas, Nazca, and Tiahuanacoid Cultural Relationships in South Coastal Peru*. Memoirs of the Society for American Archaeology 13. Society for American Archaeology, Salt Lake City.

Towle, M. 1961. *The Ethnobotany of Pre-Columbian Peru*. Aldine, Chicago.

Townsend, R. F. 1985. Deciphering the Nazca world: Ceramic Images from Ancient Peru. *Art Institute of Chicago Museum Studies* 11(2): 117–139.

Tringham, R. E. 1991. Households with Faces: The Challenge of Gender in Prehistoric Architectural Remains. In *Engendering Archaeology: Women and Prehistory*, edited by J. M. Gero and M. W. Conkey, 93–131. Blackwell, Oxford.

Trigger, B. 1990. Monumental Architecture: A Thermodynamic Explanation of Symbolic Behavior. *World Archaeology* 22: 119–132.

Valdez Cardenas, L. 1988. Los camélidos en la subsistencia Nasca: El caso de Kawachi. *Boletín de Lima* 57: 31–35.

———. 1994. Cahuachi: New Evidence for an Early Nasca Ceremonial Role. *Current Anthropology* 35(5): 675–679.

———. 1998. *The Nasca and the Valley of Acarí: Cultural Interaction on the Peruvian South Coast*. University Microfilms, Ann Arbor.

Valdez Cardenas, L., and J. E. Valdez. 1997. Reconsidering the Archaeological Rarity of Guinea Pig Bones in the Central Andes. *Current Anthropology* 38(5): 896–898.

Van Gijseghem, H. 2001. Household and Family at Moche, Peru: An Analysis of Building and Residence Patterns in a Prehispanic Urban Center. *Latin American Antiquity* 12(3): 257–273.

———. 2004. *Migration, Agency, and Social Change on a Prehistoric Frontier: The Paracas-Nasca Transition in the Southern Nasca Drainage, Peru*. University Microfilms, Ann Arbor.

———. 2006. A Frontier Perspective on Paracas Society and Nasca Ethnogenesis. *Latin American Antiquity* 17(4): 419–444.

Vaughn, K. J. 2005. Crafts and the Materialization of Chiefly Power in Nasca. In *The Foundations of Power in the Prehispanic Andes*, edited by K. J. Vaughn, D. E. Ogburn, and C. A. Conlee, 113–130. Archeological Papers of the American Anthropological Association, vol. 14. Washington, D.C.

Vaughn, K. J., C. A. Conlee, H. Neff, and K. Schreiber. 2006. Ceramic Production in Ancient Nasca: Provenance Analysis of Pottery from the Early Nasca and Tiza Cultures through INAA. *Journal of Archaeological Science* 33: 681–689.

Vaughn, K. J., and M. D. Glascock. 2005. Exchange of Quispisisa Obsidian in the Nasca Region: New Evidence from Marcaya. *Andean Past* 7: 93–110.

Vaughn, K. J., and M. Linares Grados. 2006. Three Thousand Years of Occupation in Upper Valley Nasca: Excavations at Upanca. *Latin American Antiquity* 17(4): 595–612.

Vaughn, K. J., and H. Neff. 2004. Tracing the Clay Source of Nasca Polychrome Pottery: Results from a Preliminary Raw Material Survey. *Journal of Archaeological Science* 31(11): 1577–1586.

Vaughn, K. J., H. Neff, C. A. Conlee, and K. J. Schreiber 2005. A Compositional

Analysis of Nasca Polychrome Pigments: Implications for Craft Production on the Prehispanic South Coast of Peru. In *Laser Ablation ICP-MS: A New Frontier in Archaeological Characterization Studies*, edited by R. J. Speakman and H. Neff, 138–154. University of New Mexico Press, Albuquerque.

Vaughn, K. J., D. E. Ogburn and C. A. Conlee, eds. 2005. *The Foundations of Power in the Prehispanic Andes*. Archeological Papers of the American Anthropological Association, vol. 14. Washington, D.C.

Wallace, D. T. 1971. Sitios arqueológicos del Perú (segunda entrega): Valles de Chincha y de Pisco. *Arqueológicas* 13: 4–131.

Wallerstein, I. 1974. *The Modern World System: Capitalist Agriculture and the Origins of the World Economy in the Sixteenth Century*. Academic Press, New York.

Walker, W. H., and L. J. Lucero. 2000. The Depositional History of Ritual and Power. In *Agency in Archaeology*, edited by M. Dobres and J. Robb, 130–147. Routledge, London.

Webster, S. 1971. An Indigenous Quechua Community in Exploitation of Multiple Ecological Zones. *Revista del Museo Nacional* 37: 174–183.

Wheeler, J. C. 1984. On the Origin and Early Development of Camelid Pastoralism in the Andes. In *Animals and Archaeology III: Early Herders and their Flocks*, vol. 20, edited by J. Clutton-Brock and C. Grigson, 395–410. BAR International Monographs, Oxford.

Wiessner, P. 2002. Vines of Complexity: Egalitarian Structures and the Institutionalization of Inequality Among the Enga. *Current Anthropology* 43(2): 233–269.

Wilk, R., and W. Rathje. 1982. Archaeology of the Household: Building a Prehistory of Domestic Life. *American Behavioral Scientist* 25(6).

Williams León, C. 1980. Arquitectura y urbanismo en el antiguo Peru. In *Historia del Perú: Peru republicano y procesos e instituciones*, vol. 8, edited by J. M. Baca, 389–585. Editorial Juan Mejía Baca, Lima.

Williams, S. R., K. Forgey, and E. Klarich. 2001. An Osteological Study of Nasca Trophy Heads Collected by A. L. Kroeber During the Marshall Field Expeditions to Peru. *Fieldiana: Anthropology* 33: 1–132.

Winthrop, K., and R. Winthrop. 1975. Spindle Whorls and Textile Production in Early New Mexico. *Awanyu* 3(3): 28–46.

Wolf, E. 1982. *Europe and the People Without History*. University of California Press, Berkeley.

———. 1990. Distinguished Lecture: Facing Power—Old Insights, New Questions. *American Anthropologist* 92: 586–596.

Yamamoto, N. 1982. A Food Production System in the Southern Central Andes. In *El hombre y su ambiente en los Andes Centrales*, edited by L. Millones and H. Tomoeda, 39–62. Senri Ethnological Studies, vol. 10. National Museum of Ethnology, Osaka.

# Index

A

Acarí: elites in, 173; Valley, 38, 60

Agency, human: concept of, 14–17; defined, 14; rubric of approaches, 14; and villages in the Andes, 26–27; and villages in middle-range societies, 25–26

Agency approach: and decision-making capacity, 17; at Marcaya and Cahuachi, 174–176

Agricultural cycles, ceremonies tied to, 53

Agricultural fertility: and elite power, 167; and link to polychrome pottery, 171; Nasca lines, trophy heads and, 42–43

Agriculture, in Tierras Blancas, 67

Aja river, 36

Alcalde, as ritual leader, 159–160

Allocative resources, 16. *See also* Resources

Alpaca, 58

Animals, domesticated, in Andean societies, 58–59

Antaras. *See* Panpipes

Aqueducts, 5, 40

Archaeology: and bias towards larger sites, 25; Darwinian, 14; household approach, in the Andes, 29; rural, 26

Architecture, elite, 57

Architecture in Marcaya, 69–77; doors, 70, 73; households, 74; patio groups, 73–77; variability in quality of, 75

Authoritative resources, 16

B

Batanes, 126

Beans, in ceremonial caches at Cahuachi, 48

Bowls, pottery at Marcaya, 99

Burials: analysis of human, at Marcaya, 134; analysis of textiles recovered from, 149; differences between burial and ordinary cloth, 149–151; and inequalities, 55

C

Cahuachi: agency approach at, 174–176; camelid remains at, 129; cemeteries at, 48; ceremonial caches at, 47–48; as ceremonial center of Nasca, 3–5, 39, 44–46, 153, 165; ceremonial feasts at, 46; comparison of vessel assemblages, 106; and distribution and exchange of pottery, 61–62; and Early Nasca society, 163–178 (*see also* Early Nasca society); elite residences at, 49–51; emergence as sacred place, 45; evidence for long-distance exchange at, 144; faunal remains at, 128, 142; feasting at, 46–47, 64; food storage facilities at, 164; Great Pyramid plaza at, 45, Great Temple plaza at, 45, guinea pigs at, 120; headjars in mortuary context, 102; herding activities at, 142; hunting at, 129, 141; hyperceremonialism peak, 180; panpipes cache at, 127; people of, 44–46; as permanent habitation site, 165; photo, 4; as pilgrimage center, 45–46; plainware pottery at, 104; pottery design themes, 108; pottery production at, 48–49, 64; and production of panpipes, 127; and public ritual, 175; as redistributive center for polychrome pottery, 177; rela-

tionship with Marcaya, 176; relationship with secondary ceremonial centers, 171–172; shellfish remains at, 132–133; as source of Early Nasca polychrome pottery production, 115–116; spindle whorls at, 119; subsistence economy, excavations and, 58; subsistence goods and, 177; and textile production, 148–151
Camelids: as component of Nasca subsistence, 58–59; domesticated in Nasca, 129; in excavations at Cahuachi, 128–129; as exchange product, 142–143; fibers used for textile production, 148–151; fleece used in textiles, 121; herded in Marcaya, 132, 141
Cantaros jar, at Marcaya, 102
Cavernas, as textile tradition, 38
Caxamarca, 41
Cemeteries: at Cahuachi, 48; at Marcaya, 134
Ceremonial activities. *See* Ritual
Ceremonial caches, at Cahuachi, 47–48
Ceremony, group-oriented, 63
Chalcedony drills, 118; at Marcaya, 123
Chalcedony pendant, at Marcaya, 128
Charki, production and exchange of, 143
Chavín: first appearance of, 38; and ideological integration in Early Intermediate Period, 38–39
Chiefdom: defined, 13; Nasca organized as, 12–13; and prestige-building efforts, 60; societies labeled as, 13
Chiefs, and feasting, 21
Chuquimaran, 78, 82; collomas at, 78
Clothing, women's, in ceremonial caches at Cahuachi, 47–48
Collared jars, pottery at Marcaya, 101
Collective misrecognition, 20
Collomas, at Marcaya, 78, 82–83, 139
Community perspective, 26
Compositional analysis of pottery, 109–110; results of INAA, 110–113
Cotton production, 148–151

Craft production: at Cahuachi, 168–171; elites' control over, 19; and power, 18–19
Cultures, of Nasca, 39
Cuy. *See* Guinea pig

D
Darwinian archaeology, 14
Demographic unit, social components of, 28
Design themes, of Marcaya fineware. *See* Pottery at Marcaya
Diet, Nasca, 58; agricultural component of, 140–141; camelids and, 141–143; domesticated plants and animals, 140; and marine resources, 143; self-sufficient households in, 143
Dishes, pottery, at Marcaya, 99–100
Domesticated animals, in Andean societies, 58–59
Drop spinning, 121
Drought: in ancient Nasca, 39; and Initial Period, 38; and peak of hyper-ceremonialism, 180; and pottery production, 180
Dwellings, 29. *See also* Houses

E
Early Horizon Period, 38; camelids and, 141; craft specialization in, 38
Early Intermediate Period (EIP), 38–39; and integration of Chavín, 38–39; and long-distance exchange, 173; villages dating to, 57
Early Nasca Society, 3, 162–183; and agriculture, 51–52; and Cahuachi, 163–178; characterized by small villages, 45; craft production at, 168–172; design themes on pottery of, 107; elites in, 165–166; and mixed economy, 177–178; nature of habitation at, 163–165; nature of power in, 166–168; and pottery production at Cahuachi, 48–49; power and political economy at, 172–174; and sea-

ing as indicators of, 56–57; feasts promoting, 20; formation and institutionalization of, religious ritual and, 32–33; in middle-range societies, 17–18; and power, 15, 54–58; in social formations, 15

Ingenio Valley, 42, 57, 60

Initial Period, 37–38

Instrumental neutron activation analysis (INAA): testing of obsidian sources, 126; testing of pottery at Nasca, 110–113

Integration, extra-regional, in Early Horizon period, 38

Irrigation, large-scale, and Initial Period, 37

J

Jampatilla, as source of obsidian, 124–126. *See also* Obsidian

Jars. *See* Fineware at Marcaya; Pottery at Marcaya

K

Kenya, Samia of, and feasting, 21–22

L

La Muña, 55

Late Intermediate Period (LIP): and long-distance exchange, 40–41; and marine resources in diet, 143

Late Nasca, 5; increase of conflict in, 40

La Tiza, 40–41

Lithic production, 147–148

Lithics at Marcaya, 123–128; analysis of obsidian, 124–126; chalcedony drills, 123; chipped stone artifacts, 123; flake tools, 123; ground stone, 126; Jampatilla as obsidian source, 124–126; lithic assemblage, 123; obsidian assemblages, 123–124; other artifacts, 128; panpipes, 127 (*see also* Panpipes); projectile points, 123; Quispisisa, as obsidian source, 124–126

Llama, 58–59

Local perspective, 26; in research on single communities, 27

Long-distance exchange, in Late Intermediate Period, 41. *See also* Exchange

Los Molinos, 56–57; as secondary ceremonial center, 171, 177

M

Maize, importance in subsistence economy, 58

Malacological material. *See* Shellfish

Marcaya: economic activities at, 91–92; faunal assemblage at, 141; hypothetical reconstruction of, 138; pottery at, 93–116 (*see also* Pottery; Pottery at Marcaya); as unambiguous habitation site, 165

Marcaya, as Early Nasca village, 137–161; absence of stratified middens at, 137–138; archaeological households, 137–140 (*see also* Households); conclusions, 160–161; as economically self-sufficient, 152; household organization, 138–140; mixed economy, 152; patio groups identified at, 137; political economy of, 144–161; ritual activities in, 152–153; status at, 153–160; subsistence economy in, 140–143 (*see also* Economy, subsistence)

Marcaya, investigations at, 65–92; agriculture in, 67; architectural layout, 69–77; excavations, 77–92; seasonal flooding in valley, 67–69; site boundaries and context, 69; Tierras Blancas Yunga, environment, 67–69; topographical map of, 65–66, 68

Marcaya, non-pottery artifacts at, 117–136; faunal analysis, 128–132; human remains, 134; lithics, 123–128 (*see also* Lithics at Marcaya); shellfish remains, 132–133; summary, 134–136; textiles, 117–123 (*see also* Textiles at Marcaya)

Marshall Field expedition to Peru, 43

Paracas Necropolis, as textile tradition, 38

Paredones, as retreat of Inca Emperor, 41

Pataraya, 40

Patio groups, 73–74: differences in, 90–91; distribution of pottery in, 106–107; and economic activities, 138; excavation in Marcaya of, 83–90; and ground stone artifacts at Marcaya, 139; and high-status households, 159–160; and high-status pottery, 155–160; identified at Marcaya, 137; and lithics at Marcaya, 123; as representative of prehispanic households, 137; size and architectural quality, 75–77, 154. *See also* Excavations; Excavations at Marcaya

Philippines, sixteenth century, feasting in, 20–21

Pisco Valley, 60; elites in, 173

Plainware pottery at Marcaya, 103–104. *See also* Pottery at Marcaya

Political economy: exchange and, 18–19, 144–152; and feasting, 21; and goods and services in, 32; identifying emerging, 30–31; at Marcaya, 144–161; and materialization, 23–25; in middle-range societies, 17–18; in Nasca, 51–53; production in, 18–19; and status, 31–32; and subsistence, 31–32; and villages, 25–26. *See also* Economy, political

Polychromes. *See* Pottery

Pottery: contextual analysis of motifs on, 44; as evidence of feasting, 33, 46; and first appearance of cult of Chavín, 38; as principal purveyor of ideology in Nasca society, 60; production and exchange of, 60–62; use of, Initial Period and, 37. *See also* Pottery at Marcaya

Pottery, polychrome: analysis of pigments on, 113–115; common motifs on, 43–44; distribution of, 174–175;

drought and production, 180; exchange of in political economies, 60; extent of Nasca society defined by distribution of, 41–42; as hallmark of Nasca society, 39; in Ica-Grande region, 57; and link with agricultural fertility, 171; as materialized ideology, 40; and Nasca religion, 170; photo, 4; as "power objects", 175; production at Cahuachi of, 48–49, 169–171; and status, 154–159; use of, in domestic context, 62

Pottery, production of, 108–109; analysis of pigments on, 113–115; Cahuachi, source of Early Nasca pottery production, 115–116; compositional analysis, 109–113; further compositional studies, 113–116

Pottery at Marcaya, 93–116: absence of double-spout and bridge bottle types, 95; chronology, 95; evaluations of iconography on, 153; fineware: design themes of, 107–108, 141; fineware: vessel shapes, 95–102; as grave goods, 44, 60–61; headjars, 157–158; high-status pottery, 155; hunting scenes in, 129; major categories of, 94; Nasca shape classifications, 94–95; panpipes, 158–159; plainware: vessel shapes, 94, 103–104; spatial distribution in patio groups, 106–107; and spindle whorls, 119–123; summary, 116; vessel assemblage at, 104–106

Power: and inequality, 54–58; institutions of, 15; maintenance of, feasting and ritual and, 32–33; in middle-range societies, 16, 18–19; nature of, in Nasca, 166–168; production of material symbols of, 172–173; social, 15–16; types of, 15–16; in village, 31

Power and political economy, 144–152; in middle-range societies, 17–18; in Nasca, 51–53, 172–174

Power domains, taxonomy of, 15

# About the Author

Kevin J. Vaughn is an associate professor of anthropology at Purdue University. For more than a decade (since 1996), Vaughn has worked in the Nasca region, where his work has focused on emergent sociopolitical complexity, villages, and craft production—especially ceramic production. Most recently, his work has focused on ancient mining practices in the Andes. He has also conducted archaeological fieldwork in Peru, Ecuador, the American Southwest, California, the Great Plains, and Germany. Vaughn received his B.A. from the University of Washington and his M.A. and Ph.D. from the University of California, Santa Barbara (2000). He has authored publications in international, national, and regional archaeological and scientific journals such as *Latin American Antiquity*, the *Journal of Archaeological Research*, the *Journal of Archaeological Science*, the *Journal of Anthropological Archaeology*, the *Journal of Field Archaeology*, *Antiquity*, *Andean Past*, the *SAA Archaeological Record*, as well as international materials science journals *JOM* (the journal of the Minerals, Metals and Materials Society) and *Hyperfine Interactions*. He was co-editor of a volume of *The Archaeological Papers of the American Anthropological Association* and is co-editor of a forthcoming volume to be published by the School for Advanced Research Press entitled *The Emergence of Leadership: Transitions in Decision Making from Small-Scale to Middle-Range Societies*. He has organized symposia and presented at national and international conferences in the United States, Canada, and Peru. At Purdue University, Vaughn teaches archaeology at the introductory, advanced undergraduate, and graduate level. He lives with his wife and daughter in Lafayette, Indiana.

CPSIA information can be obtained at www.ICGtesting.com
Printed in the USA
LVOW102026301111

257276LV00005B/1/P

9 780816 515943